Get started in French

French

Catrine Carpenter

Advisory editor
Paul Coggle

For UK order enquiries: please contact Bookpoint Ltd,
130 Milton Park, Abingdon, Oxon, OX14 4SB.
Telephone: +44 (0) 1235 827720. Fax: +44 (0) 1235 400454.
Lines are open 09.00–17.00, Monday to Saturday, with a 24-hour
message answering service. Details about our titles and how to
order are available at www.teachyourself.com

For USA order enquiries: please contact McGraw-Hill Customer
Services, PO Box 545, Blacklick, OH 43004-0545, USA.
Telephone: 1-800-722-4726. *Fax:* 1-614-755-5645.

For Canada order enquiries: please contact McGraw-Hill
Ryerson Ltd, 300 Water St, Whitby, Ontario, L1N 9B6, Canada.
Telephone: 905 430 5000. *Fax:* 905 430 5020.

Long renowned as the authoritative source for self-guided
learning – with more than 50 million copies sold worldwide –
the *Teach Yourself* series includes over 500 titles in the fields of
languages, crafts, hobbies, business, computing and education.

British Library Cataloguing in Publication Data: a catalogue record
for this title is available from the British Library.

Library of Congress Catalog Card Number: on file.

Previously published as *Teach Yourself Beginner's French*.

First published in UK 1992 by Hodder Education, part of Hachette
UK, 338 Euston Road, London, NW1 3BH.

First published in US 1992 by The McGraw-Hill Companies, Inc.

This edition published 2010.

The *Teach Yourself* name is a registered trade mark of
Hodder Headline.

Illustrated by Barking Dog Art, Sally Elford, Peter Labach

Typeset by MPS Limited, A Macmillan Company.

Printed in Great Britain for Hodder Education, an Hachette UK
Company, 338 Euston Road, London NW1 3BH, by CPI Cox and
Wyman, Reading, Berkshire, RG1 8EX.

The publisher has used its best endeavours to ensure that the URLs
for external websites referred to in this book are correct and active
at the time of going to press. However, the publisher and the author
have no responsibility for the websites and can make no guarantee
that a site will remain live or that the content will remain relevant,
decent or appropriate.

Hachette UK's policy is to use papers that are natural, renewable
and recyclable products and made from wood grown in sustainable
forests. The logging and manufacturing processes are expected to
conform to the environmental regulations of the country of origin.

Impression number   10 9 8 7 6 5 4 3 2 1

Year   2014 2013 2012 2011 2010

Contents

Meet the author

Born and educated in France, Dr. Catrine Carpenter is now teaching French as a Senior Lecturer at Brighton University. Having taught for over 30 years, she has acquired a wide and comprehensive experience in teaching French to both learners and teachers of French, and in publishing a whole range of learning and teaching materials. These fall into two main categories: audio, visual and web-based material, and language courses. The first language course she produced was *Teach yourself Beginner's French*, published by Hodder & Stoughton; the other two focused on undergraduate students intending to spend a year at a French university, and specialists of French in higher education. By conducting research into language learners' strategies, Dr. Carpenter has pioneered a wide range of innovative language learning and teaching approaches including projects based on email exchanges between French and British undergraduates.

Over the last 30 years, Dr. Carpenter has accrued a wealth of experience in teaching learners between the ages of 5 and 70 in the UK, and also in France, Spain, India and Africa. More recently, she has been teaching under- and post-graduate students specializing in French studies, International Business, Management and Tourism, Engineering and Architecture. She has also taught members of the public on bespoke and short courses run by the University of Brighton. These have included business people, flight crews and other professionals.

However, out of all her teaching commitments, Dr. Carpenter states that teaching beginners is the most rewarding for her, as she firmly believes that good foundations in learning a language pave the way to successful language acquisition.

Photo Credits

Front cover: © Jupiterimages/Comstock/Getty Images

Back cover and pack: © Jakub Semeniuk/iStockphoto.com, © Royalty-Free/Corbis, © agencyby/iStockphoto.com, © Andy Cook/iStockphoto.com, © Christopher Ewing/iStockphoto.com, © zebicho – Fotolia.com, © Geoffrey Holmamn/iStockphoto.com, © Photodisc/Getty Images, © James C. Pruitt/iStockphoto.com, © Mohamed Saber – Fotolia.com

Pack: © Stockbyte/Getty Images

Internal photos:

© Photodisc/Getty Images: page 6
© Imagestate Media: page 7
© Stockbyte/PhotolibraryGroup Ltd: page 14
© Imagestate Media: page 29
© Jason Holtom/Life File/Photodisc/Getty Images: page 36
© Imagestate Media: page 38
© Imagestate Media: page 42
© Imagestate Media: page 49
© Photodisc/Getty Images: page 52
© Photodisc/Getty Images: page 70
© Imagestate Media: page 81
© Imagestate Media: page 89
© Ingram Publishing Limited: page 92
© Imagestate Media: page 95
© lucwa/iStockphoto.com: page 95
© Photodisc/Getty Images: page 106
© Photodisc/Getty Images: page 111
© Imagestate Media: page 118
© Imagestate Media: page 124
© Photodisc/Getty Images: page 125
© Imagestate Media: page 134
© Imagestate Media: page 142
© Ingram Publishing Limited: page 148

© PIXFOLIO/Alamy: page 151
© Imagestate Media: page 166
© MARIA TOUTOUDAKI/iStockphoto.com: page 70
© Photodisc/Getty Images: page 171
© Imagestate Media: page 182
© Photodisc/Getty Images: page 185
© Ingram Publishing Limited: page 192
© Brand X/Jupiterimages Corporation: page 198
© David Epperson/Photographer's Choice/Photolibrary Group: page 208
© Photodisc/Getty Images: page 209
© Ingram Publishing Limited: page 217
© Ingram Publishing Limited: page 221
© ICP/Alamy: page 226
© Stockbyte/Photolibrary Group Ltd: page 242
© Imagestate Media: page 245
© Stockbyte/Photolibrary Group Ltd: page 249
© Imagestate Media: page 259
© Getty Images/Stockbyte Silver: page 262

Only got a minute?

French is spoken by about 350 million people. It is an official language in 29 countries and commonly used in many others. Replacing Latin, French became the official language of administration and court proceedings in France by the Ordinance of Villers-Cotterêts in 1539. From the 17th to the 20th centuries, France was the leading power of Europe, and French was the lingua franca of educated Europe. During the 17th and 18th centuries, it established itself in the Americas with the arrival of colonists from France. Since World War II however, French has lost most of its international significance to English with the rise of the USA as the dominant global power. Nevertheless, French is the second most-studied foreign language in the world after English.

The Normans brought their language to England in 1066. So, for 300 years French was the language of the English court, administration and culture. More than a third of all English words are derived directly or indirectly from French, and English speakers who have never studied French probably already know 15,000 French words! Once you begin *Get started in French* it won't take you long to realize that you already know many common French words because of their similarity to English words: **pardon**, **parler**, **désirer**, **café**, **journal**, **bière**, **pharmacie**, **hôpital**, **hôtel** and less common words: **instructions**, **introduire**, **téléphoner**, **organisme**, **opération**.

Language is much more than the study of vocabulary so this course will introduce basic grammatical points and provide ample opportunity to put them into use through a number of practical and communicative situations such as giving personal information, making a hotel booking, asking for directions, making travel arrangements, ordering food and drinks, shopping. These are just a few of the situations you will be able to handle once you have completed this course.

5 Only got five minutes?

French language

French is a Romance language (meaning that it originates from Latin) spoken around the world by about 77 million people as a first language (mother tongue), by 50 million as a second language, and by about another 200 million people as an acquired foreign language, with significant speakers in 54 countries. It is an official language in 29 countries most of which form what is called **La Francophonie**, the community of French-speaking nations. It is an official language of all United Nations agencies and a large number of international organizations. In the European Union, French is the most spoken second language after English and German. Before the mid 20th century, French served as the pre-eminent language of diplomacy among European and colonial powers as well as a lingua franca among the educated classes of Europe.

In France a unified official language emerged thanks to the **Académie Française** (founded in the 17th century), public education, centuries of official control and the role of media, but there remains a great deal of regional diversity. For some critics, the 'best' pronunciation occurs in Touraine (around Tours and the Loire valley).

French lost most of its international significance to English in the 20th century, especially after World War II, with the rise of the USA as the dominant global power. There is some debate in today's France about the preservation of the French language and the influence of English, especially with regard to international business, the sciences, and popular culture. Laws now require that all print ads and billboards with foreign expressions include a

French translation. Moreover, at least 40% of songs on the radio must be in French.

The grammatical points in the first part of *Get started in French*

In the first part of the book the emphasis is on the basic structures and grammatical points common to every situation. Thus Units 1–10 should be taken in order, as each builds on the previous one. The grammar section is followed by activities for practising the grammatical points introduced. Many strategies are provided to help French learners develop their own 'techniques' to become better learners. Tips are also included on how to master grammar, learn vocabulary, improve listening and reading skills and develop confidence in speaking.

In **Get started in French** the grammatical points are gradually introduced in the first part of the book in order of importance, but grammar is kept to a minimum. Unit 2 covers the definite article *the* (**le, la, l', les**), the indefinite *a, an* (**un, une, des**), and partitive article *some* (**du, de la, de l', des**) as these are the most basic nuts and bolts of the language. The articles agree in gender and number with the noun they determine. Unit 3 introduces the two most common verbs **avoir** (*to have*) and **être** (*to be*). These are irregular, as in English, but need to be learnt by heart because they are essential for talking about oneself: **Je suis canadien** (*I am Canadian*), **je suis marié** (*I am married*), and for asking other people questions about themselves and their family: **Vous êtes anglais?** (*Are you English?*), **Vous avez des enfants?** (*Do you have any children?*). Unit 3 also includes the negative form **ne... pas** so that responses such as **Non, je n'ai pas d'enfants** (*No, I don't have any children*) can be given and understood. The possessive adjectives (**mon, ma, mes,** etc.) are introduced in Unit 4 to make it easier to talk about one's family. The three different ways of asking simple questions in French are introduced in Unit 5, the easiest consisting of making a statement and raising the voice on the last syllable: **Vous êtes français?** (*You are French?*). Common prepositions such as **avant, près de, à côté de, entre, dans,** used in front of nouns, are taught in Unit 6. Prepositions make directions and distances clearer: **La poste est en face du café** (*The post office is opposite the café*), **la gare est près de chez moi** (*the station is near my home*). Adjectives are introduced in Unit 7. These are describing words and agree in gender and number with the noun they modify. The adjective's masculine singular form is its default form. The feminine singular of most adjectives is formed from the masculine by adding **-e** (**grand, grande**). Most adjective plurals are formed from their corresponding singulars by adding **-s** (**grands, grandes**). By the end of Unit 10, the French learner will have been introduced to other irregular common verbs such as **aller, partir, faire, prendre, sortir, venir, pouvoir** and **vouloir**. The first six are useful when talking about everyday activities at home or at work: **Je fais des courses avec mes amies** (*I go shopping with my girlfriends*), **je vais au bureau à neuf heures du matin** (*I go to the office at nine in the morning*), while the last two are useful when asking for help. Start with **Vous pouvez** (*Can you*) and raise the voice on the last word: **Vous pouvez me dire ...?** (*Can you tell me ...?*).

Everyday situations in the second part of *Get started in French*

The second part of the book (Units 11–19) deals with everyday situations such as shopping, eating, booking a room, travelling, and gives the French learner the opportunity to practise the language acquired in the first part. These units may be taken in any order. I have chosen the topics for their relevance to a tourist or business traveller. In each unit the key words and phrases containing the basic vocabulary of the topic are introduced. There are several short dialogues, each dealing with a different aspect of the topic. Some units have more key words than others, but I have tried not to overload the learner with too many! For example in Unit 11, Shopping, I have included the most common vocabulary (**pain, jambon, saucisson, café, thé, fromage, journaux, pantalon,**

chemise) but deliberately left many other words out. Instead I included sentences such as **Où est-ce que je peux acheter/trouver?** (*Where can I buy/find?*) and **Vous avez autre chose de moins cher?** (*Have you got anything cheaper?*) to help the learner find what he/she is looking for. Unit 13, Eating and drinking well, introduces the three simplest but most useful phrases to talk about food and drinks: **Qu'est-ce que vous avez à manger/boire?** (*What do you have to eat/drink?*), **Je vais prendre** (*I'll take/have*) and **Vous pouvez me conseiller pour ...?** (*Can you advise me about ...?*). With these structures one should be able to cope with most eating and drinking situations. Similarly in Unit 16, Going out, I introduce two phrases which are useful for finding out what there is to see/do in a French town/region: **Qu'est-ce qu'il y a comme ...?** (*What sort of ... is/are there?*) and **Qu'est-ce qu'on peut faire?** (*What can I/we/one do?*). What is most important for the learner in each situation is to know how to communicate his/her needs with a simple question, and then to understand the key information in the answer. Developing listening skills is as important as knowing how to ask. Remember to listen to the dialogues first and use the pause button to practise the new words and phrases out loud. The course is best used together with the accompanying recording, but is not dependent upon it. There are many additional listening exercises in this fifth edition, so French learners have even more opportunities to practise their listening and speaking skills in meaningful situations. Learners without the recording should use the **Pronunciation guide** at the beginning of the book. This gives approximate English equivalents for the French sounds. It is important to try to pronounce the correct sounds from the beginning, but remember that the main aim is to be understood.

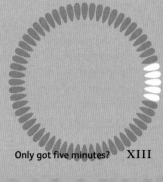

10 Only got ten minutes?

The French language spoken in the world

French is a descendant of the Latin language of the Roman Empire, as are national languages such as Portuguese, Spanish, Italian and Romanian, and minority languages ranging from Catalan and Occitan to Neapolitan and many more. Its development was also influenced by the native Celtic languages of Roman Gaul and by the Germanic language of the post-Roman Frankish invaders. French is spoken around the world by about 77 million people as a first language (mother tongue), by 50 million as a second language, and by about another 200 million people as an acquired foreign language, with significant speakers in 54 countries. Most native speakers live in France. The rest live essentially in Canada (particularly Quebec), Belgium, Switzerland, francophone Africa, Luxembourg and Monaco. Most second-language speakers of French live in francophone Africa, the Democratic Republic of the Congo being the francophone country with the largest population.

Europe

In Switzerland, French is one of the three official languages and is spoken in the part of Switzerland called **Romandie**. French is the native language of about 20% of the Swiss population. Apart from small differences involving some numbers, most of Swiss French is compatible with the standard French spoken in France. In Belgium, French is the official language of **Wallonia** and one of the two official languages along with Dutch of the Brussels-capital region where it is spoken by the majority of the population. In total, native French speakers make up about 40% of the country's population, while the remaining 60% speak Dutch as a first language. Of the latter over half of them claim to speak French as a second language. In Malta,

17% of the population speak French, a language which originated with the arrival of the **Ordre des Hospitaliers** in 1530. French is the official language in Monaco, 47% of its population being French. French is also the official language along with Italian in the province of Aosta Valley in Italy. While Catalan is the official language in Andorra, French is commonly used because of its proximity to France. French is one of the three official languages in Luxembourg with German and Luxembourgish. In the United Kingdom, French is a large minority language with over 300,000 French-born people in the UK. It is the most popular foreign language taught in schools. French is understood by 23% of the UK population. French is an official language in the Channel Islands. Both use French to some degree, mostly in an administrative or ceremonial capacity.

Americas

In Canada, French is the second most common language after English, and both are official languages at the federal level. French is the sole official language in the province of Quebec, being the mother tongue for some 6 million people. In Haiti, French is an official language, although it is mostly spoken by the upper class, while Haitian Creole (a French-based Creole language) is more widely spoken as a mother tongue. French is also the official language in France's overseas territories of French Guiana, Guadeloupe, Martinique, Saint Barthélemy, Saint Martin and Saint-Pierre and Miquelon. Although it has no official recognition at federal level, French is the third most-spoken language in the United States, after English and Spanish, and the second most-spoken language in the states of Louisiana, Maine, Vermont and New Hampshire. Louisiana is home to many distinct dialects, of which Cajun French has the largest number of speakers.

Africa

According to the 2007 report by the Organisation Internationale de la Francophonie, an estimated 115 million African people spread across 31 francophone African countries can speak French as either a first or a second language. French is an official language in many African countries, most of them consisting of former French or Belgian colonies such as Cameroon, Chad, Congo, Côte d'Ivoire, Djibouti, Gabon, Niger, Senegal. In the Maghreb states of Algeria, Mauritania, Morocco and Tunisia, French is an administrative language and commonly used though not on an official basis. In Egypt, while the predominant European language is English, French is considered by the Egyptian upper-middle classes to be a more sophisticated language. French is also the official language of Mayotte and Réunion, two overseas French territories located in the Indian Ocean, as well as an administrative and educational language in Mauritius, along with English.

Asia

French is the official language in Lebanon, along with Arabic. French is widely used by the Lebanese, especially for administrative purposes, and is taught in many schools as a primary language. In Syria, French is no longer official, but still spoken by educated groups, both elite and middle-class.

Southeast Asia, India and Oceania

French is an administrative language in Laos and Cambodia, although its influence has waned in recent years. In colonial Vietnam, French used to be spoken by the elite and those who worked for the French. The language was also spoken by the elite in the leased territory Guangzhouwan in southern China. In Burma, French is gaining popularity amongst university students and the tourism sector. The Alliance Française has active centres in Rangoon and Mandalay. French has *de jure,* official status in the Indian Union Territory of Puducherry (formerly Pondicherry), along with the regional languages Tamil and Telugu. French is a second official language of the Pacific Island nations of Vanuatu and Wallis and Futuna.

In France's territories of French Polynesia and New Caledonia, 90% of speakers have French as either their native or secondary language.

Regional and minority languages spoken in Metropolitan France

The sole official language of France is French. However, several regional languages (including Alsatian, Basque, Breton, Catalan, Corsican, Flemish, Franco-Provençal dialects, Gascon, Lorraine German dialect, Occitan, and some Oïl dialects – e.g. Picard) are also occasionally understood and spoken, mostly by elderly people, and are the mother tongue of about 15% of the population, but the French government and state school system discouraged the use of any of them until recently. These historical regional languages have been known as **patois**, though this has been considered depreciative. They are now taught at some schools, though French remains the only official language in use by the government, local or national. Some languages spoken by immigrants are also frequently spoken, especially in large cities: Portuguese, Maghreb Arabic, several Berber languages, several languages of Sub-Saharan Africa, Turkish, several spoken variants of Chinese, Vietnamese, and Khmer are the most frequently spoken.

Language differences: French and English

French is an Indo-European language and part of the Romance family, along with Spanish and Italian. The English language was influenced by the introduction of French during of the Norman invasion of Britain in the 11th century. The two languages share many grammatical features and contain many cognates (similar words).

The French alphabet contains the same 26 letters as the English alphabet, plus the letters with diacritics: **é** (acute accent), **è à ù** (grave accent), **ç** (cedilla), **â ê î ô û** (circumflex), **ë ï ü ö** (diaeresis). Learners may find the French accents baffling as they first encounter them, because they tend to change the way the letter is pronounced. French accents are simpler than they first appear and the **Pronunciation guide** at the beginning of the book and on the recording provides clear examples for the learner to repeat. Two letters in the French alphabet are a little confusing: **e** and **g**. If wrongly pronounced to sound like the letters in the English alphabet, they could be mistaken for the French letters **i** and **j**.

There are other differences in the sound systems of the two languages that may impede learners' comprehension and speech production. Usually, however, it is the speed with which the French 'link' their words which makes the comprehension difficult. Moreover, to make the French words run more smoothly, the final consonants of words, which are usually silent, are sounded when the next word starts with a vowel or **h**, e.g. **très_important** (*very important*). This is called a **liaison**. In some cases, liaisons are essential; in other cases they are optional. To help the learners of French recognize when the liaisons are essential they have been indicated with a linking mark (_) in Units 1–10. The French **r** is pronounced differently from the English but this difficulty can quickly be overcome if sounded like the Scottish sound *ch* in *loch*. The French tend to use their facial muscles more than the English and this needs to be done if the French vowels **u i e o** are to be clearly understood. Final consonants in words (**vous, anglais, nuit, dames, messieurs**) tend not to be sounded in French. While this may result in spelling errors when writing in French or mispronunciation in speech production, learners of French will quickly become accustomed to it. Another feature of French is that the **h** is silent. Thus there is no need to pronounce it in words such as **théâtre** or **thé**. The pronunciation of the French nasal sounds **ein in ain on un en** is more of a challenge as it is totally alien to English speakers. To be successful, students of French need to 'feel' the sounds through their nose as they are practised.

English learners typically have problems with the stress pattern of French words. Unlike most English words, it is the last part of the word that bears a heavy stress in French (**res-tau-rant, par-don, im-por-tant**). However, when the word finishes with a consonant followed by **e** (**té-lé-pho-ne, pe-ti-te, o-ran-ge**) the last syllable is unstressed and the penultimate syllable takes the stress.

In grammar, French and English have considerable areas of overlap, particularly with regard to verbs. While only the present (**je parle, tu parles, il parle** etc.) and immediate future tenses (**je vais parler**) are introduced in this book, both languages have auxiliaries, participles, active/passive voice, past/present/future tenses.

In English, the auxiliary *do* used in asking questions is replaced by **est-ce que** in French. Both structures **est-ce que** and **qu'est-ce que** may seem complex to use because of their 'unfriendly' spelling. To make it easier, learners of French need to think of both structures as sounding like **esker** or **kesker**, and remember that while the answer to an **est-ce que** question will start with **oui** or **non**, a **qu'est-ce que** question may have an infinite number of answers.

Although English and French share the same basic Subject-Verb-Object syntax, there are numerous variations in the word order of sentences. Adverbs come after the verbs in French: **je travaille souvent** (*I often work*) and not before as in English. On the contrary most French pronouns come before the verb: **il le lui donne** (*he gives it to her*). It is a little more complicated with adjectives. Short and common adjectives are placed before the nouns: **la grande maison** (*the big house*), **le vieil homme** (*the old man*) whereas long adjectives and those specifying colours and nationalities are placed after the nouns: **il porte un pull vert** (*he is wearing/wears a green jumper*), **il a un père anglais** (*he has an English father*).

A large number of words in the two languages have the same Latin roots and are mutually comprehensible, although this applies more to academic/technical words than to everyday vocabulary. The concomitant problem, however, is the significant number of false friends. Here are just a few examples: **cave** (*cellar*), **isolation** (*insulation*), **demander** (*ask*), **rester** (*stay*), **assister** (*attend*).

Don't let these difficulties deter you from learning French. I will be guiding you through all the essentials of the language, giving you all the tools you need to communicate successfully with French speakers.

About the course

Get started in French is the right course for you if you are a complete beginner or wanting to make a fresh start. It is a self-study course which will help you to understand, read and speak most of the French you will need on holiday or a business trip.

TWO KEY ELEMENTS

The book has two parts. The first ten units introduce you to the basic structures and grammatical points you'll need in everyday situations. Units 1–10 should be taken in order, as each builds on the previous one. Units 11–19 deal with everyday situations such as shopping, eating, booking a room, travelling and give you the opportunity to put into practice the language you've acquired in the first part. These units may be taken in any order.

The course is best used together with the accompanying recording, but is not dependent upon it. You are recommended to obtain and use the recording if possible. The recorded dialogues and audio exercises give you plenty of practice in understanding the basic language; they will help you develop an authentic accent and increase your confidence in saying simple phrases. Readers without the recording will find that some units include one activity that cannot be done with the book alone, but in such cases the material is always adequately covered by the other activities in the unit.

ABOUT UNITS 1–10

The first page of each unit tells you what you are going to learn and there is an easy exercise, *Essayez!* **Have a go!** which gets you speaking straight away.

Key words and phrases contain the most important words and phrases from the unit. Try to learn them by heart. They will be practised in the rest of the unit and the later units.

Dialogue Listen to the dialogue once or twice without stopping or read through it without looking anything up; try to get the gist of it. The notes underneath each dialogue will help you to understand it. Then, using the pause button, break the dialogue into manageable chunks and try repeating each phrase aloud. This will help you acquire a more authentic accent. Words and phrases listed in bold appear in the subsequent vocabulary box.

Insight

These boxes provide you with advice on how make progress and tips on how to maintain your confidence in learning.

Grammar In this section, you may want to start by reading the example(s) then work out the grammatical point, or you may prefer to read the **Grammar** section first and see how the rule applies. Once you feel confident about a particular grammar point, try to create your own examples.

Activities Each activity in this section allows you to practise one of the points introduced in the **Grammar** section. In some activities you will need to listen to the recording. It is not essential to have the recording in order to complete this course, as most of the activities are not dependent on it. However, listening to the recording will make your learning much easier.

Things to remember At the end of Units 1, 2, 4, 5, 8 and 9, you are presented with a list of short questions to help you to remember the most important structures from each unit.

Self-test You can test yourself at the end of Units 3, 7 and 10 and see how well you did in the short self-assessment tasks. A space is provided for you to keep your own score.

ABOUT UNITS 11–19

The first page of each unit tells you what you are going to learn. There is also a checklist of structures which you have already learnt and will be practising in the unit. You'll also find in most units a short text in French about the topic.

Key words and phrases contains the basic vocabulary you'll need when coping, in real life, with practical situations such as checking into a hotel, ordering a snack, asking for a train timetable, going on an excursion.

Dialogues There are several short dialogues, each dealing with a different aspect of the topic. Remember to listen to the dialogues first and use the pause button to practise the new words and phrases out loud.

Insight
The boxes will help you make progress in your language learning through a range of useful tips and advice.

Activities The activities are mostly based on authentic French material. Here you can develop a feel for how things work in France, as well as practising your reading skills. You will then have more confidence to cope with the real situations.

Things to remember At the end of Units 11, 12, 14, 15, 17 and 18, you are presented with a list of short questions to help you to remember the most important structures from each unit.

Self-test You can test yourself at the end of Units 13, 16 and 19 and see how well you did in the short self-assessment tasks. A space is provided for you to keep your own score.

KEY TO THE EXERCISES AND TESTS

The answers to the questions on the **Dialogues** in Units 1–10, **Activities**, *Essayez!* **Have a go!**, *Pratiquez!* **Practise!**, **Things to remember**, **Self-tests** can be found at the back of the book.

BE SUCCESSFUL AT LEARNING LANGUAGES

1 Do a little bit every day, between 20 and 30 minutes if possible, rather than two or three hours in one session.

2 Try to work towards short-term goals, e.g. work out how long you'll spend on a particular unit and work within this time limit.

3 Revise and test yourself regularly using the **Things to remember** or **Self-test sections** at the end of each unit.

4 Make use of the tips given in the book and try to say the words and phrases out loud whenever possible.

5 Use every opportunity to speak the language. Attend some classes to practise your French with other people, get some help from a French speaker or find out about French clubs, societies, etc.

6 Don't worry too much about making mistakes. The important thing is to get your meaning across and remember that making mistakes in French will not stop a French person understanding you. Learning can be fun particularly when you find you can use what you have learnt in real situations.

AT THE BACK OF THE BOOK

At the back of the book is a section which contains:

- ▶ A **Taking it further** section to direct you to further sources of French.
- ▶ **Key to the exercises and tests.**
- ▶ An **Appendix** list of numbers
- ▶ **Rôle-play scripts** for Units 4–10 and **Self-tests.**
- ▶ A **French–English vocabulary** list containing all the words in the course.
- ▶ An **English–French vocabulary** list with the most useful words you'll need when expressing yourself in French.
- ▶ An **Index** to enable you to look things up in the book.

SYMBOLS AND ABBREVIATIONS

◆) This indicates that the recording is needed for the following.

(m)	masculine	(pl)	plural
(f)	feminine	(lit.)	literally
(sing)	singular		

Pronunciation guide

The **Pronunciation guide** is on the recording at the end of Unit 1.

◆) CD1, TR 5

1 HOW TO SOUND FRENCH

Here are a few rules that will help you to sound French right from the beginning:

1 In French, unlike in most English words, it is the last part of the word that bears a heavy stress:

res-tau-**rant**, o-**range**, ca-**fé**, té-lé-**phone**

2 French words that are spelt like English words are almost always pronounced differently:

pardon, important, parking, sandwich, ticket

3 In general, consonants at the end of a word such as **d g p s t x z**, and the letter **h**, are silent.

vous   anglais   nuit   dames   messieurs   hôtel

2 FRENCH SOUNDS

Here is the list of the **French vowels** with a rough English equivalent sound. You'll see that an accent on an **e** or an **o** changes the way the letter is pronounced.

letter	rough English sound	French example
a à	cat	madame
e	1 above	le ne
	2 best (before two consonants or x)	merci
	3 may (before z, r)	parlez
é	may	café
è ê	pair	père fête
i î y	police	merci diner typique
o	dot	olive
u	a sound not found in English – first say **oo**, but then keeping the lips in that position try saying **ee**	une du
ai	as è ê above	lait s'il vous plaît
ô au eau	pronounced as **o** but with rounded lips	hôtel autobus beaucoup
eu œu	sir	leur sœur
oi	the **wa** sound at the beginning of **one**	bonsoir
ou	moo	vous

◀)) **CD1, TR 6**

Many **consonants** are similar to English, with a number of exceptions and variations:

letter	rough English sound	French example
ç	sit	ça français
ch	shop	chic

g	leisure (before **i, e**)	Brigitte
gn	onion	cognac
h	not pronounced	hôtel hôpital
j	leisure	je bonjour
l ll	yes (often when **i** precedes **l, ll**)	fille travail
qu	care	question
r	pronounced at the back of the throat with the tongue touching the bottom teeth	rat Paris
s	desert (between vowels)	mademoiselle
t	(before **ion**) pass	attention
th	tea	thé
w	1 what	whisky
	2 van	wagon-restaurant

Here are the **nasal sounds** formed usually with vowels followed by **m** or **n**. Speak through your nose when you pronounce them and listen carefully to the recording.

ein im in ain	} bang (stop before the g) }	frein important vin train impossible
en an	long (stop before the g)	encore Jean restaurant
on	as above but with lips pushed forward	pardon on non
un um	similar to **ein im in ain**	parfum un

◄» **CD1, TR 6, 01:55**

3 HOW TO LINK THE SOUNDS TOGETHER

To make the words run more smoothly, the final consonants of words which are usually silent are sounded when the next word starts with a vowel or **h**, e.g. **très_important** (trayzimportan). This is called a liaison. In some cases, as above, liaisons are essential; in other cases they are optional. To help you recognize when the liaisons are essential they'll be indicated with a linking mark (_) in Units 1–10.

When making liaisons, all French people:

1 pronounce **s** and **x** like **z**: les_oranges   deux_heures

2 pronounce **d** and **t** like **t**, but the **t** of **et** (*and*) is never sounded: le grand_homme   c'est_ici   un café et une bière

3 link **n** in the nasal **un** when the next words starts with a vowel or a silent **h**: un_enfant   un_hôtel

4 A FEW TIPS TO HELP YOU ACQUIRE AN AUTHENTIC ACCENT

It is not absolutely vital to acquire a perfect accent. The aim is to be understood. Here are a number of techniques for working on your pronunciation:

1 Listen carefully to the recording or a native speaker or a teacher. Whenever possible repeat aloud, imagining you are a native speaker of French.

2 Record yourself and compare your pronunciation with that of a native speaker.

3 Ask native speakers to listen to your pronunciation and tell you how to improve it.

4 Ask native speakers how a specific sound is formed. Watch them and practise at home in front of a mirror.

5 Make a list of words that give you pronunciation trouble and practise them.

6 Study the sounds on their own then use them progressively in words, sentences and tongue-twisters.

Try this one! **Panier-piano, panier-piano, panier-piano** (**panier** is a basket in French).

5 AND NOW PRACTISE …

Starting with **Paris** on the following map, go round anti-clockwise saying each of the 14 towns out loud. Pause after each town and check your pronunciation with the recording.

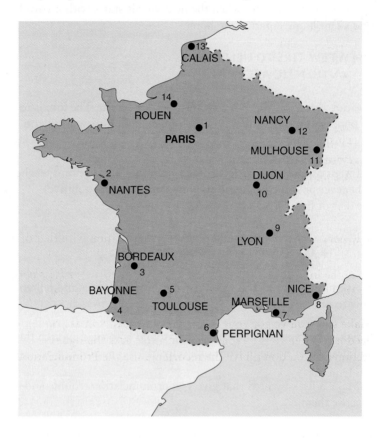

1

Bonjour
Hello

In this unit you will learn how to
- *Say 'hello' and 'goodbye'*
- *Exchange greetings*
- *Observe basic courtesies*
- *Ask people to speak more slowly*

Before you start

Read the **Introduction** to the course. This gives some useful advice on studying alone and how to make the most of the course.

Make sure you've got your recording ◀» next to you as you'll need it to listen to the **Pronunciation guide** and **Dialogues** sections. If you don't have the recording, use the **Pronunciation guide** in the book.

Study tips

Remember that studying for 20 minutes regularly is better than occasionally spending two hours in one go.

1 Listen to the **Dialogues** once or twice without the book (read them if you haven't got the recording).

2 Go over each one, bit by bit, in conjunction with the **Key words and phrases** and notes underneath the dialogues.

3 Read the **Grammar** section very carefully and study it.

4 Read the tips on **How to learn vocabulary** and **How to pronounce.**

5 Go back to the **Dialogues** and **Key words and phrases** for more listening and studying, this time using the pause button and repeating aloud after the recording.

6 Do the **Activities** including **Things to remember**, check your answers in the **Key to the exercises and tests** and test yourself with the **Self-tests.**

Essayez! **Have a go!** Can you think of any French words you know such as the words for 'hello' and 'thank you'? Say them out loud, and then look at the **Key words and phrases** to check the answers.

Key words and phrases

bonjour	*good morning/afternoon, hello*
bonsoir	*good evening* (after 5.00 p.m.)
bonne nuit	*good night* (when going to bed)
au revoir	*goodbye*
bonjour, Madame	*good morning (Madam)*

bonjour, Mademoiselle	*good morning (Miss)*
bonsoir, Monsieur	*good evening (Sir)*
au revoir, Messieurs-dames	*goodbye ladies and gentlemen*
oui	*yes*
non, merci	*no, thank you*
merci	*thank you*
merci beaucoup	*thank you very much*
s'il vous plait	*please*
d'accord	*OK*
pardon	*sorry* (to apologize), *excuse me*
comment ça va? ça va (informal)	*how are things? fine*
(très) bien merci	*(very) well thank you*
comment vas-tu?	*how are you?*
comment_allez-vous? (formal)	*how are you?*
je vais bien et toi?	*I am well – how about you?*
et vous? (formal)	*and you?*
vous parlez_anglais?	*do you speak English?*
parlez plus lentement	*speak more slowly*

Insight

When you see a linking mark '_' between two words, sound the last letter of the first word as though it were attached to the next word: **vous parlez_anglais?**

Dialogues

Listen to the recording and hear people practising saying 'hello' and greeting each other in French.

Press the pause button after each sentence and repeat aloud.

Insight

Pay particular attention to the way the 's' in **Messieurs** and **Monsieur** is pronounced. It should sound as in *pass* and not as in *shop*.

DIALOGUE 1 SAYING 'HELLO'

CD1, TR 2

Jane	Bonjour, Messieurs-dames.
Michel	Bonjour, Mademoiselle.
Jane	Bonjour, Monsieur.
Roger	Bonsoir, Madame.
Nathalie	Bonsoir, Monsieur.
Roger	Comment ça va, Jane?
Jane	Très bien, et toi?
Roger	**Moi aussi**, ça va bien.
Rosine	Comment vas-tu?
Jane	Je vais très bien Rosine, et toi?
Mme Dubois	Comment_allez-vous, Monsieur Dubosse?
M. Dubosse	Très bien merci, et vous?
Mme Dubois	Très bien.

DIALOGUE 2 SAYING 'GOODBYE'

CD1, TR 3

Michel	Au revoir, Madame et … merci beaucoup.
Nathalie	Au revoir, Monsieur.

DIALOGUE 3 WHEN THINGS GET DIFFICULT …

CD1, TR 4

Jane	Pardon, Monsieur, vous parlez_anglais?
Garçon	Ah, non, **je regrette** …
Garçon	Bonjour, Madame. **Qu'est-ce que vous désirez?**
Nathalie	Parlez plus lentement, s'il vous plaît.
Garçon	D'accord … Qu'est-ce que vous désirez?

moi *me, I*
aussi *also, too*
garçon *waiter*
je regrette *I'm sorry*
Qu'est-ce que vous désirez? (lit.) *What do you wish?* but used in shops it means *Can I help you?*

HOW TO PRONOUNCE ...

▶ As a general rule don't pronounce **d g p s t x z** at the end of a word, e.g. beaucoup vous nuit plaît.
▶ The letter **e** often gets swallowed as in **mad'moiselle**.
▶ The stress, in French, is on the last part of the word: par-**don** mer-**ci** mad'-moi-**selle** mon-**sieur**.
▶ **ç** placed before **o, u, a** is pronounced **s** as in *sit*: garçon, ça va?
▶ The s in **monsieur** is pronounced as **ss** in *pass*.

Grammar

1 SIMPLE QUESTIONS

The simplest way of asking something in French is to raise your voice on the last syllable (part of a word):

Vous parlez_an**glais**?   **Par**don?   Ça **va**?

Now practise saying par**don**? (to have something repeated) and

pardon (to apologize or attract someone's attention).

2 REFUSING POLITELY IN FRENCH

If you want to refuse something in France, you can say **non merci** or **merci** on its own.

3 CALLING THE WAITER'S ATTENTION

Although **garçon** is the word for waiter, today you would usually say **Monsieur** to attract his attention. For a waitress, you say **Madame** or **Mademoiselle** as you think fit or just look expectant and say **s'il vous plaît**.

> **Insight**
>
> Don't forget to shorten **Mademoiselle** to **Mad'moiselle** to make it sound more French!

4 HOW TO BE COURTEOUS

In France when you're talking to someone you don't know very well, it's polite to add **Monsieur, Madame, Mademoiselle** particularly after short phrases like **oui, non, bonjour** or **merci**.

The French shake hands with good friends and acquaintances every time they meet or say goodbye. Kissing (on both cheeks) is reserved for family and close friends.

5 WHEN TO USE **TU** (YOU) AND WHEN TO USE **VOUS** (YOU)

The equivalent of *you* in French can be either **tu** or **vous**. French people use **tu** when speaking to children, teenagers, relations and close friends. They use **vous** in work and business situations or when speaking to senior or old people: **vous** is also used to address a group of people to whom one might say **tu** individually. The best advice is to say **vous** until you are addressed as **tu** or asked to use the **tu** form: **on se tutoie?** *shall we call each other* **tu?**

HOW TO LEARN VOCABULARY

There are several ways of learning vocabulary. Find the way that works best for you; here are a few suggestions:

- ▶ Say the words out loud as you read them.
- ▶ Write the words over and over again.
- ▶ Listen to the recording several times.
- ▶ Study the list from beginning to end then backwards.
- ▶ Associate the French words with similar sounding words in English, e.g. **parlez** with *parlour*, a room where people chat.
- ▶ Associate the words with pictures or situations, e.g. **bonjour, bonsoir** with shaking hands.

- ▶ Use coloured pencils to underline/group the words in a way that will help you to remember them.
- ▶ Copy the words on to small cards or slips of paper, English on one side, French on the other. Study them in varying order giving the French word if the card comes out with the English on top, or vice versa.

Activities

1 How would you say *hello* or *good night* in the following situations? Remember to add **Monsieur, Madame, Mademoiselle**. Write your answer underneath each picture.

a. _____ b. _____ c. _____

d. _____ e. _____ f. _____

2 You're arriving late at a hotel one evening; greet the person behind the reception desk by choosing the right phrase in the box below.

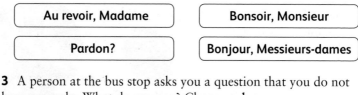

| Au revoir, Madame | Bonsoir, Monsieur |
| Pardon? | Bonjour, Messieurs-dames |

3 A person at the bus stop asks you a question that you do not hear properly. What do you say? Choose **a**, **b** or **c**.

a s'il vous plaît   **c** pardon?
b non merci

4 You are staying the night with some friends. It's late and you decide to go to bed. You say:

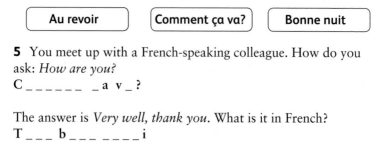

| Au revoir | Comment ça va? | Bonne nuit |

5 You meet up with a French-speaking colleague. How do you ask: *How are you?*

C _ _ _ _ _ _ _ a v _ ?

The answer is *Very well, thank you.* What is it in French?

T _ _ _ b _ _ _ _ _ _ _ i

6 Use the clues to complete the grid. When you've finished, the vertical word will be what you say if you step on someone's foot!

a The French translation for *please*
b Your answer to a friend who asks how you are
c *Goodbye*
d Calling the waitress' attention
e Greeting someone after 5 p.m.
f Refusing politely

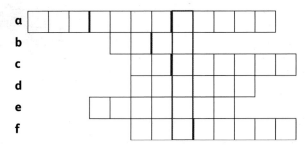

7 Choose the appropriate word or group of words.

a How would you greet several people?
  i Bonjour Madame
  ii Au revoir
  iii Bonjour Messieurs-dames

b How would you refuse politely?
  i D'accord
  ii Non merci
  iii Pardon

c To ask someone if s/he speaks English you say:
  i Parlez plus lentement
  ii Au revoir Messieurs-dames
  iii Vous parlez_anglais?

d To wish someone good night you say:
  i Bonjour
  ii Bonsoir
  iii Bonne nuit

Remember to check your answers at the end of the book. If you have a number of wrong answers look back at the tips for learning vocabulary.

THINGS TO REMEMBER

You've arrived at the end of Unit 1. Now you know how to say 'thank you' and exchange greetings and you've also learnt a little about French sounds. Do you remember how to say the following in French?

1 Good morning (Madam).

2 How are things? Fine.

3 Do you speak English?

4 Speak more slowly.

5 How would you ask to have something repeated?

You'll find the answers to **Things to remember** in the **Key to the exercises and tests** at the end of the book. If they are correct you are ready to move to Unit 2. If you found the test difficult, spend more time revising Unit 1.

2

....

C'est combien?
How much is it?

In this unit you will learn how to
- *Count up to ten*
- *Ask for something*
- *Say how much you want*
- *Ask the price*

_____

Before you start

In this unit we will show you that it is nearly always possible to ask for what you want with just two words, **je voudrais** (*I would like*) and **s'il vous plaît** at the end.

The dialogue is short but there are a lot of new words including useful things you may need in France. Try to learn the words by heart using one of the techniques described in Unit 1 in the section **How to learn vocabulary.**

Essayez! **Have a go!** You are in a **pâtisserie** (*cake shop*) in France to buy a **baguette** (*French stick*). How would you greet the woman behind the counter? How would you ask for a French stick?

Key words and phrases

For you to say	
un café	*a coffee/a café*
un thé	*a tea*
un coca-cola	*a coca-cola*
un_euro	*a euro*
un journal	*a newspaper*
un plan	*a map, plan*
une baguette	*a French stick*
une bière	*a beer*
une chambre	*a room*
une pharmacie	*a chemist's*
une station-service	*a petrol station*
le timbre	*the stamp*
la carte postale	*the postcard*
la gare	*the station*
l'hôtel (m)	*the hotel*
l'hôpital (m)	*the hospital*
l'eau minérale (f)	*the mineral/bottled natural water*
gazeuse/plate	*sparkling/still*
l'addition (f)	*the bill*
les toilettes	*the toilets*
je voudrais	*I would like*
vous_avez …?	*do you have …?*
ça	*this/that*
du pain	*some bread*
du vin	*some wine*
de la limonade	*some lemonade*
de l'aspirine (f)	*some aspirins*
des sandwiches	*some sandwiches*
c'est combien?	*how much is it? (lit. it is how much?)*
un kilo	*one kilo*
un demi-kilo	*half a kilo*
un paquet	*one pack*
une bouteille	*one bottle*
une boîte	*one tin, box*

For you to understand	
fermé	*shut*
je n'en_ai pas	*I haven't got any*
avec ça?	*will that be all?* (lit. *with that?*)
c'est tout?	*is that all?*

NUMBERS 1–10

1	**un**	6	**six**
2	**deux**	7	**sept** (the **p** is not pronounced)
3	**trois**	8	**huit**
4	**quatre**	9	**neuf**
5	**cinq**	10	**dix**

Dialogue

Jane is in **une alimentation** *(grocer's shop). What does she want to buy? Does she get what she wants? Listen to the recording first, answer the questions, then check your answers.*

Jane	Vous_avez de la bière?
Vendeuse	Ah non, je regrette, je n'en_ai pas.
Jane	Et du vin?
Vendeuse	Euh oui. **Quel vin** désirez-vous?
Jane	Je voudrais une bouteille de Muscadet.
Vendeuse	Oui, **voilà** … et avec ça?
Jane	Deux bouteilles d'eau minérale.
Vendeuse	De la gazeuse ou de la plate?
Jane	De la plate.
Vendeuse	Bon, très bien. C'est tout?
Jane	Oui, merci. C'est combien?
Vendeuse	Pour le Muscadet, c'est **6€50** et pour l'eau minérale, **1€30** la bouteille.

la vendeuse *the shop assistant* (female)
quel vin? *which wine?*
voilà *there you are*
six_euros cinquante *six euros fifty*
un_euro trente *one euro thirty*

HOW TO PRONOUNCE ... **SIX ET DIX**

▶ When **six** and **dix** are on their own as numbers the **x** is pronounced as **s** and they rhyme with 'peace': **vous_avez des timbres? Oui, six.**

▶ When followed by a word starting with a consonant the **x** is not pronounced and they sound like 'dee' and 'see': **dix kilos, six bières.**

▶ When followed by a word starting with a vowel or **h** pronounce the **x** and **s** as **z**: **six_euros, dix_hôtels.**

Grammar

1 *WORDS FOR 'A', 'AN':* **UN, UNE**

The word *a* or *an* is **un** in front of a masculine noun and **une** in front of a feminine noun. All French nouns belong to one of the two groups: masculine or feminine. Sometimes it is obvious as in **un Français** *a Frenchman*, **une Française** *a Frenchwoman* while at other times it is not obvious as in **un café** but **une bière**.

There is no rule to tell you to which group a noun belongs, although the ending of a noun often acts as a guide. For example:

▶ words ending in **-age**, **-ment** are often masculine, as in **le village**, **le moment**.

▶ words ending in **-lle**, **-tte**, **-ion**, **-ée** are often feminine as in **une bouteille, une cigarette, une alimentation, une année.**

2 *WORDS FOR 'THE'*: **LE, LA, L', LES**

There are four different ways of saying *the*:

le with masculine nouns	**le** timbre
la with feminine nouns	**la** gare
l' with nouns starting with a	**l'**hôtel (m)
vowel or an **h**	**l'**eau (f)
les with plural nouns	**les** toilettes

Insight

Plural nouns usually take an **s** at the end. Make a habit of learning words together with **le** or **la** before them. If they start with a vowel or **h**, they are followed by (m) or (f) in **Key words and phrases** to indicate whether they are masculine or feminine.

---

3 VOUS AVEZ ...? *DO YOU HAVE ...?*

To check if they have what you want, start your request with **vous avez** (*do you have*). To indicate that it is a question raise the voice on the last syllable of the sentence:

Vous_avez un plan?   *Do you have a street map?*

4 WORDS FOR 'SOME', 'ANY': *DU, DE LA, DE L', DES*

When **de** (*of*) is used in combination with **le, la, l', les** it changes its form and can mean *some* or *any* according to the context:

de + le becomes **du**	**de l'** remains unchanged
de la remains unchanged	**de + les** becomes **des**

Compare the examples below:

Je voudrais **du** vin.	*I would like **some** wine.*
Je voudrais **le** vin.	*I would like **the** wine.*
Vous_avez **de la** bière?	*Do you have **any** beer?*

Vous_avez **la** bière?	*Do you have **the** beer?*
Vous_avez **de** l'eau minérale?	*Have you **any** mineral water?*
Vous_avez **l'**eau minérale?	*Do you have **the** mineral water?*
Je voudrais **des** timbres.	*I would like **some** stamps.*
Je voudrais **les** timbres.	*I would like **the** stamps.*

Insight

In English we often omit the word *some*. In French, **de** + the definite article (**le, la, l'** or **les**) is almost always used.

5 UN KILO DE *A KILO/ONE KILO OF*

To ask for one of something use **un** with masculine nouns and **une** with feminine nouns:

un kilo de sucre	*one kilo of sugar or a kilo of sugar*
une boîte de sardines	*one tin of sardines or a tin of sardines*

6 C'EST COMBIEN? *HOW MUCH IS IT?*

You need only two words to ask for the price: **C'est combien?** *How much is it?* (lit. *it is how much*) followed by whatever you want to know the price of:

C'est combien la carte postale?	*How much is the postcard?*
C'est combien la baguette?	*How much is the French stick?*

Insight

You will come across **C'est** a lot more in the next few units. It is a useful word which can mean any of the following: *he is, she is, it is.*

HOW TO ORGANIZE YOUR LEARNING

It may help you to remember the new vocabulary, pronunciation and grammar rules that you learn in the book if you create your own system to organize this information, perhaps using one or more of the following ideas.

- ▸ You could group new words under:
  - **a** generic categories, e.g. *food*, *furniture*.
  - **b** situations in which they occur, e.g. under *restaurant* you can put *waiter*, *table*, *menu*, *bill*.
  - **c** functions: greetings, parting, thanks, apologizing, etc.
- ▸ When organizing the study of pronunciation you could keep a section of your notebook for pronunciation rules and practise those that trouble you.
- ▸ To organize your study of grammar you may like to write your own grammar glossary and add new information as you go along.

Activities

1 Look at the objects below, and write their names in French preceded by **un**, **une** or **des**.

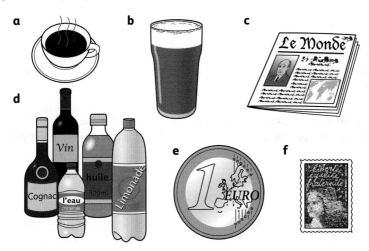

2 You've arrived at a French hotel; you would like three things. What are they? You will find them hidden in the string of letters below:

> **motunechambrepozowiuncafémoghttunjournaldfc**

3 Before you leave the hotel you want to buy a few things: how would you ask for them in French?

    a I would like four cards, please.

    ....

    b Do you have four stamps for England?

    .... **pour l'Angleterre?**

    c And some aspirin, please.

    et ....

    d How much is it?

    ....

4 All the numbers 'one' to 'ten' are listed in this wordsearch except for one. Which is missing? Read horizontally or vertically, either forwards or backwards.

E	Y	Q	N	I	C
R	S	E	P	T	R
T	M	I	D	I	X
A	O	N	E	U	F
U	L	U	U	H	I
Q	S	H	X	I	S

5 Match the words in the left-hand column with the ones in the right.

    a deux bouteilles   **i** chewing gum

    b un kilo   de   **ii** sardines

    c une boîte   **iii** vin

    d un paquet   **iv** sucre

6 Michel, sitting at a café, is ordering some drinks with his friends. He then asks for the bill. Using the words in the box, complete the script then check your version with the recording and/or the **Key to the exercises and tests.**

a Garçon	Bonjour	café
b Michel	Je voudrais_un ....et vous, Marie?	voudrais
c Marie	Moi, une.........................	addition
d Sylvie	Je .... une limonade.	Messieurs-dames
e Michel	Et je voudrais_aussi l' ....s'il vous plaît.	bière

◀) **CD1, TR 10**

7 As numbers are very important, here's another chance to practise them. Write your answers to the following sums (in words, not figures).

a deux + trois =
b cinq + quatre =
c neuf + un =
d six + trois =
e dix − huit =
f sept − trois =
g trois × trois =
h quatre × deux =

Check your answers by listening to the recording, Activity 7.
If you do not have the recording, check them in the the **Key to the exercises and tests**.

THINGS TO REMEMBER

You've arrived at the end of Unit 2. Now you know how to ask for something, say how much you want and ask the price. Do you remember how you say the following in French?

1 I would like ....

2 some bread

3 some water

4 some lemonade

5 some stamps

6 Do you have...?

7 a newspaper

8 one pack of coffee

9 How much is it?

10 It is six euros.

You'll find the answers to **Things to remember** in the **Key to the exercises and tests** at the end of the book. If they are correct you are ready to move to Unit 3. If you found the test difficult, spend more time revising Unit 2.

3

Je m'appelle ... et vous?

My name is ... what's yours?

In this unit you will learn how to
- *Count up to 20*
- *Talk about yourself and your family*
- *Say that things are not so*
- *Say how old you are*

Before you start

Speaking about yourself and your family in French is fairly easy once you know the vocabulary to describe your home and family and you know how to say what you do or don't have (**j'ai, je n'ai pas**) and what you are or aren't (**je suis, je ne suis pas**).

As we said in the introduction, to be successful at learning languages try to work towards short-term goals. In this unit concentrate on mastering **avoir** and **être**, the two most useful verbs in French. Keep practising them out loud: in the car, the bus, the bath. Aim at saying them without thinking.

Essayez! **Have a go!** You've just arrived in France. You stop at **une alimentation** to buy something to drink. How would you ask for two bottles of beer and one kilo of oranges? **Je ...**

Key words and phrases

quel est votre nom?	*what is your name?*
je m'appelle ... et toi/vous	*my name is ... what's yours? (formal)?*
tu es français?	*are you French? (to a man)*
vous_êtes française?	*(to a woman, formal)*
je suis_anglais/anglaise	*I'm English (a man/a woman)*
tu es marié?	*are you married? (to a man)*
vous_êtes mariée?	*(to a woman, formal)*
non, je ne suis pas marié	*no, I am not married*
je suis divorcé/e	*I am divorced (man/woman)*
Jane a un copain/petit_ami	*Jane has a boyfriend*
il a une copine/petite_amie	*he has a girlfriend*
vous_avez des_enfants?	*do you have any children?*
oui, deux filles et un garçon	*yes, two girls (or daughters) and a boy*
ils_ont dix et six ans	*they are ten and six years old*
non, je n'ai pas d'enfants	*no, I have no children*
la fille/le fils	*daughter/son*
la sœur/le frère	*sister/brother*
le père/la mère	*father/mother*
les parents/les grands-parents	*parents/grandparents*
le grand-père/la grand-mère	*grandfather/grandmother*
j'habite en_Angleterre	*I live/I'm living in England*
avec ma famille	*with my family*
je travaille à New York	*I work in New York*
je viens/suis de Vancouver	*I am/come from Vancouver*
elle est secrétaire/comptable	*she is a secretary/an accountant*
elle travaille dans une banque	*she works in a bank*
il travaille pour IBM	*he works for IBM*
à mi-temps/à temps plein	*part-time/full-time*

Insight

In English *a* is used before a profession. In French it is always omitted:

Elle est professeure. *She is a teacher.*

Some professions are still used in their masculine form in French. Thus you will often encounter the following: **Elle est professeur.**

◀) CD1, TR 11

NUMBERS 11–20

11	onze	16	seize
12	douze	17	dix-sept
13	treize	18	dix-huit
14	quatorze	19	dix-neuf
15	quinze	20	vingt (pronounced as French **vin**)

Dialogue

Jane is sitting on the terrace of a café reading an English magazine. A Frenchwoman has struck up a conversation with her. Listen to the recording or read the dialogue below. Does the Frenchwoman work? Has she got any children? Is Jane married?

CD1, TR 12

Frenchwoman	Vous_êtes_anglaise?
Jane	Je suis_anglaise et **irlandaise**. J'ai un père anglais et une mère irlandaise.
Frenchwoman	Ah c'est bien. Et vous_habitez Londres?
Jane	Non. Je suis de Londres mais j'habite Brighton.
Frenchwoman	C'est où ça, Brighton?
Jane	Dans le sud de l'Angleterre. Et vous, vous_êtes française?

(Contd)

Frenchwoman	Oui, je suis de Lille dans le nord de la France, mais j'habite Paris avec ma famille.
Jane	Vous_êtes mariée?
Frenchwoman	Divorcée, mais **je vis**_avec un copain **depuis cinq ans**.
Jane	Et vous_avez des_enfants?
Frenchwoman	Oui, j'ai trois_enfants, une fille et deux garçons.
Jane	Ils_ont quel âge?
Frenchwoman	La fille a dix_ans et les garçons ont huit_ans et six_ans.
Jane	Ah, très bien.
Frenchwoman	Et vous, vous_êtes mariée?
Jane	Non, je ne suis pas mariée, mais moi **aussi** j'ai un petit_ami.
Frenchwoman	Il est_anglais?
Jane	Non, il est_américain. Il travaille pour IBM en Angleterre.
Frenchwoman	Ah c'est bien. Et vous, vous travaillez?
Jane	Oui, je suis dentiste.
Frenchwoman	Moi aussi, je travaille à mi-temps dans_**une agence de voyages**.
Jane	C'est bien votre travail?
Frenchwoman	Oui, très. Je parle beaucoup anglais avec les touristes. Mais vous, vous parlez très bien français.
Jane	Non, **seulement un petit peu** …

QUICK VOCAB

irlandais/e *Irish*
je vis … depuis cinq ans *I have been living … for five years*
aussi *also*
une agence de voyages *a travel agency*
seulement un petit peu *only a little*

HOW TO PRONOUNCE …

▶ **nom** (*name*) is pronounced like **non** (*no*).
▶ **fille** is pronounced 'fee-ye' and **fils** is pronounced 'fee-sse'.

▶ To pronounce **secrétaire** French people will tend to pinch their lips for **se**, open the mouth up for **cré** and relax the mouth for **taire**. If you haven't got the recording check with the **Pronunciation guide**.

Look at the **Key words and phrases** section and try to practise linking the words with a linking mark, e.g. **vous_êtes** (pronounce 'vou zêtes').

Insight

Some liaisons are essential, others are optional. For example, in the question **Vous_avez des_enfants?** both liaisons are essential. In **Vous_êtes_anglais** you need to link **Vous_êtes** but you can say either **êtes_anglais** or **êtes anglais**. Today the French tend to drop their liaisons.

Grammar

1 *REGULAR VERBS ENDING IN* **-ER**, *E.G.* **PARLER**, *TO SPEAK*

In English *to speak* is the infinitive of the verb (this is the form of the verbs you find in the dictionary). In French the equivalent infinitive is **parler**. It follows the same pattern as many other verbs with infinitives ending in -er. Here is the present tense of **parler**:

parler *to speak*

je	parl**e**	*I speak, I'm speaking*
tu	parl**es**	*you speak, you're speaking*
il/elle/on	parl**e**	*he/she/one speaks, is speaking*
nous	parl**ons**	*we speak, we're speaking*
vous	parl**ez**	*you speak, you're speaking*
ils/elles	parl**ent**	*they speak, they're speaking*

▶ The present tense in French makes no distinction between *I speak* and *I'm speaking*.

- Before a vowel or **h**, **je** becomes **j'**: **j'habite** *I live.*
- **On** is commonly used in French when people talk about themselves. In a general sense it is the equivalent of *one, you, we.*
- **Ils** is used when the group of people is mixed or all males.
- **Elles** is for an all-female group.
- Pronunciation: the **je tu il elle on ils elles** forms of the present tense of any regular **-er** verb sound the same. Do not pronounce the 3rd person plural ending **-ent**. If you do, people may not understand you.

Pratiquez! **Practise!** Can you work out the present tense of **travailler?** Write it down and read it aloud. Remember the pronunciation tips above.

2 TWO IMPORTANT VERBS: **AVOIR** TO HAVE; **ÊTRE** TO BE

Avoir and **être** are irregular, i.e. they do not follow the normal pattern. They are the two most common verbs in French and need to be learnt individually:

avoir *to have*		**être** *to be*	
j'ai	*I have*	**je suis**	*I am*
tu as	*you have*	**tu es**	*you are*
il/elle/on_a	*he/she/ one has*	**il/elle/on_est**	*he/she/ one is*
nous_avons	*we have*	**nous sommes**	*we are*
vous_avez	*you are*	**vous_êtes**	*you are*
ils/elles_ont	*they have*	**ils/elles sont**	*they are*

Pratiquez! **Practise!** Practise the verbs **avoir** and **être** in sentences using some of the key words you already know. Remember that for a question, you need to raise the voice on the last syllable. For example:

J'**ai** un_enfant.

Je **suis** marié.

Tu **as** des_enfants?

Tu **es**_anglaise?

Il **a** trois frères.

Elle **est** professeure.

Nous_**avons** ...

3 *THE NEGATIVE FORM:* **NE … PAS**

To say something is not so in French, you put **ne … pas** round the verb.

Je ne comprends **pas.** *I don't understand.*

Ne becomes **n'** if the following verb starts with a vowel or **h.**

Je **n'**habite **pas** Paris.　　*I don't live in Paris.*

After a negative form, **du, de la …** becomes **de:**

Je **n'**ai **pas de** vin.　　*I don't have any wine.*

but

J'ai **du** vin.　　*I have some wine.*

Insight

Today **ne** is often omitted in French conversations: **Je parle pas anglais.**

4 ADJECTIVES: HOW THEY AGREE

To describe things in detail or talk about yourself you need to add descriptive words (called adjectives) to nouns; an adjective describing a masculine noun has a masculine form, and one describing a feminine noun has a feminine form. As a general rule, feminine adjectives end in -e and the plural adjectives take an -s, but it is not pronounced:

J'ai un_ami américain.	*I have an American friend.*
J'ai un**e** amie améric**ain**e.	*I have an American friend.*
Me**s**_ami**s** sont_ américain**s**.	*My friends are American.*

5 CAPITAL LETTERS

In French, adjectives of nationality and names of languages are not written with a capital letter (unless they start a sentence):

Vous parlez **f**rançais?	*Do you speak French?*
Je suis **c**anadien.	*I am Canadian.*
but: un(e) **A**nglais(e)	*an Englishman/woman*
un(e) **A**méricain(e)	*an American*
un(e) **Français(e)**	*a Frenchman/woman*

6 QUEL EST VOTRE NOM? *WHAT'S YOUR NAME?*

Quel, meaning *what* or *which*, is a useful word to remember; it is always pronounced 'kel' but it is spelt differently to agree with the noun to which it refers:

Quel est votre nom**?**	*What's your name?*

Nom is a masculine noun.

Que**lle** est votre ***adresse?***	*What's your address?*

Adresse is a feminine noun.

Que**ls vins?**	*Which wines?*

Vins is a masculine plural noun.

Que**lles bouteilles***?*	*Which bottles?*

Bouteilles is a feminine plural noun.

7 SAYING HOW OLD YOU ARE

Start with **j'ai** (not **je suis**), add your age followed by **ans** (*years*):

Vous_avez quel âge?	*How old are you?*
J'ai dix-sept ans.	*I am 17.*

BE ACTIVE IN YOUR LEARNING

As all language teachers will assure you, the successful learners are those students who overcome their inhibitions and get into situations where they must speak, write and listen to the foreign language. Here are some useful tips to help you practise French:

Rehearse in the foreign language.

▸ Hold a conversation with yourself, using the dialogues of the units as models and the structures you have learnt previously.
▸ After you have conducted a transaction with a salesperson, clerk or waiter in your own language, pretend that you have to do it in French, e.g. buying petrol, groceries, ordering food, drinks and so on.
▸ Look at objects around you and try to name them in French.
▸ Look at people around you and try to describe them in detail.

Activities

◂) **CD1, TR 13**

1 On the recording, you will hear some numbers between 1 and 20. Repeat and write them down in figures.

a _____
b _____
c _____
d _____
e _____
f _____
g _____
h _____
i _____
j _____

2 This time practise these sums aloud and write the answers in words. (+ is **plus** in French and – is **moins**)

 a 10 + 3 =
 b 7 + 8 =
 c 15 + 5 =
 d 4 + 9 =
 e 13 + 6 =
 f 19 – 8 =
 g 11 – 6 =
 h 16 – 10 =
 i 12 – 8 =
 j 15 – 3 =

3 Look at the family tree below and fill in the sentences:

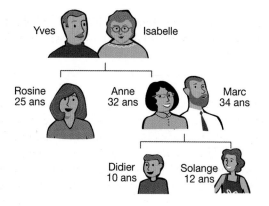

Yves   Isabelle

Rosine
25 ans

Anne
32 ans

Marc
34 ans

Didier
10 ans

Solange
12 ans

 a Isabelle .... mariée avec Yves.
 b Ils .... deux filles.
 c .... s'appellent Rosine et Anne.
 d Anne et Marc ont deux ...., une fille et .... fils.
 e Rosine .... d'enfants.
 f Elle .... mariée.
 g Didier a .... ans.
 h Solange .... douze ....

4 You are being very negative and answer **non ...** to all the following questions using **ne ... pas:**

   a Vous_avez des timbres? Non, je...
   b Elle a du café? Non, elle...
   c Il est marié? Non, il...
   d Elle est secrétaire? Non, elle..
   e Vous_avez une chambre? Non, je..................................
   f Ils_ont quatre enfants? Non, ils....................................
   g Brighton est dans le nord de l'Angleterre?
     Non, Brighton..
   h Vous parlez français? Non, je.......................................
   i Il a 18 ans? Non, il..

◀) CD1, TR 14

5 As you listen to (or read if you haven't got the recording) the passage on **la famille Guise,** look back at the family tree in Activity 3 to help you understand it better.

La famille Guise
Monsieur et Madame Guise sont français. Ils_habitent Chaville, 15 rue de la Gare et ils travaillent à Paris. Yves est comptable et Isabelle travaille dans la publicité. Monsieur et Madame Guise ne parlent pas anglais. Ils_ont deux filles: Rosine qui a vingt-cinq ans et Anne qui a trente-deux ans. Rosine travaille dans_une banque, elle est divorcée. Anne est secrétaire et travaille à mi-temps. Elle est mariée avec Marc qui est professeur de math dans_une école. Ils_ont deux_enfants: une fille, Solange et un fils, Didier. Solange a douze_ans, Didier a dix_ans. Anne et Marc parlent anglais tous les deux.

Rôle-play
Now imagine you're Anne and that you've been asked to take part in a survey. What would you reply to the interviewer?

   a Comment vous_appelez-vous?
   b Vous_êtes célibataire?
   c Vous_avez des_enfants?

d Des filles ou des garçons?
e Ils_ont quel âge?
f Où habitez-vous?
g Vous travaillez?

Merci beaucoup, Madame.

6 This time you are the interviewer, questioning a man. Here are his replies. What were your questions?

a .... Non, je suis divorcé.
b .... Non, je n'ai pas d'enfants.
c .... Oui, je suis professeur.
d .... Oui, j'habite Paris.
e .... Oui, j'ai deux frères et une sœur.
f .... Ils_ont 20 ans, 17 ans et 12 ans.
g .... Non, je suis canadien.
h .... Oui, je parle anglais.

> ## Insight
>
> Spend extra time on activities 3–6 because they are a little
> more challenging as they require you to use different verbs.
> The pronunciation is also a little tricky: **ai**, **es**, **est** (**j'ai**, **tu es**,
> **il est**) are pronounced as in *may*, but **as** and **a** (**tu as**, **il a**) are
> pronounced as in *apple*.

Before going on to Unit 4 take the **Self-test 1** (Units 1–3). Check
your answers in **Key to the exercises and tests** and the **Rôle-play
scripts**, and write your score in the box provided.

SELF-TEST 1

UNITS 1–3   POINTS: /50

This **Self-test** covers a series of short self-assessment tasks which use the main vocabulary and phrases, skills and language points in Units 1–3. When the questions require individual responses, we usually give you model answers to guide you. We indicate the number of points allocated to each answer, so that you can keep your own score (out of a total of 50 points per test).

1 Can you do the following? Say the answers out loud and write them down. Two points for each correct answer. Check your pronunciation with the **Pronunciation guide**.

   a Introduce yourself and ask someone to introduce themselves.

   b Ask someone for their name using the formal way.

   c Ask a friend how he/she is.

   d Answer the previous question and return the question (informally).

   e Tell someone what you do in life.

   f Ask someone what their job is.

   g Say where you live (town and country).

   h Say what nationality you are and what language(s) you speak.

   i Say whether you are married or single and whether you have children.

   j Say that you don't understand.

   k Ask someone if they speak English.

   l Ask someone to speak more slowly.

   m Say your age.

Points: _____ /26

2 Fill in the blanks with the right endings of the verbs *to have* or *to be*. One point for each correct answer:

Je **a** ……. anglais mais ma mère **b** …… française. Mon père et ma mère **c** …… mariés depuis 50 ans. J' **d** ….. trois frères qui ne **e**

.... pas mariés et une sœur qui **f** ..... deux enfants. Ils
g .... quinze et dix ans. Ma sœur et moi **h** ..... un mari anglais et
nous **i** .... professeures de français en Angleterre. Je n' **j** .... pas
d'enfants.

Points: _____/10

◀)) **CD1, TR 15**

3 Rôle-play

You are travelling on the train to Paris. The person sitting next
to you strikes up a conversation. You are happy to practise your
French. Take part in the conversation.

One point for each correct sentence. Two points when your answer
consists of two correct sentences.

Points: _____/14

You will find the answers to the test questions in the **Key to
the exercises and tests** and the **Rôle-play scripts**. Here are a few
guidelines to help you grade your performance:

40–50 points	Congratulations! You are ready to start the next units.
30–40 points	Very good. You have mastered most of the points covered in the last units. Try to identify the areas which still need some work and go over them again.
20–30 points	Well done, but it might be advisable to revise the areas where you are not quite so confident before moving on to the next units.
Below 20 points	Not bad, but we would strongly advise you to go back over the last units. When you have done so, take the test again and see how much you have improved.

So if you score between 40 and 50 points, you can go straight on to Unit 4. If your score is between 20 and 40 points, you need to spend more time revising the areas which require more work. Below 20 points, go back over Units 1, 2 and 3 and take the test again to see how much you have improved.

Self-test 1 score (Units 1–3)

Points: _____/50

Insight

Always remember that learning a new language may take more time than you think. If you feel that it seems a bit difficult, don't be discouraged. Look back at the tips in the section **Be successful at learning languages** in the introduction to the course as well as those in limits 1–3 and try to put them into practice. They do work!

4

Vous habitez où?
Where do you live?

In this unit you will learn
- *Numbers from 20 to 70*
- *Simple and useful questions and their likely answers*
- *How to say that things are yours or someone else's*
- *How to understand prices*

Before you start

In this unit you will meet some simple questions which you will find useful when coping with everyday situations in France. Some are formed simply by raising the voice at the end of a statement, others by including a question word in the statement: **c'est loin, la gare?** *how far is the station?*, **c'est combien, le billet?** *how much is the ticket?*

Essayez! **Have a go!** At a party you meet a friend of a friend who only speaks French. You want to be friendly and try out your French. You know he/she is married and has a family. Can you think of at least four questions you could ask in French?

Key words and phrases

vous vous_appelez comment?	*what's your name?*
je m'appelle …	*my name is …*
vous_habitez où?	*where do you live?*
le magasin est_ouvert?	*is the shop open?*
non, il est fermé	*no, it's closed*
c'est loin?	*is it far?*
c'est_au bout de la rue	*it is at the end of the street*
c'est près d'ici	*it is nearby*
c'est_à 50 mètres d'ici	*it is 50 metres away* (lit. *50 m from here*)
c'est_à cinq minutes à pied	*it is five minutes away on foot*
c'est_une grande ville	*it is a big town*
c'est_une petite piscine	*it is a small swimming pool*
c'est gratuit, la brochure?	*is the brochure free?*
non, il faut payer	*no, you must pay* (lit. *it's necessary to pay*)
c'est combien, le billet?	*how much is the ticket?*
c'est où, l'arrêt d'autobus?	*where is the bus stop?*
c'est où, la station de métro?	*where is the tube (subway) station?*
c'est quand, le départ?	*when is the departure?*
c'est_à quel étage?	*what floor is it on?*
c'est_au premier étage	*it's on the first floor*
c'est cher/bon marché?	*it's expensive/ cheap?*
il y a un car pour Caen?	*is there a coach for Caen?*
oui, il y en_a un	*yes, there is one*
il y a un train direct pour Paris?	*is there a direct train to Paris?*
non, il n'y en_a pas	*no, there isn't any*
un restaurant dans l'hôtel	*a restaurant in the hotel*
beaucoup de …	*a lot of …*

NUMBERS 20–70

20	vingt	28	vingt-huit	50	cinquante
21	vingt_et un	29	vingt-neuf	51	cinquante et un
22	vingt-deux	30	trente	52	cinquante-deux
23	vingt-trois	31	trente et un	60	soixante
24	vingt-quatre	32	trente-deux	61	soixante et un
25	vingt-cinq	40	quarante	62	soixante-deux
26	vingt-six	41	quarante et un	70	soixante-dix
27	vingt-sept	42	quarante-deux		

Insight

Numbers need to be learnt by heart as they are so useful! They are probably the single most useful language item you will need to say and understand if you travel by yourself in France. Notice how for 21, 31, 41, 51, 61, one says **vingt et un** *(twenty and one)*, **trente et un** *(thirty and one)* etc., but for 22, 23, 24, 25, etc., one replaces **et** with a hyphen: **vingt-deux**, **vingt-trois**, **vingt-quatre**.

Dialogue

Jane has been invited to an office party. She strikes up a conversation with one of her friend's colleagues. Does he work? Does he live near Paris? Is he married? Has he got any children?

Jane	Vous vous_appelez comment?
Jean Durand	Je m'appelle Jean Durand et vous?
Jane	Moi, Jane Wilson. Vous_habitez où?
Jean Durand	**Dans la banlieue** de Paris, à Chatou.
Jane	Et … c'est loin Chatou?
Jean Durand	C'est_à 45 minutes en train. Il y a un train direct Paris–Chatou.
Jane	Et … vous travaillez?

(Contd)

Jean Durand	Oui, je suis_**homme d'affaires** et vous?
Jane	Moi, je travaille en_Angleterre, à Brighton … je suis dentiste.
Jean Durand	Et vous_êtes_**en vacances**?
Jane	Oui, je suis_ici **depuis deux semaines. J'aime** beaucoup Paris. Vous_êtes marié?
Jean Durand	Oui.
Jane	Vous_avez des_enfants?
Jean Durand	J'ai trois_enfants: deux filles et un garçon.
Jane	Il y a **une école** à Chatou?
Jean Durand	Oui. Il y en_a une à dix minutes à pied.
Jane	**Votre femme** travaille?
Jean Durand	Oui, elle est professeure à l'école de Chatou.
Jane	C'est_une grande ville, Chatou?
Jean Durand	Oui, c'est grand. Il y a beaucoup de magasins, deux banques, une pharmacie, **un parc** et une piscine.
Jane	Il y a un cinéma?
Jean Durand	Non, il n'y en_a pas.

dans la banlieue in the suburbs
un_homme d'affaires a businessman
en vacances on holiday
depuis deux semaines for two weeks
j'aime I like/love
une école a school
votre femme your wife
un parc a park

Grammar

1 HOW TO ASK SIMPLE QUESTIONS

As you already know, the easiest way to ask a question is to make a statement and raise the voice on the last syllable:

Vous_êtes marié?   *Are you married?*

2 C'EST ...? *IS IT ...? IS THAT ...?*

You can start the question with **c'est** (lit. *it is ...*) and raise the voice at the end of the sentence. To say that *it isn't* use **ce n'est pas:**

C'est loin?   *Is is far?*
Non, ce n'est pas loin.   *No, it isn't far.*

3 IL Y A ...? *IS THERE ...? ARE THERE ...?*

You can also start the question with **il y a** (*there is*, *there are*) and raise the voice at the end of the sentence. To say *there is no ...* or *there are no ...*, use **il n'y a pas de ...**

Il y a un restaurant dans   *Is there a restaurant in*
l'hôtel?   *the hotel?*
Non, il n'y a pas de restaurant ici.   *No, there is no restaurant here.*

....
Insight
    Il y a and **c'est** are two easy French phrases which you can
    often start a sentence or a question with. Get into the habit
    of using them!
....

4 SOME LIKELY ANSWERS: YES, THERE IS; NO,
    THERE ISN'T

To the question **il y a une banque près d'ici?** *is there a bank nearby?* most people in France would answer **oui, il y en_a une** *yes there is one* or **non, il n'y en_a pas** *no there isn't (one)*; **en** which means *one*, *some*, *of it*, *of them*, can be omitted in English but not French:

Il y a *une banque à Chatou?*   *Is there a bank at Chatou?*
Oui, il y en_a une.   *Yes, there is one.*
Il y a *une cabine téléphonique*   *Is there a telephone box near*
    près d'ici?   *here?*
Non, il n'y en_a pas.   *No, there isn't one.*

5 MORE ANSWERS: YES, I HAVE; NO, I HAVEN'T

Similarly, to the question **vous_avez un/une ...** you will hear the answer **oui, j'en_ai un/une** or **non, je n'en_ai pas**:

Vous_avez un timbre?	*Do you have a stamp?*
Oui, j'en_ai un.	*Yes, I have.*
Vous_avez une voiture?	*Do you have a car?*
Oui, j'en_ai une.	*Yes, I have.*
Non, je n'en_ai pas.	*No, I haven't.*

6 OTHER QUESTIONS

You can form other questions starting with **c'est** or giving a statement and adding the question word afterwards:

C'est comment, le musée?	*What is the museum like?*
C'est combien, le billet?	*How much is the ticket?*
C'est où, l'arrêt d'autobus?	*Where is the bus stop?*
C'est quand, les vacances?	*When are the holidays?*
Les magasins ferment **quand?**	*When do the shops shut?*
Les magasins ouvrent **quand?**	*When do the shops open?*

7 MON, TON, SON *MY, YOUR, HIS*

Thing possessed	*my*	*your*	*his/her/ its/one's*	*our*	*your*	*their*
masc. sing.	**mon**	**ton**	**son**	**notre**	**votre**	**leur**
fem. sing.	**ma**	**ta**	**sa**	**notre**	**votre**	**leur**
masc. & fem. pl.	**mes**	**tes**	**ses**	**nos**	**vos**	**leurs**

Like all adjectives in French, these agree with the noun they refer to:

mon mari	*my husband*
ma femme	*my wife*
mes enfants	*my children*

Insight

Take care when using **son** and **sa** to make them agree with the thing being owned, and not the owner:

le fils de M. Durand becomes **son fils** (*his son*)
le fils de Mme Durand becomes **son fils** (*her son*)
la fille de M. Durand becomes **sa fille** (*his daughter*)
la fille de Mme Durand becomes **sa fille** (*her daughter*)

CREATE EVERY OPPORTUNITY TO IMMERSE YOURSELF IN THE LANGUAGE

▶ Try to practise your French with other learners or French speakers.

Find out about French societies, clubs or circles in your area (the library is a good place to find out information). They provide an opportunity to meet other people with whom you can practise your newly acquired language.

▶ Listen to some French regularly.

Not only will it sharpen your comprehension skills but it will help you improve your pronunciation.

▶ Read something in French.

Buy a French magazine and read the French press online and see how many words you can recognize. Try to get the gist of short articles by concentrating on the words you know, getting clues from photographs if there are any and using some guesswork.

▶ For more details refer to the **Taking it further** section at the end of the course.

Activities

1 Match the questions in the left-hand column with the answers on the right.

a	C'est gratuit?	**i**	Non, c'est Monsieur Durand.
b	C'est M. Martel?	**ii**	Non, c'est bon marché.
c	C'est_ouvert?	**iii**	Non, c'est_à dix minutes à pied.
d	Il y a des timbres?	**iv**	Oui, c'est tout près.
e	C'est loin?	**v**	Non, il faut payer.
f	C'est cher?	**vi**	C'est 50€4.
g	C'est combien?	**vii**	Non, c'est fermé.
h	C'est près?	**viii**	Non, il n'y en_a pas.

2 You've just arrived at a hotel. At the reception you find out about the hotel and the amenities in the area. Can you reconstruct the conversation?

a ....
Non, Monsieur, il n'y a pas de restaurant dans l'hôtel.

b ....
Oui, il y a une pharmacie au bout de la rue.

c ....
Oui, il y a beaucoup de magasins près d'ici.

d ....
Non, Monsieur, la banque est fermée maintenant.

e ....
Oui, il y a un train direct pour Paris.

f ....
Non, la gare n'est pas loin. Elle est_à cinq minutes à pied.

g ....
Les toilettes sont_au premier étage:

3 That night you have a nightmare; you are in town doing some shopping but it is a very strange town. Using the example as a model, describe what you see to your friend:

Example: Il y a des cartes postales mais il n'y a pas de timbres.

a .... une pharmacie .... aspirine.

b .... pâtisserie .... croissants.

c .... une gare .... trains.
d .... un arrêt d'autobus .... bus.
e .... un bar .... bière.
f .... une cabine téléphonique .... téléphone.

4 You overhear one side of a woman's conversation in a café. These are the answers, but what were the questions?
  a Oui, je suis_en vacances.
  b Oui, je suis mariée.
  c Non, je n'ai pas d'enfants.
  d Non, je n'habite pas Londres, j'habite Manchester.
  e Je travaille comme secrétaire.

5 Fill in the gaps using one of the following question words:
où, quand, comment, combien.

a C'est .... le journal?	C'est 2€11.
b C'est .... l'arrêt d'autobus?	C'est_au bout de la rue.
c C'est .... les vacances?	C'est_en juin.
d C'est .... le Sacré-Cœur?	C'est_au nord de Paris.
e C'est .... la Pyramide?	C'est près du Louvre.
f C'est .... le film?	C'est super.

◀) CD1, TR 18

6 Listen to how much each item costs and fill in the price tags in euros.

a _____ **b** _____ **c** _____ **d** _____
e _____

◀) CD1, TR 19

7 Rôle-play

You are stopped by a French tourist in your home town. She needs some information on the amenities of the town. Answer her.

THINGS TO REMEMBER

You've arrived at the end of Unit 4. Now you know simple and useful questions, how to say that things are yours and you can understand prices.

Ask someone:

1 his/her name

2 his/her age

3 Where he/she lives

4 Whether he/she has any children

5 Whether there is a bank nearby

6 Whether it is far

7 Where the bus stop is

8 How much the ticket is

9 Which floor it is on

Say to someone that:

10 Your daughter has no children

11 Your son is twenty-two years old

12 Your children work in Paris

You'll find the answers in the **Key to the exercises and tests** at the end of the book. If your answers are correct you are ready to move to Unit 5. If you found the test difficult, spend more time revising Unit 4.

5

....

Quelle heure est-il?
What time is it?

In this unit you will learn
- *The days of the week*
- *The months of the year*
- *Some useful expressions of time*
- *Numbers from 70 to 90*
- *How to say what you want to do*
- *How to ask what you can or cannot do*
- *How to ask for help*
- *The dates*
- *How to tell the time*

_____

Before you begin

For a successful holiday or business trip in France you need to know when things are happening or when shops open. You also need to be able to say what you want to do, find out if it can be done and ask for help. You will be able to achieve all this with the few structures introduced in this unit. You'll also be introduced to quite a lot of vocabulary: days, dates and times.

Essayez! **Have a go!**

1 You are in **l'office de tourisme** (*tourist office*) in Paris. How would you ask for a street map? Ask if there are a bank and telephone box nearby? Can you think of other questions to ask?

2 Revise the following numbers: say them aloud.

41 – 22 – 68 – 15 – 5 – 55 – 14 – 29 – 31 – 47 – 60 – 11

◀) **CD1, TR 20**

Check your answers and your pronunciation with the recording. If you do not have the recording, check with **Appendix: Numbers** at the back of the book.

Key words and phrases

à quelle heure …	*at what time …*
***quand est-ce que l'avion part?**	*when does the aircraft leave?*
***quand est-ce que le bus arrive?**	*when does the bus arrive?*
***quand est-ce qu'on rentre?**	*when do we come back?*
***quand est-ce qu'on peut prendre le petit déjeuner?**	*when can we have breakfast?*
***quand est-ce qu'il y a un métro?**	*when is there a (tube, subway) train?*
***quand finit le concert?**	*when does the concert finish?*
quelle heure est-il?	*what time is it?*
il est …	*it's …*
qu'est-ce que vous faites dans la vie?	*what's your job* (lit. what do you do in life?)
dans dix minutes	*in ten minutes' time*
à dix heures du soir	*at ten o'clock in the evening*
je travaille …	*I work …*
tous les jours de la semaine	*every day of the week*
sauf le samedi et le dimanche	*except Saturdays and Sundays*
le lundi, le mardi	*on Mondays, Tuesdays*
et le mercredi	*and Wednesdays*

le jeudi et le vendredi	on Thursdays and Fridays
jusqu'à midi/minuit	until lunch/midnight
depuis dix heures du matin	since ten in the morning
pendant l'après-midi	during the afternoon
je regarde la télévision ...	I watch TV ...
quelquefois	sometimes
souvent	often
toujours	always
aujourd'hui	today
demain	tomorrow
maintenant	now

Insight

As you have already learnt in Unit 4, you can make the same questions easier by placing the question word afterwards:

L'avion part quand? — *When does the plane leave?*

Le bus arrive quand? — *When does the bus arrive?*

Pratiquez! **Practise!** Can you work out a simpler way of asking the other questions marked with an asterisk in **Key words and phrases**?

Insight

Before carrying on, have a quick recap of the new vocabulary you have just learnt. Without looking at the book, imagine you are telling someone about your typical working week or your television habits!

◀) **CD1, TR 20, 00:38**

LES MOIS DE L'ANNÉE *THE MONTHS OF THE YEAR*

QUICK VOCAB

janvier *January*
février *February*
mars *March*
avril *April*
mai *May*
juin *June*

juillet *July*
août *August*
septembre *September*
octobre *October*
novembre *November*
décembre *December*

◀) **CD, TR 20, 01:01**

NUMBERS 70–90

soixante-dix	*70*	**quatre-vingts**	*80*
soixante et onze	*71*	**quatre-vingt-un**	*81*
soixante-douze	*72*	**quatre-vingt-deux**	*82*
soixante-treize	*73*	**quatre-vingt-trois**	*83*
soixante-quatorze	*74*	**quatre-vingt-quatre**	*84*
soixante-quinze	*75*	**quatre-vingt-cinq**	*85*
soixante-seize	*76*	**quatre-vingt-six**	*86*
soixante-dix-sept	*77*	**quatre-vingt-sept**	*87*
soixante-dix-huit	*78*	**quatre-vingt-huit**	*88*
soixante-dix-neuf	*79*	**quatre-vingt-neuf**	*89*
		quatre-vingt-dix	*90*

Insight

The French sometimes have a tendency to complicate things! 90 in French is four twenty ten. In the next unit you will learn that for 99 you need to say four twenty ten nine!

Dialogue

Jane is asking Mme Durand about her working week. Listen to the recording several times. At what time does Mme Durand start in the mornings and finish in the evenings? Where does she go for lunch?

Jane	Mme Durand, qu'est-ce-que vous faites dans la vie?
Mme Durand	Je suis professeure de biologie.
Jane	Vous travaillez tous les jours?
Mme Durand	Oui, je travaille à temps plein, **donc** tous les jours sauf le dimanche.
Jane	À quelle heure est-ce que vous commencez le matin?
Mme Durand	**Ça dépend**, le lundi, le mercredi et le vendredi, je commence à huit heures et demie, mais le mardi et le jeudi je ne travaille pas le matin.
Jane	À quelle heure finissez-vous l'après-midi?
Mme Durand	Je finis à cinq heures et demie le lundi, le mardi, le jeudi et le vendredi. Le mercredi après-midi je ne travaille pas **mais je reste** dans mon **bureau**. Le samedi, l'école finit à midi et c'est le week-end jusqu'au lundi matin.
Jane	Où est-ce que vous déjeunez à midi?
Mme Durand	Mes_enfants et moi, nous déjeunons_à l'école. Il y a une cafétéria **qui est_ouverte** toute la journée de neuf heures à cinq heures.
Jane	Et le week-end, qu'est-ce que vous faites?
Mme Durand	Ah, le week-end c'est **formidable** mais_**il passe trop vite**. Samedi après-midi je regarde souvent le football à la télévision avec mon **mari** et mes_enfants. Dimanche **on va** toujours à la piscine de Chatou.

donc *therefore*
ça dépend *it depends*
mais je reste *but I stay*
le bureau *the office*
qui est_ouverte *which is open*
formidable *great*
il passe trop vite *it goes too quickly*
mari *husband*
on va *we go*

Grammar

1 SAYING WHAT YOU WANT/WANT TO DO

Instead of saying **je veux** (*I want*), it's more polite to start with
je voudrais (*I would like*). To say what you want to do, put the
infinitive next. (**Je veux** and **je voudrais** are part of the verb **vouloir**.)

Je voudrais_une chambre pour   *I would like a room for tonight.*
ce soir.
Je voudrais_acheter un timbre   *I would like to buy a stamp for*
pour l'Angleterre.   *England.*

2 ASKING WHAT YOU CAN DO; ASKING FOR HELP

To ask if you can do something, use **je peux** or **on peut** followed by
the infinitive describing what you want to do. To ask for someone's
help, use **vous pouvez**. (**Je peux, on peut, vous pouvez** are part of
the verb **pouvoir**.)

Je peux changer de l'argent?	*Can I change some money?*
On peut prendre le petit déjeuner à quelle heure?	*At what time can I/we have breakfast?*
Vous pouvez répéter?	*Can you repeat that?*

3 THREE DIFFERENT WAYS TO ASK A QUESTION

a By giving a questioning tone to what is really a statement:

Tu es française? *Are you French?*

b By leaving the verb as it is and using **est-ce que** (pronounced *esker*) which is the equivalent of the English *do, does,* in sentences such as *do you speak English?*

Est-ce que tu travailles?	*Do you work?*
Où est-ce que tu habites?	*Where do you live?*

c By turning the verb round and joining the two parts with a hyphen:

Travailles-tu? *Do you work?*

Out of the three different ways of asking a question, the safest one is **b** as there are no situations in which **est-ce que** cannot be used; **a** is common in conversation but less so in written French; **c** is not usually used with **je**.

4 QUESTIONS STARTING WITH **QU'EST-CE QUE** ...? *WHAT* ...?

Many questions start with **qu'est-ce que** ...? *what* ...?

Qu'est-ce que c'est?	*What's that?*
Qu'est-ce que vous désirez?	*What would you like?* (in a shop)
Qu'est-ce que vous faites dans la vie?	*What's your job?* (lit. *what do you do in life?*)

Qu'est-ce que can also be replaced by **quoi** and placed at the end like other question words (**quand, où, comment**):

C'est **quoi?**	*What's that?*
Vous désirez **quoi?**	*What would you like?*
Vous faites **quoi** dans la vie?	*What's your job?*

Insight

When you start the question with **est-ce que** (think of it as *do* or *does*) the answer will be 'yes' or 'no'. When you start the question with **qu'est-ce que** (*what* ...) expect a wide range of replies.

5 *VERBS ENDING IN* **-IR** *AND* **-RE**

There are three main groups of regular verbs in French:

verbs ending in **-er** e.g. **travailler**

verbs ending in **-ir** e.g. **finir**

verbs ending in **-re** e.g. **attendre**

To work out the present tense of **-ir** and **-re** verbs, knock the **-ir** and **-re** off the infinitives and then add the following endings:

finir	*to finish*	attendre	*to wait*
je	fin**is**	j'	attend**s**
tu	fin**is**	tu	attend**s**
il/elle/on	fin**it**	il/elle/on	attend
nous	fin**issons**	nous	attend**ons**
vous	fin**issez**	vous	attend**ez**
ils/elles	fin**issent**	ils/elles	attend**ent**

À quelle heure **finissez-vous?**	*At what time do you finish?*
Je finis à 5h.30.	*I finish at 5.30.*
L'école finit à midi.	*School finishes at lunchtime.*
J'attends le train de 7h.30.	*I'm waiting for the 7.30 train.*
Elle attend son petit_ami.	*She's waiting for her boyfriend.*

Remember not to pronounce the last letters in: finis/finit/finissons/
finisse**nt**; atten**ds**/atten**d**/atten**dons**/attende**nt**.

6 GIVING THE DATE

The English talk about the 1st, 2nd, 3rd, 4th, etc. ... of the month.
The French say 'the 1st' (**le premier** or **1er**) but 'the two', 'the three',
'the four', etc. ... of the month:

Quelle est la date?	*What's the date?*
Nous sommes **le 1er_octobre.**	*It's the 1st October.*
Aujourd'hui c'est **le deux_avril.**	*Today is the 2nd of April.*

7 TELLING THE TIME

a The 24-hour clock is used widely in France to distinguish
between a.m. and p.m.

il est treize heures	*it's 1 p.m.*
il est quatorze heures quinze	*it's 2.15 p.m.*
il est quinze heures trente	*it's 3.30 p.m.*
il est seize heures quarante-cinq	*it's 4.45 p.m.*
il est dix-sept heures cinquante	*it's 5.50 p.m.*
il est dix-huit heures cinquante-deux	*it's 6.52 p.m.*
il est dix-neuf heures cinquante-cinq	*it's 7.55 p.m.*

b The 12-hour clock. To reply to the question **Quelle heure est-il?** *What time is it?*, one is more likely to use the 12-hour clock:

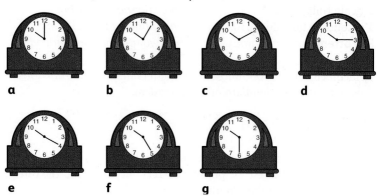

a   b   c   d

e   f   g

- **a** il est dix heures
- **b** il est dix heures cinq
- **c** il est dix heures dix
- **d** il est dix heures et quart *(lit. ten hours and a quarter)*
- **e** il est dix heures vingt
- **f** il est dix heures vingt-cinq
- **g** il est dix heures et demie *(lit. ten hours and half)*

h   i   j   k   l

- **h** il est onze heures moins vingt-cinq (lit. *eleven hours minus twenty-five*)
- **i** il est onze heures moins vingt
- **j** il est onze heures moins le quart (lit. *eleven hours minus the quarter*)
- **k** il est onze heures moins dix
- **l** il est onze heures moins cinq

To distinguish between 9 a.m. and 9 p.m. people say:

| il est neuf heures **du matin** | *it's 9 a.m.* |
| il est neuf heures **du soir** | *it's 9 p.m.* |

Pronounce the **f** of **neuf** as a **v** when it is followed by a vowel or an **h**.

Noon and midnight are however distinguished from each other:

| il est **midi** | *it's (12 p.m.) midday* |
| il est **minuit** | *it's (12 a.m.) midnight* |

8 FAIRE *TO DO/TO MAKE*

Faire is an irregular verb as it does not follow the pattern of **attendre**. It is used in a number of expressions in French (can you think of a recent one you've seen?). Here is a new one: **faire la cuisine** *to do the cooking*:

je fais	**nous faisons**
tu fais	**vous faites**
il/elle/on fait	**ils/elles font**

Insight
Faites, **êtes** and **dites** (from **dire** *to say*) are the only verbs which do not take **ez** in the **vous** person.

9 PRENDRE *TO TAKE*

Prendre is also an irregular verb and needs to be learnt on its own. **Apprendre** *to learn* and **comprendre** *to understand* follow the same pattern as **prendre**:

je prends	**nous prenons**
tu prends	**vous prenez**
il/elle/on prend	**ils/elles prennent**

EXPERIMENT WHILE LEARNING

Get a feel for the language

Learning a language is like learning any other skill. Take swimming for example: it is only when you go into the water and put into practice what you've read or been told, that real learning starts.

Experiment with grammar rules: sit back and reflect on some of the rules you've been learning. See how they compare with your own language or other languages you may already speak. Try to find out some rules on your own and be ready to spot the exceptions. By doing this you'll remember the rules better and get a feel for the language.

Experiment with words: use the words that you've learnt in new contexts and find out if they are correct. For example, you've learnt that **passe** can mean go in the context of time, e.g. **le dimanche passe trop vite.** Experiment with **passe** in new contexts. **Les vacances passent trop vite; la semaine passe** ... etc. Check the new phrases either in this book, a dictionary or with French speakers.

Activities

1 See how many sentences you can make using the verbs in the boxes below and adding a few words.

je voudrais je peux on peut vous pouvez	+	déjeuner .... habiter .... prendre .... acheter .... finir .... commencer .... apprendre ....

2 Put the correct endings to the verbs in brackets.
  a Le matin je (prendre) le train à 7.30.
  b Mes_enfants (commencer) l'école à 8.30.

c Le train (arriver) à huit heures du matin.

d Il (apprendre) le français depuis deux mois.

e À midi on (déjeuner) à la cafétéria.

f Qu'est-ce que vous (prendre) pour le petit déjeuner?

g De huit heures à neuf_heures je (faire) la cuisine.

h Quelle heure (être)-il?

i Le mercredi, la journée (finir) à midi.

j Qu'est-ce que vous (faire) dans la vie?

k Nous_(attendre) à l'arrêt d'autobus.

l Ils (comprendre) l'anglais.

3 Complete the questions by selecting the appropriate endings.

a	Comment	**i** vous faites dans la vie?
b	Quel âge	**ii** une banque près d'ici?
c	C'est où	**iii** vous_appelez-vous?
d	Qu'est-ce que	**iv** commencez-vous le matin?
e	Il y a	**v** la cabine téléphonique?
f	À quelle heure	**vi** combien d'enfants?
g	Vous_avez	**vii** ont-ils?

4 Below is M. Durand's timetable for a typical day. However, the lines got muddled up. Can you put them in the right order, starting with the sentence in bold type?

a Il arrive au travail à 9 heures.

b Le soir, il regarde la télévision jusqu'à 22 heures.

c Il travaille de 9.15 à 13 heures.

d Il finit la journée à 17.30.

e Il prend le train à 7 heures du matin.

f Il prend le petit déjeuner à 6.30 du matin.

g À midi il déjeune au restaurant avec ses collègues.

h Il rentre à la maison vers 19.15.

Insight

Short words can be the most useful ones and the ones that tend to be left out. Notice in Activity 4 the following ones: **jusqu'à** (*until*), **de ... à ...** (*from ... to*), **avec** (*with*), **vers** (*around*).

5 Using the pictures to help you, fill in the missing words.

a Je .... le petit déjeuner.
b Ils .... le train.
c Elle ...... le travail à 9h.
d Il .... jusqu'à midi.
e À midi il .... à la cafétéria.
f Le soir il .... le travail à 17.30.
g Elle .... la cuisine.
h Ils .... la télévision.

6 Give the following dates in French:

1st May	10th June	3rd February	13th October
21st March	30th September	15th July	6th August

🔊 **CD1, TR 22**

7 Listen to the recording. Michel is talking about what he's going to do this week. Fill in the gaps with the correct day of the week in French (**aller** = *to go*).

    a .... je déjeune au restaurant avec Sophie
    b .... je prends le train pour Manchester
    c .... je regarde la télévision avec ma famille
    d .... je réserve une chambre à l'Hôtel Nelson
    e .... j'achète des fleurs pour ma femme
    f .... je voudrais_aller au cinéma avec mes_enfants
    g .... je travaille au bureau toute la journée

8 What time is it? Write out your answers in full, using the 12-hour clock. To differentiate between a.m. and p.m. you can use **du matin/de l'après midi/du soir**. Use also **midi** and **minuit** to distinguish between the middle of the day and the middle of the night.

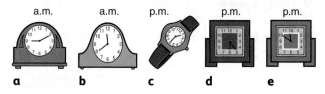

  a.m.   a.m.   p.m.   p.m.   p.m.

    a   **b**   **c**   **d**   **e**

🔊 **CD1, TR 23**

9 Rôle-play

A journalist interviews you on your typical week. Take part in the interview.

THINGS TO REMEMBER

In unit 5 you have learnt the days of the week, the months of the year, some useful expressions of time, new irregular verbs, how to ask what you can or cannot do and how to ask for help. You have also learnt the dates and how to tell the time. Can you do the following?

1 Say the days of the week

2 Say the months of the year

3 Ask a man in three different formal ways whether he is French

4 Give the endings of the three main groups of regular verbs in French

5 Say: Today is the 12th of August

6 Express in French the difference between 10 a.m. and 10 p.m. using suitable words.

7 Say: every day of the week except Saturdays and Sundays

8 Say: today, tomorrow, sometimes, often, always

You'll find the answers in the **Key to the exercises and tests** at the end of the book. If they are correct you are ready to move to Unit 6. If you found the test difficult, spend more time revising Unit 5.

6

Pour aller à ...?
The way to ...?

In this unit you will learn
- *How to count from 90 upwards*
- *How to ask for and understand directions*
- *Useful verbs to describe what you do every day*

Before you start

In **Key words and phrases**, Unit 4, you learnt to say how far somewhere is and how long it takes to go somewhere on foot and by train. Revise these structures as you will need them to understand the dialogue in this unit.

You now know how to ask where things are: **Où est ...?** or **C'est où ...?** Asking the way is also very simple; you start your question with the phrase **pour aller à** and raise the voice at the end of the statement.

Understanding the answer can be more tricky and you'll need to pick out the few essential words such as **tout droit, à gauche, à droite** out of the flow of other words.

As people give you directions, repeat after them, to make sure you have understood. If you do not understand, ask them to repeat or slow down.

Essayez! **Have a go!**

1 Ask someone:
  a to speak more slowly
  b to repeat

2 Talk about your typical day. Use the verbs in the box below to make it exciting and busy.

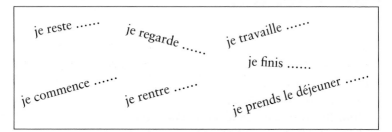

je reste ......   je regarde ......   je travaille ......

je finis ......

je commence ......   je rentre ......   je prends le déjeuner ......

Key words and phrases

To go straight on	
pour_aller à ...	*the way to ...*
(vous) allez tout droit	*(you) go straight on*
continuez	*carry on*
descendez la rue	*go down the street*
montez l'avenue	*go up the avenue*
passez le magasin	*go beyond the shop*
traversez la place	*cross the square*
prenez la route de ...	*take the road to ...*
To turn	
(vous) tournez à gauche	*(you) turn left*
tournez à droite	*turn right*
vous_allez prendre ...	*you're going to take ...*
la première rue à droite	*the first street on the right*
la deuxième sur votre gauche	*the second on your left*

Where it is	
la place du marché est située ...	the market place is ...
au coin de la rue	at the corner of the street
à côté du supermarché	next to the supermarket
en face de la boulangerie	opposite the baker's
au centre ville	in the town centre
sur votre gauche	on your left
sur, sous	on, under
devant, derrière	in front of, behind
dans	in, inside
entre	between
il faut combien de temps?	how long does it take?
il faut environ 25 minutes	you need about 25 minutes

◀) CD1, TR 24

NUMBERS OVER 90

quatre-vingt-dix	90	cent	100
quatre-vingt-onze	91	cent un	101
quatre-vingt-douze	92	cent deux	102
quatre-vingt-treize	93	cent vingt-trois	123
quatre-vingt-quatorze	94	cinq cent trente-quatre	534
quatre-vingt-quinze	95	mille	1000
quatre-vingt-seize	96	mille neuf cent quinze	1915
quatre-vingt-dix-sept	97	deux mille	2000
quatre-vingt-dix-huit	98		
quatre-vingt-dix-neuf	99		

Dialogue

Jane passe la journée chez les Durand. L'après-midi, elle décide d'aller au centre ville de Chatou.

Jane is spending the day with the Durands. She decides to go to the town centre in the afternoon.

While you listen to the recording, look at the street map (le plan de ville) of Chatou with Activity 2. How do you get from M. Durand's house to the park and how long does it take to walk there?

Jane	M. Durand, avez-vous un plan de Chatou? Je voudrais_aller **d'abord** au parc et puis, **si j'ai le temps**, dans les magasins …
M. Durand	**Voici** le plan. Vous pouvez **le garder** car j'en_ai deux.
Jane	Merci beaucoup. Où est le parc de Chatou?
M. Durand	**Voyons**, nous sommes_ici sur le plan. Vous tournez à gauche **en sortant de la maison**, vous_allez jusqu'au bout de la rue Vaugirard, vous tournez à droite dans la rue Vincennes et puis c'est sur votre gauche à 200 mètres.
Jane	Bon, alors, à gauche en sortant puis je tourne à droite et c'est sur ma gauche … C'est loin à pied?
M. Durand	Non, pas très loin; il faut environ 25 minutes.
Jane	Oh là là, c'est **trop loin** pour moi. Euh, on peut y aller en_autobus?
M. Durand	Oui, oui. L'arrêt d'autobus est situé juste au coin de la rue Vaugirard. C'est très pratique et il y a un autobus toutes les dix minutes.
Jane	Je voudrais aussi **faire des_achats** pour moi et acheter quelques souvenirs pour ma famille en Grande-Bretagne et au Canada.
M. Durand	Eh bien, vous pouvez_aller au **centre commercial**. Il est sur la place du marché à côté de la gare. Vous_avez un_autobus direct. Il va du parc au centre commercial.
Jane	Bon, je pars tout de suite … j'ai beaucoup de choses à acheter et … je voudrais rentrer vers 19 heures.

d'abord *firstly*
si j'ai le temps *if I have the time*
voici *here is …*
le garder *keep it*
voyons *let's see*
en sortant de la maison *as you leave the house*
trop loin *too far*
faire des_achats *to do some shopping*
le centre commercial *the shopping centre*

Grammar

1 ASKING THE WAY AND GIVING DIRECTIONS

Pour_aller à (*to get to*) is a very useful structure to remember. Used in a questioning tone it means *How do I/we get to …?*

Pardon, Monsieur, pour_aller à Gordes?	*Excuse me, Sir, how do we get to Gordes?*
Pour_aller à Gordes, prenez la route pour St. Saturnin.	*To get to Gordes, take the road to St Saturnin.*

2 ALLER *TO GO* PARTIR *TO LEAVE*

Here are two very useful verbs. Both verbs are irregular, and **aller** is particularly useful as it is used when speaking about the future (explained in Unit 10):

aller *to go*	**partir** *to leave*
je vais	je pars
tu vas	tu pars
il/elle/on va	il/elle/on part
nous allons	nous partons
vous allez	vous partez
ils/elles vont	ils/elles partent

Vous **allez** jusqu'au bout de la rue.	You go to the end of the road.
Je voudrais aller à la banque.	I would like to go to the bank.
Je pars tout de suite.	I'm leaving immediately.

3 UNDERSTANDING DIRECTIONS

Understanding directions can be trickier than asking the way as the directions can sound complicated, so it is important to pick out the essential words:

a As an answer to your question, you'll probably hear one of the following constructions:

prenez	descendez	tournez à	allez	montez
take	go down	turn	go	go up

Il faut prendre ...	You have to (lit. it's necessary to) take
Il faut descendre ...	You have to go down ...
Il faut tourner ...	You have to turn ...
Il faut aller ...	You have to go ...
Il faut monter ...	You have to go up ...

b The **t** in **droite** *right* is sounded but it is not in **droit** *straight*. Droit is usually preceded by **tout**: **tout droit** *straight on*. Droite is preceded by à or **sur la**: à droite, sur la droite:

Il faut aller **tout droit.**	You have to go straight on.
La gare est **sur la droite.**	The station is on the right.

c You may be unlucky when asking directions and find that you are asking a tourist! His answer would be **je ne sais pas** (*I don't know*), or **je ne suis pas d'ici** (*I am not from here*).

d If you don't understand the information, e.g. the address, the street name, or the number of the building you are given, use the structure **c'est quel(le) ...?** (Unit 3) to have the information repeated:

C'est quelle rue?	*Which street is it?*
C'est quel numéro?	*Which number is it?*
C'est quelle adresse?	*Which address is it?*

Insight

Out of this whole section the most useful expression for you to remember is **Pour aller à ...** when you want to ask the way. To make sure that you understand the directions, repeat them aloud as they are given to you. You can always ask people to repeat or slow down.

4 *WHEN TO USE* **À**; *WHEN TO USE* **EN**

To say that you are in town or you are going/want to go to a town, always use **à** (with an accent to differentiate it from **a** *has*). Study the examples below:

Je suis à Bordeaux.	*I'm in Bordeaux.*
Nous_allons à Bordeaux.	*We're going to Bordeaux.*

To say that you are in a country or you're going to a country, use **en** with feminine countries (often finishing with an **-e**) and **au/aux** with the others:

Je suis en_Australie.	*I am in Australia.*
Je vais en_Angleterre.	*I'm going to England.*
Vous_allez au Canada.	*You're going to Canada.*

The country is preceded by its article in sentences such as:

Je connais bien la Suisse.	*I know Switzerland quite well.*
J'aime beaucoup le Portugal.	*I like Portugal a lot.*

Insight

So... it's easy! Use **à** before towns and **en** before countries, or **au** with the few masculine ones.

5 WHEN À *(AT, TO, IN, ON) IS FOLLOWED BY* **LE, LA, L', LES** ...

The preposition à followed by a definite article (**le, la, l', les**) changes its form in the following way:

à + le   becomes   **au**
à + la   remains   **à la**
à + l'   remains   **à l'**
à + les   becomes   **aux**

Pour_aller **au musée** du Louvre, s'il vous plaît?
Which way to the Louvre Museum please?

Nous_allons **à l'église** St. Paul.
We are going to St Paul's Church.

Il arrive **à la gare** à huit heures du matin.
He arrives at the station at eight o'clock in the morning.

Il va **aux_États-Unis** deux fois par mois.
He goes to the United States twice a month.

6 LOCATING THE EXACT SPOT

Remember that when **de** is used in combination with **le, la, l', les** in expressions such as **en face de** *opposite*, **à côté de** *next to*, **au coin de** *at the corner of*, **près de** *near*, you need to change its form (Unit 2):

au coin **du parc**
at the corner of the park

près **des grands magasins**
near the department stores

en face **de la piscine**
opposite the swimming pool

à côté **de l'office du tourisme**
next to the tourist office

7 PREMIER, DEUXIÈME, TROISIÈME *FIRST, SECOND, THIRD*

If you are directed to the 3rd floor, the 2nd street and so on, the numbers end in **-ième**:

deuxième	*second*	**quatrième**	*fourth*
troisième	*third*	**dixième**	*tenth*

But, *first* is **premier** before all masculine nouns, and **première** before all feminine nouns:

Vous montez au **premier** étage.	*You go up to the first floor.*
C'est la **première** porte.	*It is the first door.*
Vous prenez la **deuxième** à gauche.	*You take the second on the left.*
C'est le **troisième** bâtiment.	*It's the third building.*

SELF-EVALUATION

▶ How well are you doing with speaking French? The revision of the last six dialogues, at the end of this unit, will give you the opportunity to test your overall speaking performance. If you experience some difficulties, look back at the last five units. They give advice on how to organize the study of vocabulary and grammar and how to create opportunities to practise your French.

▶ How well are you doing with understanding: are you listening to some French every day? Look at **Learn to guess the meaning** at the end of Unit 9 and read about the various ways in which you can improve your understanding. If you have the recording, listen to the dialogues again and again, pausing and repeating until you feel familiar with the passages. When listening to a passage, pick out the most important key words.

Activities

1 You are Jane, visiting Chatou for the first time. How would you ask a passer-by the way to:

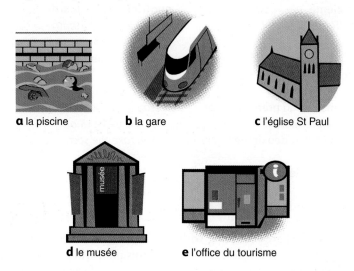

a la piscine   **b** la gare   **c** l'église St Paul

d le musée   **e** l'office du tourisme

◄)) **CD1, TR26**

2 Now listen to the replies of the passers-by on the recording and work out which letter on the map represents each of these places. If you haven't got the recording, read the replies below:

  a C'est très facile. Vous montez la rue Vincennes et vous prenez la première à gauche. La piscine se trouve sur votre droite, en face du parc.

  b Bon, pour la gare, continuez tout droit, toujours tout droit. Juste avant le pont, tournez à droite et vous_êtes dans la rue Thiers. La gare est_à côté du centre commercial.

  c L'église St Paul? Eh bien, c'est tout droit, à 100 mètres d'ici, sur votre droite, au coin de la rue Fleurus.

  d Euh – attendez voir – il faut tourner tout de suite à droite puis descendez la rue Fleurus et le musée est_à 10 minutes à pied sur votre gauche à côté de l'Hôtel Colbert.

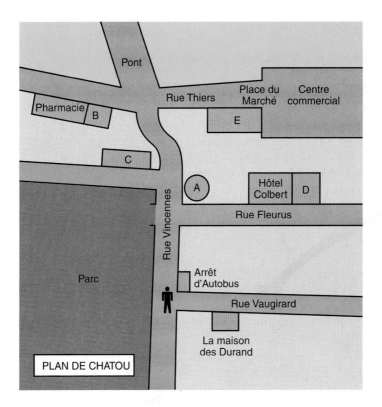

PLAN DE CHATOU

e Vous_allez tout droit jusqu'au pont. Juste avant le pont tournez à gauche et l'office du tourisme se trouve à côté d'une pharmacie.

3 Now it's your turn to practise giving directions. Use the text above as a model but you don't have to answer exactly like it; for example instead of **vous montez/descendez la rue** you can say (**vous**) **allez/continuez tout droit**. (The answers are not given in **Key to the exercises and tests**.) Here are the questions:

   a Pardon Monsieur, pour_aller à la piscine?

   b S'il vous plaît Madame, je voudrais aller au musée; pouvez-vous me dire où il se trouve?

   c Pardon Monsieur, savez-vous où est l'office du tourisme?

   d Pardon Mademoiselle, je ne suis pas d'ici … euh, il y a un centre commercial à Chatou?

4 Choose the right answer.

Jane habite à Brighton?/en Brighton?/de Brighton?

Elle et son petit_ami passent leurs vacances en France/
au France/France

mais_ils préfèrent Allemagne./l'Allemagne./en Allemagne.

Jane est restée une semaine à Berlin/Berlin/en Berlin et trois jours
Bonn./au Bonn./à Bonn.

Cet_été (*this summer*) elle va au Danemark/Danemark/en
Danemark où elle a des_amis.

Son petit_ami va souvent en États-Unis/aux_États-Unis/les_États-
Unis et au Japon./en Japon./Japon.

Il est_homme d'affaires (*businessman*) et travaille en Londres./
à Londres./Londres.

5 Look at the **centre commercial de Chatou** and fill in the blanks
using the words from the list below.

a La poste est .... café.
b Le café est .... pâtisserie.
c L'office du tourisme est .... la place
François 1er.
d La pharmacie est .... la poste et la
banque.
e L'église est .... la rue Thiers.
f Les .... sont en face du supermarché.
g Le .... est à côté de l'hôtel.
h La .... est entre le café et l'office du
tourisme.
i La pharmacie est .... Thiers.
j Le supermarché est .... François 1er.

à côté de la
en face du
dans la rue
entre
grands magasins
pâtisserie
sur la place
au coin de
au bout de
bar

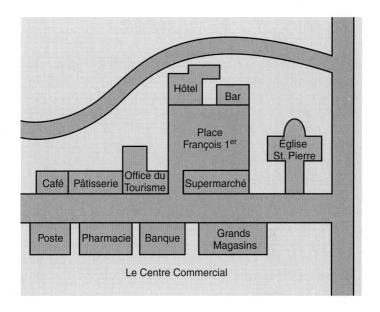

6 Numbers

Test yourself. Pick numbers from the box below and say them
aloud in French. Check your answers at the back of the book
where all the numbers are listed. Repeat the exercise over a number
of days and see if you can improve your performance.

72	24	80	92	65	43	75	61
76	68	15	66	17	96	87	70
19	21	49	55	65	56	13	77

◀) **CD1, TR 27**

7 Rôle-play

You are in the shopping centre in Chatou. A French passer-by
stops you and asks about the shops. Look at the street map in
Exercise 5 above and answer her.

THINGS TO REMEMBER

In this unit, **Things to remember** is replaced by a revision of the last six dialogues: try translating the dialogues from Units 1 to 6 into English and then from English retranslate them orally into French. Check your answers with the book. You might like to record yourself, imagining that you're French. If you have the original recording, compare your own recording with it. How different is yours from the original? Try in your recording to match the speed, the accent and intonation on the original recording.

Insight

While this exercise may seem difficult, it is well worth doing. You have learnt a great deal of French so far ... more than you probably realize. Now is the time to consolidate it. Take your time over the exercise, and do it thoroughly. It will save time later.

7

C'est comment?
What is it like?

In this unit you will learn
- *How to describe things and people*
- *How to say precisely what you want*
- *How to compare people and objects*
- *Colours*

Before you start

In Unit 2 you've already seen how to ask for things using just a few words. Getting precisely what you need may involve giving a few more details. This unit will provide you with some of the key words you'll need to describe what you are looking for, specifying colours, materials, quantities, prices, etc. There is a lot of new vocabulary in this unit, appearing in the sections **Key words and phrases**, **Grammar** and **Activities**. It will be useful to you when doing Unit 11 which concentrates on the topic of shopping in France.

Essayez! **Have a go!** Fill in the blanks in the sentences below with some of the prepositions you met in the last unit.

1 Les fleurs sont .... (*in*) le vase.
2 Le croissant est .... (*on*) l'assiette.
3 Le journal est .... (*between*) le vase et l'assiette.
4 Le jus d'orange est .... (*next to the*) journal.
5 La carte postale est .... (*under*) l'assiette.
6 Les clefs sont .... (*in front of*) le jus de fruit.
7 Les aspirines sont .... (*behind*) le vase.

Key words and phrases

For you to say	
faire des_achats, des courses, du shopping	*to do some shopping*
dépenser	*to spend*
qu'est-ce que vous_avez comme ...	*what do you have in the way of ...*
souvenirs/cadeaux?	*souvenirs/presents?*
qu'est-ce que c'est?	*what is it?*

vous_avez autre chose?	*do you have anything else?*
ça coûte/ça fait combien?	*how much is it?*
c'est de quelle couleur?	*what colour is it?*
je cherche quelque chose …	*I'm looking for something …*
grand/moyen/petit	*big/medium/small*
un peu plus grand	*a little bigger*
un peu moins cher	*a little less expensive*
meilleur marché	*cheaper*
spécial/différent	*special/different*
pour réparer, ouvrir	*to repair, open*
je vais prendre le plus petit	*I'll take the smallest*
rouge, blanc, vert, marron/brun, bleu, jaune	*red, white, green, brown, blue, yellow*
faire un paquet-cadeau	*to gift-wrap*
qui est-ce?	*who is it?*
c'est_une personne sympathique	*he/she is a nice person*
c'est_un jeune homme français	*he's a young Frenchman*
c'est_une jeune fille anglaise	*she's a young English girl*
c'est quelqu'un de grand/petit/ gros/mince	*it's someone tall/small/ big/thin*
il porte des lunettes de soleil	*he wears/is wearing sunglasses*
il a les cheveux noirs et raides	*he has black, straight hair*
elle porte une chemise unie	*she wears/is wearing a plain shirt*
elle a les yeux marron	*she has brown eyes*

For you to understand

je vais vous montrer	*I'll show you*
il vaut mieux prendre	*you should take* (lit. *it is better to take*)
si vous voulez bien me suivre	*would you come this way*
payez à la caisse	*pay at the till*

Dialogue

Jane fait des courses dans un grand magasin de Chatou.

Jane is shopping in a department store in Chatou. She is looking for something special to take back to her mother in the UK.

Listen to the recording or read the dialogue in the book: Why does Jane buy the small scarf? She asks for it to be gift-wrapped. What does she say in French?

● CD1, TR 28

Vendeuse	Vous désirez?
Jane	Je cherche un souvenir pour ma mère ... euh quelque chose de spécial pour **ramener** en Angleterre.
Vendeuse	Bon, très bien. Alors si c'est pour votre mère, je peux vous montrer des **foulards en soie** avec des scènes typiquement françaises.
Jane	Oh, ils sont très **jolis** et leurs couleurs sont vraiment superbes. C'est combien?
Vendeuse	Alors, les grands coûtent 68€50 et 53€ et les petits 46€.
Jane	Je peux voir **ceux qui** sont à 46€?
Vendeuse	Mais bien sûr. Ils représentent les monuments **célèbres** de Paris. **Certains** sont rouges et bleus, **d'autres** verts et jaunes.
Jane	Je préfère les grands, mais_ils sont trop chers et je ne veux pas trop dépenser.
Vendeuse	Alors, il vaut mieux prendre un petit à 46€.
Jane	Oui, je vais prendre **ce petit** qui représente l'Arc de Triomphe. Ses couleurs bleues et rouges sont superbes et il n'est pas trop cher. **Je crois que** ma mère **sera** très **contente**. Vous pouvez me faire un paquet-cadeau, s'il vous plaît?
Vendeuse	Oui, un instant ... si vous voulez bien me suivre? *(The shop assistant wraps the present up.)* Et maintenant vous payez_à la caisse.
Jane	Ah bon, merci bien, Madame.

QV

ramener *to bring back*
foulard (m) *scarf*
en soie *made of silk*
joli(e) *pretty*

ceux qui ... *the ones which ...*
célèbres *famous*
certains ... d'autres *some ... others*
ce petit *this small one*
je crois que *I believe that*
sera contente *will be pleased*

Grammar

1 CE, CET, CETTE, CES *THIS, THAT, THESE, THOSE*

Ce, cet, cette all mean *this* or *that*; ces means *these* or *those*.
Ce comes before masculine singular nouns, **cet** before masculine
singular nouns beginning with a vowel or silent **h**, **cette** before
feminine singular nouns and **ces** before plural nouns:

	masculine	*masc. (before a vowel or silent **h**)*	*feminine*
singular	**ce**	**cet**	**cette**
plural	**ces**	**ces**	**ces**

ce foulard	*this/that scarf*
cet_homme	*this/that man*
cette femme	*this/that woman* (**femme**, pronounced 'fam', also means 'wife')
ces_enfants	*these/those children*

2 SAYING PRECISELY WHAT YOU WANT

You already know how to ask for something (Unit 5),
e.g. **je voudrais cette bouteille.** This is the most general
way of asking for things, but you may want to give more
information.

a How much? Expressions of quantity are linked with **de**:

Combien **d'**enfants?	*How many children?*
beaucoup **d'**enfants	*lots of children*
un verre **de** vin	*a glass of wine*
une boîte **de** haricots	*a tin of beans*

b Made of what? You can use **de** or **en** to say what things are made of:

une chemise **de** coton	*a cotton shirt*
une robe **en** soie	*a silk dress*

c What kind? Add adjectives to describe in more detail:

un verre de vin **rouge**	*a glass of red wine*
une boîte de **petits** pois **français**	*a tin of French peas*
un kilo de raisins **noirs**	*a kilo of black grapes*

d What's in/on it? Special features such as patterns, flavours or key ingredients are linked with **à**:

un yaourt **à** l'abricot	*an apricot yoghurt*
un sandwich **au** fromage	*a cheese sandwich*
une glace **à** la vanille	*a vanilla ice cream*
une tarte **aux** pommes	*an apple pie*

Don't forget to change the **à** to **au** or to **aux** if the following noun is masculine or plural.

e With/without. Put **avec** (*with*) or **sans** (*without*) in front of what you want or don't want:

une chambre **avec** télévision	*a room with (a) television*
un hôtel **sans** parking	*a hotel without car park*

3 HOW ADJECTIVES WORK

As explained in Unit 3, adjectives change according to what they are describing; they may take masculine, feminine or plural forms:

	masculine	feminine
singular	**petit**	**petite**
plural	**petits**	**petites**

ce **petit** foulard — *this little scarf*
c'est_une **bonne** école — *it's a good school*
les **petits** pois sont verts — *peas are green*
avec des scènes **françaises** — *with French scenes*

a Adding an -e to the masculine (if it has not already got an -e) to form the feminine often changes the pronunciation, as in **petit** (m), **petite** (f), but not always, e.g. **noir** (m), **noire** (f), **bleu** (m), **bleue** (f). The -s in the plural is not sounded.

b Brun is used almost exclusively to refer to the colour of someone's hair, complexion or brown ale (**bière brune**). For most brown objects, use **marron**, which is an invariable form.

c A few adjectives have two masculine forms: the second one is used in front of nouns beginning with a vowel or silent **h**:

le **nouveau** garçon — *the new boy*
le **nouvel**_élève — *the new pupil*
le **vieux** port — *the old harbour*
le **vieil**_hôtel — *the old hotel*

d Here are some common adjectives with irregular endings. You will pick up others as you go along:

masc. 1	masc. 2	fem.	masc. pl.	fem. pl.
beau	bel	belle	beaux	belles
nouveau	nouvel	nouvelle	nouveaux	nouvelles
vieux	vieil	vieille	vieux	vieilles

e Adjectives are usually placed after the noun:

un café **noir**	*a black coffee*
une bière **brune**	*brown ale*

except with common ones such as: **petit** (*small*), **bon(ne)** (*good*), **beau** (*beautiful*), **grand** (*tall*), **jeune** (*young*), **vieux** (*old*), **mauvais** (*bad*), **joli** (*beautiful*), **tout** (*all*):

un **grand** café	*a large coffee*
une **bonne** bière	*a good beer*

f If there are two or more adjectives they are placed after the noun and linked with **et**, or they are placed either side of the noun:

des cheveux **blonds et longs**	*long, blond hair*
un **grand** homme **mince**	*a tall, slim man*

Insight

This section provided you with more details on how to ask things. While it may all seem a little complex, rest assured, however, that if you get the adjectives' endings muddled up or forget to change **à** to **au** or to **aux** you will still be understood.

4 MAKING COMPARISONS

To say that something is *more ... than* or *less ... than* use:

plus ... que	*more ... than*
moins ... que	*less ... than*

Le train est **plus rapide que** la voiture.	*The train is faster than the car.*
Il est **moins grand que** moi.	*He's less tall than I.*

The -s of **plus** is not pronounced except in the following cases:

▶ before a vowel or silent **h**, -s is sounded **z**: **plus_âgé**
▶ whenever the word means **plus** (+), -s is sounded **s**:

Il y a du beurre **plus** du lait dans la recette.
There is some butter plus some milk in the recipe.

▶ when it is followed directly by **que** to produce **plus que** *more than*, -s is sounded s:

Il travaille **plus que** moi.
He works more than I.

Saying 'better'
To say that something/someone is *better*, use **meilleur** (e); to say that you do something *better* use **mieux**:

Le film est **meilleur** que le livre.
The film is better than the book.

Elle parle français **mieux** que moi.
She speaks French better than I.

Insight

What may seem a little confusing is that because in English there is only one word *better* when there are two in French. It is easy to differentiate between them, however. **Meilleur** goes with things, e.g. books, films, food, whereas **mieux** goes with how you do things.

LEARNING TO COPE WITH UNCERTAINTY

▶ **Don't over-use your dictionary.**
When reading a text in the foreign language, don't be tempted to look up every word you don't know. Underline the words you do not understand and read the passage several times, concentrating on trying to get the gist of the passage. If after the third time there are still words which prevent you from getting the general meaning of the passage, look them up in the dictionary.

▶ **Don't panic if you don't understand.**
If at some point you feel you don't understand what you are told, don't panic or give up listening. Either try and guess

what is being said and keep following the conversation or, if you cannot, isolate the expression or words you haven't understood and have them explained to you. The speaker might paraphrase them and the conversation will carry on.

▶ **Keep talking.**
The best way to improve your fluency in the foreign language is to talk every time you have the opportunity to do so: keep the conversation flowing and don't worry about the mistakes. If you get stuck for a particular word, don't let the conversation stop; paraphrase or replace the unknown word with one you do know, even if you have to simplify what you want to say. As a last resort use the word from your own language and pronounce it in the foreign accent.

Activities

1 À la gare routière: fill in the blanks with **ce, cet, cette** or **ces**. To check if the words are masculine or feminine look at the French–English vocabulary.

Touriste	Pardon Monsieur, ... autobus va à Quimper?
Homme	Oui, Madame, tous ..... autobus vont à Quimper.
Touriste	Je voudrais partir ..... matin. A quelle heure partent les_ autobus?
Homme	Bon, ... deux_autobus partent pour Quimper ..... matin. Le premier part à 8.30 et arrive à 12.00 et le deuxième part à 9.15 et arrive à 13.15 ..... après-midi.
Touriste	Très bien. Je veux rentrer ..... nuit. À quelle heure rentre le dernier_autobus de Quimper?
Homme	Alors ..... semaine, le dernier bus quitte Quimper à 20.30.

2 Using the grid below and M. Durand's description as a model, write down in a few sentences what Mme Durand and Jane look like. Make sure that the adjectives agree with the nouns they describe. Check the vocabulary with the drawings below or in the vocabulary list at the back of the book. Then write a few sentences describing yourself.

	M. Durand	**Mme Durand**	**Jane**
sexe	homme	femme	femme
âge	40 ans	35 ans	23 ans
cheveux	noirs/raides	blonds/longs	bruns/courts
yeux	marron	verts	bleus
taille	1,78 mètre	1,70 mètre	1,62 mètre
poids	79 kg	65 kg	55 kg
signes particuliers	moustache	lunettes rondes	–
vêtements	costume bleu marine, cravate jaune, chaussures noires	ensemble vert uni, chemise blanche, chaussures légères	jean bleu pâle, pull-over blanc, bottes noires

Monsieur Durand a 40 ans. Il a les cheveux noirs et raides et les yeux marron; il fait 1 mètre 78 et pèse 79 kg. Il a une moustache. Il porte un costume bleu marine, une cravate jaune et des chaussures noires.

a  b  c

Look in the **Key** at the back of the book and check that what you've written is correct. Using as a model M. Durand's description on the recording, read aloud what you've written.

3 How would you ask for all the items on the list? The words in the box will help, though they aren't all there!

a a tin of French peas	baba (m) vanille (f)
b an apple tart	petits pois (m)
c a rhum baba	vin (m)
d a vanilla ice cream	pommes (f) fromage (m)
e a lemon sorbet	citron (m)
f a big glass of red wine	sucre (m)
g a white coffee without sugar	sandwich (m) poulet (m)
h a chicken at 6€80	verre (m) lait (m)
i a small black coffee	tarte (f) rhum (m)
j a cheese sandwich	glace (f)
k a bottle of milk	sorbet (m) café (m)
	boîte (f) bouteille (f)

4 Sally is spending Christmas and New Year in France with a French family. She writes to her friend Isabelle. Can you fill the gaps with the words from the box (below Sally's letter)? You may have to look up some of the words in the **Vocabulary** at the back of the book.

(a) .... Isabelle,
Je suis depuis une semaine avec la (b) .... Guise. Ici (c) ....
le monde est très (d) .... et je passe de très (e) .... vacances.
La maison est (f) .... et (g) .... Je fais de (h) ....
promenades presque tous les (i) .... La cuisine française est (j)
.... que la cuisine (k) .... et je mange trop. Je parle (l) ....
le français maintenant. Je retourne chez moi la semaine (m) ....

Joyeux Noël et Bonne Année
Sally

meilleure	longues	tout	jours	confortable
prochaine	famille	bonnes	grande	anglaise	mieux
	Chère	sympathique		

5 You are in a café with four of your friends. The waiter arrives and you order (**vous commandez**):

	Garçon	Bonjour, Messieurs-Dames. Qu'est-ce que vous désirez?
a	**You**	*A large black coffee.*
	Garçon	Un grand café, oui…
b	**You**	*Two draught beers*
	Garçon	Oui.
c	**You**	*And a small white coffee.*
	Garçon	Alors un grand crème, deux limonades et un petit café noir, c'est ça?
d	**You**	*No. Two draught beers, a small white coffee and a large black coffee.*
	Garçon	Bon très bien. Excusez-moi.
e	**You**	*Have you got some croissants?*
	Garçon	Vous_en voulez combien?
f	**You**	*Say you want four.*
	Garçon	Très bien, Monsieur.

◄》 **CD1, TR 30**

6 Rôle-play

You have organized a trip to Paris to meet your French penfriend whom you have never met. He has offered to meet you at the station. He phones you to find out about your arrival. Take part in the conversation.

Before going on to Unit 8, do the **Self-test** 2 (Units 4–7). As in Unit 3, record your score. If your score is between 40 and 50 points, you can go straight on to Unit 8. If it is between 20 and 40 points, revise the points and areas which require more work. Below 20 points, you need to go back over Units 4, 5, 6 and 7, and take the test again to see how much you have improved.

SELF-TEST 2

UNITS 4–7   POINTS: /50

This test covers the main vocabulary and phrases, skills and language points in Units 4–7. For how to read your score, refer back to the first Self-test at the end of Unit 3. You can check your answers in the **Key to the exercises and tests** and the **Rôle-play scripts. Bonne chance!**

1 Can you ask and say the following? Say the answers out loud and write them down. One point for each correct answer.
   a Is it far?
   b No, it is not far.
   c Is there a bank nearby?
   d No, there is not a bank nearby.
   e Have you a stamp?
   f No, I haven't any.
   g What is the film like?
   h Where is the bus stop?
   i It is ten minutes away on foot.
   j When does the shop open?

Points: ____/10

2 Complete the questions by selecting the appropriate endings. One point for each correct answer.
   a Il y a   **i** c'est'?
   b Quel âge   **ii** vous appelez-vous?
   c Qu'est-ce que   **iii** commencez-vous le matin?
   d À quelle heure   **iv** ont-ils?
   e Comment   **v** une cabine téléphonique près d'ici?

Points: ____/5

3 Using the example overleaf as a model, say these dates out loud in French, then write them out in full for practice. One point for each correct answer.

Tuesday, the 9th of November: **le mardi neuf novembre**

a Sunday, the 31st of March
b Wednesday, the 2nd of June
c Friday, the 18th of January
d Tuesday the 24th of October
e Saturday, the 11th of May
f Monday, the 23rd of August
g Thursday, the 19th of September

Points: ____/7

4 Can you say the following in French? Say the answers out loud and write them down. Two points for each correct answer.
 a I have breakfast at 8.00 in the morning.
 b My mother does the cooking every day.
 c My husband and I often take the train on Mondays.
 d What are you doing this weekend?
 e She always works until lunchtime.
 f At what time do you finish work?
 g Today he goes home around 20.00.
 h You have been watching TV since 10 in the morning.
 i I never work on Sundays.

Points: ____/18

◄» **CD1, TR 31**

5 Rôle-play

This is the continuation of the conversation you started in **Self-test 1** (Units 1–3) on the train to Paris. Give yourself one point for each correct answer and two when your answer consists of two correct sentences.

Points: ____/10

Self-test 2 score (Units 4–7)

Points: _____/50

8

Vous aimez le sport?
Do you like sport?

In this unit you will learn how to
- *Ask and talk about likes and dislikes*
- *Say what you and others do as a hobby*
- *Talk about the weather*

Before you start

Once you know a French person well enough you'll find yourself wanting to express your likes and dislikes and talk about your hobbies; here are the structures you'll need:

j'adore	*I adore, I love*
j'aime beaucoup	*I like very much*
je n'aime pas	*I don't like*
je déteste	*I hate*
je joue	*I play*
je fais	*I do*

Talking about the weather is a particularly important aspect of the British way of life; you may find it useful to enquire about the weather forecast if you are planning some kind of outdoor activity.

Essayez! **Have a go!** You are in a shop in France looking for a corkscrew. However, you don't know the French word for it. How would you say that you're looking for something to open bottles of wine?

You	....
Shopkeeper	**Ah! Vous voulez un tire-bouchon** *(a corkscrew)*?

Key words and phrases

For you to say	
qu'est-ce que vous faites/pratiquez comme sport?	*what sport do you do?*
vous faites quoi pendant vos loisirs?	*what hobbies do you have?*
vous_aimez faire du sport?	*do you like doing sport?*
quelle est votre cuisine préférée?	*which cooking do you prefer?*
j'adore aller au restaurant	*I love going to the restaurant*
mon sport préféré est la natation	*swimming is my favourite sport*
je fais de la natation	*I swim*
j'aime (beaucoup) …	*I like (very much) …*
jouer au squash	*playing squash*
la cuisine française	*French cooking*
écouter de la musique	*listening to music*
regarder la télévision	*watching television*
je n'aime pas …	*I don't like …*
la planche à voile	*windsurfing*
la musique classique	*classical music*
me promener à pied	*going for a walk*
je déteste faire la cuisine	*I hate cooking*
je joue au tennis	*I play tennis*
je joue du piano	*I play the piano*
je préfère l'équitation	*I prefer riding*

For you to understand

moi, ce que j'aime c'est	*what I really like is going out*
sortir avec mes_amis	*with my friends*
moi, ce que je déteste c'est	*what I really dislike is*
la viande saignante	*rare meat*
Le temps	*The weather*
quel temps fait-il?	*what's the weather like?*
il fait beau, mauvais	*the weather is fine, bad*
il fait chaud, froid	*it is hot, cold*
le soleil brille	*the sun shines*
il pleut	*it's raining*
il neige	*it's snowing*

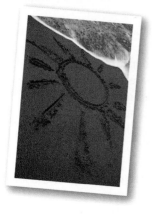

Insight

Out of this list of phrases, the three most useful to remember are:

Je fais du ... when speaking about hobbies
Je joue au ... when talking about sports
Je joue du ... when playing an instrument.

Dialogue

Jane parle de sports et de loisirs avec les Durand.

Jane and the Durands are talking about sport and hobbies.

Listen to the recording or read the dialogue and then answer the following questions: What's Mrs Durand's favourite hobby? What sports does Mr Durand do?

CD1, TR 32

Jane	Mme Durand, qu'est-ce que vous faites pendant vos loisirs?
Mme Durand	Moi, j'adore faire la cuisine, **surtout** la cuisine française.
Jane	Et dans la cuisine française, quels sont vos **plats favoris**?
Mme Durand	Eh bien, j'aime beaucoup faire tous les plats en sauce, en particulier **le bœuf bourguignon** ou **le coq au vin**. **Vous savez**, mon mari aime bien manger et bien boire; c'est un gourmet et il **apprécie** ma cuisine … alors **ça fait plaisir**!
Jane	Et vous, Monsieur Durand, vous_aimez faire la cuisine?
M. Durand	Moi, **je laisse la cuisine** à ma femme. Elle la fait très bien. Je préfère le sport.
Jane	Quels sports **pratiquez**-vous?
M. Durand	Je joue au squash deux fois par semaine après mon travail et **quand j'ai le temps**, je fais de la natation avec les_enfants le samedi, à la piscine de Chatou.
Mme Durand	Tu aimes bien aussi faire de la planche à voile **en_été**.
M. Durand	Oui, **c'est vrai**. J'aime beaucoup la planche à voile surtout quand_il y a du **vent**, mais je déteste en faire quand_il fait froid ou quand_il pleut.

| **Mme Durand** | Et vous Jane, qu'est-ce que vous faites comme sport? |
| **Jane** | Oh moi, je pratique un peu tous les sports: le badminton, le tennis et quelquefois l'équitation, mais je n'ai pas beaucoup de temps pour faire du sport. |

surtout *mainly*
plats favoris *favourite dishes*
le bœuf bourguignon *beef stew with wine*
le coq au vin *chicken cooked in wine*
vous savez *you know*
boire *to drink*
il apprécie *he appreciates*
ça fait plaisir *it is a pleasure*
je laisse la cuisine *I leave the cooking*
pratiquer *to do*
quand j'ai le temps *when I have the time*
en_été *in summer*
c'est vrai *it's true*
le vent *the wind*

QUICK VOCAB

Grammar

1 ASKING AND SAYING WHAT YOU DO AS A HOBBY

In French to answer questions such as **qu'est-ce que vous faites comme sport?** *what do you do in the way of sport?* or **qu'est-ce que vous faites pendant vos loisirs?** *what are your hobbies?* use **je fais de ...** or **je joue à ...** if it is a game. If you play a musical instrument use **je joue de.**

Je fais **de la** natation et **du** surf.
I swim and I surf.

Je joue **au** tennis et **à la** pétanque.
I play tennis and petanque (kind of bowls played in the South of France).

Je joue **du** piano et **de la** trompette.
I play the piano and the trumpet.

2 LIKES AND DISLIKES

To express your tastes and feelings, you can use **aimer** (*to like, to love*) or the two extremes **adorer** and **détester**:

j'adore	aller au restaurant
j'aime (beaucoup)	jouer au squash
	cuisiner
	écouter des disques
	regarder la télé
je n'aime pas	la planche à voile
	la musique classique
	me promener à pied
je déteste	faire la cuisine

To say what you like/dislike doing, add the infinitive after **j'aime, j'adore, je déteste, je préfère: je déteste faire de la bicyclette:** *I hate cycling.*

Include the article **le, la, les** when making generalizations:

J'aime **les** fromages français.	*I like French cheese.*
L'histoire est plus_intéressante que **la** géographie.	*History is more interesting than geography.*

When stating likes/dislikes you will often hear French people use the following structures: using **ce que**

> **Moi, ce que j'aime c'est** sortir avec mes_amis.
> **Moi, ce que je déteste c'est** la viande saignante.
> **Moi, ce que j'adore c'ut** sortir le samedi soir.

3 *PRONOUNS:* **LE, LA, LES** *IT, HIM, HER, THEM*

The pronouns **le** (*it, him*), **la** (*it, her*), **les** (*them*) are used to avoid
unnecessary repetitions of nouns; they are placed before the verb to
which they refer:

Vous connaissez **M. Durand?**	*Do you know Mr Durand?*
Oui, je **le** connais.	*Yes, I know him.*
Vous prenez **la carte postale?**	*Are you taking the postcard?*
Oui, je **la** prends.	*Yes, I'm taking it.*
Vous_achetez **ces foulards?**	*Are you buying these scarves?*
Oui, je **les**_achète.	*Yes, I'm buying them.*
Vous_aimez **le thé?**	*Do you like tea?*
Oui, je l'aime.	*Yes, I like it.*

L' replaces **le** or **la** when the next word starts with a vowel or silent
h. In a negative sentence, **l', le, la, les** come between the **ne** or **n'**
and the verb:

Vous préférez le tennis?	*Do you prefer tennis?*
Non, je **ne le préfère pas**.	*No, I don't prefer it.*

4 MORE NEGATIVES

You saw in Unit 3 how to make a statement negative in French,
using **ne ... pas**:

Je **n'**ai pas **d'**enfants.	*I have no children.*

There are other negatives you can use:

ne … plus	no more/no longer
ne … rien	nothing
ne … jamais	never
ne … que	only
Je n'ai plus de vin.	I have no more wine.
Il ne veut rien.	He wants nothing.
Il n'a jamais d'argent.	He never has any money.
Je n'ai que dix_euros.	I've only got ten euros.

5 'TO KNOW': WHEN TO USE SAVOIR, WHEN TO USE CONNAÎTRE

There are two verbs for *knowing*: **savoir** and **connaître**.

a Use **savoir** (on its own) to say that you *know* or *don't know* a fact:

Je sais à quelle heure part le train.	I know when the train leaves.
Je ne sais pas où est l'arrêt d'autobus.	I don't know where the bus stop is.

b Use **savoir** followed by the infinitive to say that you *know how to do* something:

Je sais faire la cuisine.	I know how to cook.
Vous savez faire du ski?	Do you know how to ski?

c Connaître is used to say that you *know people and places*:

Je connais Paris.	I know Paris.
Depuis combien de temps est-ce que vous le connaissez?	How long have you known him?

6 QUEL TEMPS FAIT-IL? *WHAT'S THE WEATHER LIKE?*

The easiest way to talk about the weather is to start with **il fait**:

il fait beau, mauvais	*it's fine, the weather is bad*
il fait froid, chaud	*it's cold, hot*
il fait du vent	*it's windy*
il fait du brouillard	*it's foggy*
il fait (du) soleil	*it's sunny*
il pleut	*it's raining*
il neige	*it's snowing*
le soleil brille	*the sun is shining*

Pratiquez! **Practise!**
How would you answer the question:
Quel temps fait-il aujourd'hui? **Aujourd'hui il ...**

LEARN FROM YOUR ERRORS

▶ Don't let errors interfere with getting your message across. Making errors is part of any normal learning process, but some people get so worried that they won't say anything unless they are sure it is correct. This leads to a vicious circle as the less they say, the less practice they get and the more mistakes they make.

▶ Note the seriousness of errors. Many errors are not serious as they do not affect the meaning; for example if you use the wrong article (**le** or **la**), wrong pronoun (**je l'achète** for **je les achète**) or wrong adjective ending (**blanc** or **blanche**). So concentrate on getting your message across and learn from your mistakes.

Activities

◀) CD1, TR 33

1 Roger Burru has agreed to take part in a survey and is ready to talk about himself. Can you ask him in French the questions on the right? Then listen to the whole survey on the recording and check your answers (or check them in the **Key to the exercises and tests**).

a	Nom	Roger Burru	*What's your name?*
b	Âge	35	*How old are you?*
c	Marié(e)	oui	*Are you married?*
d	Enfant(s)	non	*Have you any children?*
e	Profession	professeur	*What's your job?*
f	Depuis ...	10 ans	*Since when?*
g	Adresse	Lille	*Where do you live?*
h	Sport	natation	*What sport do you do?*
i	Loisir	faire la cuisine	*What are your hobbies?*

Now it's your turn to take part in a survey. Can you answer in French the same questions? (The answers are not included in **Key to the exercises and tests**.)

◀) CD1, TR 34

2 On the recording you will hear Chloé talk about her likes and dislikes. Listen carefully and put a tick in the appropriate box:

	adore	aime beaucoup	n'aime pas	déteste
a Playing volleyball	☐	☐	☐	☐
b Working on Sundays	☐	☐	☐	☐
c Going out in the evenings	☐	☐	☐	☐
d Watching TV	☐	☐	☐	☐
e Listening to music	☐	☐	☐	☐
f Shopping	☐	☐	☐	☐
g Eating out	☐	☐	☐	☐

h Cooking ☐ ☐ ☐ ☐

Now it's your turn to tell Chloé what you like and dislike. Can you think of any more likes/dislikes you could add to the list?

3 Answer the following questions using the example as a model. You may have to revise the verbs ending in -er (Unit 3, Section 1), -ir and -re (Unit 5, Section 5), **prendre** (Unit 5, Section 9) and **faire** (Unit 5, Section 8).

a	Vous_achetez les_oranges?	Oui nous les_achetons.
b	Vous prenez le train?	Oui, je …
c	Je connais M. Durand?	Oui, vous …
d	Elle a les timbres?	Oui, elle …
e	Vous_avez l'adresse de Claude?	Oui, je …
f	Ils_aiment le coq au vin?	Oui, ils …
g	Vous faites la cuisine?	Oui, je …
h	Vous_attendez l'autobus?	Oui, nous …
i	Il regarde la télé?	Oui, il …
j	Vous_écoutez les disques?	Oui, nous …

4 Find the right ending for each sentence:

a	Il ne va …	**i**	jamais de sport.
b	Il n'écoute …	**ii**	plus de viande. Il est végétarien.
c	Elle ne veut …	**iii**	pas du piano.
d	Il ne mange …	**iv**	rien faire.
e	Elle ne boit …	**v**	qu'une fille.
f	Je ne regarde …	**vi**	plus comme secrétaire.
g	Il ne joue …	**vii**	jamais de musique.
h	Elle ne travaille …	**viii**	pas dans les musées.
i	Il n'a …	**ix**	que de l'eau.
j	Elle ne fait …	**x**	plus la télé.

◀) **CD1, TR 35**

5 Listen to the weather report while looking at the map on the following page; some of the statements (a–l) are true (**vrai**), others are false (**faux**). Put an x in the appropriate boxes.

		vrai	faux
a	Il fait beau à Newcastle.	☐	☐
b	À Brighton, il pleut.	☐	☐
c	Il pleut à Calais.	☐	☐
d	Le soleil brille à Nice.	☐	☐
e	Il pleut à Strasbourg.	☐	☐
f	Il fait froid en Espagne.	☐	☐
g	Il fait du vent à Malaga.	☐	☐
h	Il fait très chaud en Italie.	☐	☐
I	Il fait du vent à Rome.	☐	☐
j	En Suisse il fait chaud.	☐	☐
k	Il neige à Ostende.	☐	☐
l	Le soleil brille à Bruxelles.	☐	☐

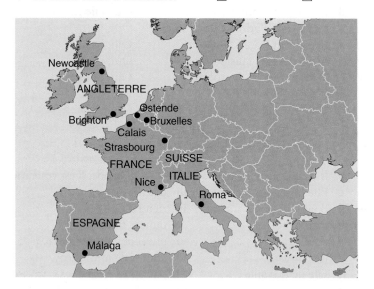

◀) **CD1, TR 36**

6 Rôle-play

You take part in a phone-in radio programme. The interviewer asks you questions on your likes and dislikes and those of your partner.

THINGS TO REMEMBER

In this unit you have learnt to talk about your likes and dislikes, your hobbies and the weather. You've also learnt more negatives words and the difference between **connaître** and **savoir**. See how much you remember and say the following in French:

1 What sport do you do?

2 I windsurf when it is sunny in summer.

3 When the weather is bad I play squash.

4 What hobbies do you have?

5 I like cooking very much.

6 I never watch television.

7 My son plays trumpet at school.

8 On Saturdays I love going out with my friends.

9 I do not know him well.

10 Do you know what time the film starts?

You'll find the answers in the **Key to the exercises and tests** at the end of the book. If your answers are correct you are ready to move to Unit 9. If you found the test difficult, spend more time revising Unit 8.

9

Qu'est-ce qu'il faut faire?
What should I do?

In this unit you will learn
- *A few useful linking words*
- *How to ask for assistance*
- *How to use* pouvoir *and* vouloir
- *How to give and understand instructions*

Before you start

This unit prepares you to cope with difficulties you may encounter in France. It gives you the few structures you need to let people know that you're having a problem: **je suis perdu, je ne comprends pas, la machine ne marche pas,** and also to ask for help: **vous pouvez me montrer? qu'est-ce qu'il faut faire?** (see **Key words and phrases**).

Essayez! **Have a go!**

1 How would you ask someone politely to:
  a repeat?
  b speak more slowly?

2 How would you answer the question:
  Quel temps fait-il aujourd'hui?

Key words and phrases

For you to say

pardon Monsieur, Madame …	*excuse me*
je suis perdu	*I'm lost*
je ne sais pas …	*I don't know …*
je ne comprends pas …	*I don't understand …*
vous pouvez m'aider, s'il vous plaît?	*can you help me please?*
qu'est-ce qu'il faut faire?	*what must I/we do?*
la machine ne marche pas	*the machine does not work*
utiliser l'Internet	*to use the Internet*
excusez-moi de vous déranger	*sorry to disturb you*
d'abord	*firstly*
et puis	*and then*
après ça	*after that*
finalement	*finally*

For you to understand

il faut_introduire …	*you must insert …*
il faut vérifier le niveau d'huile	*you have to check the oil level*
vous devez composter le billet	*you must date-stamp the ticket*
je vais m'en_occuper	*I'll attend to it*
ne pas déranger	*do not disturb*
en dérangement/en panne	*out of order* (machine, telephone)
hors de service	*out of order*

Dialogues

Jane est au garage. Elle demande au mécanicien de vérifier le moteur de son auto qui fait un drôle de bruit.

Jane is at the garage, asking the mechanic to check the engine of her car which is making a strange noise.

Jane	Ah, bonjour Monsieur. Voilà … Depuis ce matin il y a un drôle de bruit dans le moteur de ma voiture. Je ne sais pas ce que c'est. Je ne comprends pas, la voiture marche bien mais …
Mécanicien	Oui, bien sûr! Avez-vous vérifié le niveau d'huile? Le niveau d'eau? Il fait très chaud aujourd'hui et peut-être que **le moteur chauffe trop**.
Jane	Euh … non. Je ne sais pas ce qu'il faut faire. Vous pouvez vérifier tout ça, s'il vous plaît?
Mécanicien	Bon, allez … d'accord, **repassez** dans trois_heures, je m'en_occupe.

le moteur chauffe trop *the engine is heating up too much*
repassez *come back*

Jane est sur le quai de la gare. Elle essaie de composter son billet pour le valider mais sans succès. Elle arrête une passante.

Jane is on the platform at the station. She is trying to date-stamp her ticket but she is having difficulties. She stops a passer-by:

Jane	Pardon, Madame, je ne sais pas comment marche cette machine. Vous pouvez m'aider, s'il vous plaît?
Passante	Mais oui, Mademoiselle, c'est très facile; il faut introduire votre billet sous **la flèche verte**.
Jane	C'est ce que j'ai fait et ça ne marche pas.
Passante	Alors il faut peut-être tourner le billet **dans l'autre sens**?
Jane	(*she hears a click*) Ah, bien, le billet est maintenant composté. Merci, Madame, et excusez-moi de vous avoir dérangée.
Passante	**De rien**, Mademoiselle.

la flèche verte *the green arrow*
c'est ce que j'ai fait *that's what I've done*
dans l'autre sens *the other way round*
de rien *don't mention it* (lit. *for nothing*)

Grammar

1 ASKING FOR ASSISTANCE

There are several ways of asking a favour, depending on how polite you want to be and how well you know the person.

The easiest but perhaps least polite way of asking is to use the verb in the 2nd person plural (i.e. **vous** person) deleting the **vous**:

Faites le plein, s'il vous plaît.   *Fill the car up with petrol, please (lit. make the full, please).*

A more polite way of asking is to start with **vous pouvez** (*can you*) and raise the voice on the last word:

Vous pouvez me montrer, s'il vous plaît?   *Can you show me, please?*

Some likely answers:

Oui, avec plaisir	*Yes, with pleasure*
Certainement	*Certainly*
D'accord	*OK*
Bien sûr	*Of course*

Like the verbs **aimer, détester, adorer** (Unit 8), **vous pouvez** is followed by a verb in the infinitive:

Vous pouvez vérifier le niveau d'huile, s'il vous plaît?   *Can you check the oil level, please?*

2 TWO VERY USEFUL VERBS: **POUVOIR** *TO BE ABLE TO,* **VOULOIR** *TO WANT*

Pouvoir and **vouloir** are two verbs used very frequently in French:

pouvoir *to be able to, can*	**vouloir** *to want*
je peux	je veux
tu peux	tu veux
il/elle/on peut	il/elle/on veut
nous pouvons	nous voulons
vous pouvez	vous voulez
ils/elles peuvent	ils/elles veulent

Insight

As we saw in the examples given above, the most useful form of the verb **pouvoir** is **Vous pouvez** followed by **me** and a verb in the infinitive. In the second part of the book there will be many opportunities to use it in everyday situations.

3 GIVING AND UNDERSTANDING INSTRUCTIONS

a The simplest and most commonly used way to give instructions is to use the **vous** or **tu** forms of the present tense:

Pour téléphoner en Grande Bretagne, **vous composez** le 00, **vous attendez** la tonalité, **vous faites** le 44 puis l'indicatif de la ville sans le 0.	*To phone Great Britain, dial 00, wait for the dialling tone, dial 44 then the local code without the zero.*

b In written instruction, a verb is often in the infinitive:

Introduire votre billet sous la flèche verte, le **glisser** vers la gauche jusqu'au déclic; si la mention 'tournez votre billet' apparaît, **présenter** l'autre extrémité.	*Insert your ticket under the green arrow and slide it to the left until there is a click; if the sign 'turn your ticket' appears, insert the other end.*

c Qu'est-ce qu'il faut ...? To find out what needs to be done, use **qu'est-ce qu'il faut** followed by the appropriate verb in the infinitive:

Qu'est-ce qu'il faut faire pour composter son billet?	*What do you have to do to date-stamp your ticket?*

d Il faut + a verb. Followed by a verb in the infinitive, **il faut** (which is only used in the 3rd person) means any of the following, depending on the context: *it is necessary, I/we/you have to, must, one has to, must*:

Il faut décrocher l'appareil.	*You must lift the receiver.*
Il faut attendre la tonalité.	*One must wait for the dialling tone.*
Il faut composter le billet.	*You must date-stamp your ticket.*

···

> ### Insight
> There is another way of saying *must* in French by conjugating the verb **devoir**. Thus you would say: **Je dois composter mon billet** if you say what you must do, and **Vous devez composter votre billet** if you tell someone what he/she must do. Using **Il faut ...** is simpler as it applies to everybody.

···

e Il faut + a noun. Followed by a noun, **il faut** means *you need/one needs/I need*. The pronouns **me** (*to me*), **lui** (*to him, to her*), **nous** (*to us*) can be inserted to make it more personal:

Il lui faut **une télécarte pour téléphoner.**	*He needs a phone card to phone.*
Il me faut_**un passeport pour aller en France.**	*I need a passport to go to France.*

Activities

1 Using the words in the box, say what is needed in each case. Practise the questions and answers aloud:

Qu'est-ce qu'il faut

a	pour ouvrir une bouteille?	**i**	une station-service
b	pour prendre le train?	**ii**	le livre *Get started in French*
c	pour envoyer une lettre?	**iii**	une raquette et des balles
d	pour faire une omelette?	**iv**	un passeport
e	pour jouer au tennis?	**v**	un tire-bouchon
f	pour jouer de la musique?	**vi**	des_œufs
g	pour apprendre le français?	**vii**	un billet
h	pour aller en France?	**viii**	un_instrument
i	pour acheter de l'essence?	**ix**	un timbre

2 Below is a list of things you need to do *to keep fit* **pour être en pleine forme**. Match them up with the appropriate verbs on the left. You may need to look up some of the words in the vocabulary list at the back of the book.

Pour être en pleine forme il faut

a	boire	**i**	un sport
b	manger	**ii**	les sucreries et le sel
c	pratiquer	**iii**	son travail
d	dormir	**iv**	peu d'alcool
e	diminuer	**v**	beaucoup de légumes et de fruits
f	aimer	**vi**	huit heures par jour

3 Here is a recipe from a children's cookery book. Match the instructions with the corresponding drawings then answer the questions:

Omelette

(pour quatre personnes)

a D'abord tu bats sept œufs dans un grand bol.

b Puis tu poivres et tu sales.

c Ensuite tu fais fondre dans la poêle 30 grammes de beurre.

d Quand le beurre est chaud, tu verses les œufs.

e Après trois ou quatre minutes, tu mélanges avec une fourchette.

f Finalement, quand l'omelette est cuite, tu sers immédiatement.

   i How many eggs are needed?

  ii What do you do after beating the eggs?

 iii What do you melt in the frying pan?

  iv When is the egg mixture poured into the frying pan?

   v What do you use to mix the mixture?

4 To know what to do to check your emails in a French cybercafé, you need to understand some key words and phrases. See if you can put the following lines in a sequential order starting with **c**.

a Donc, il faut appuyer sur le bouton «marche/arrêt» sur le clavier.
b ... et sélectionner l'Internet.
c Il faut mettre l'ordinateur en marche.
d Ça y est! Vous pouvez commencer à vérifier vos courriels.
e Vous devez donc cliquer dessus avec la souris.
f Ensuite, il faut aller dans «Menu».

◀) **CD1, TR 39**

5 Rôle-play

You are now ready to check your emails using a computer in a French cybercafé. Follow the prompts.

LEARN TO GUESS THE MEANING

Here are three tips to help your general listening and reading comprehension:

▶ **Imagine the situation.**
When listening to the recording try to imagine where the scene is taking place and who the main characters are. Let your experience of the world help you guess the meaning of the conversation, e.g. if a dialogue takes place in a snack bar you can predict the kind of vocabulary that is being used.

▶ **Concentrate on the main part.**
When watching a foreign film you usually get the meaning of the whole story from a few individual shots. Understanding a foreign conversation or article is similar. Concentrate on the main parts to get the message and don't worry about individual words. When conversing with French speakers look out for clues given by facial expressions and body language; they can tell you a lot about the mood and atmosphere of the conversation.

▶ **Guess the key words; if you cannot, ask.**
When there are key words you don't understand, try to guess what they mean from the context. If you're listening to a

French speaker and cannot get the gist of a whole passage because of one word or phrase, try to repeat that word with a questioning tone; the speaker will probably paraphrase it, giving you the chance to understand it. If for example you wanted to find out the meaning of the word **voyager** (*to travel*) you would ask **Que veut dire voyager?**

Pratiquez! **Practise!** The notice below is situated in the grounds of a museum of sculptures in Paris. There are strict rules about what you can and cannot do! What are they? (Check your answers with the translation in **Key to the exercises and tests.**)

IL EST EXPRESSÉMENT DÉFENDU:
– de photographier avec pied ou flash
– de dégrader les sculptures, vases
– de cueillir des fleurs ou des fruits
– d'escalader les sculptures
– de marcher sur le gazon et de monter sur les bancs
– de déjeuner hors de la zone réservée à la cafétéria
– d'introduire des animaux
– de circuler à bicyclette
– de jouer avec des balles et ballons
– de déposer ou de jeter des ordures ailleurs que dans des
  corbeilles à papier

THINGS TO REMEMBER

This unit has prepared you to cope with difficulties you may encounter in France. It gave you only a few but useful structures which can be used in many situations. Can you remember them? Say in French:

1 I don't know.

2 I don't understand.

3 Can you help me please?

4 The machine does not work.

5 What must I do?

6 I need a passport to go to France.

7 One needs to drink a lot.

You'll find the answers in the **Key to the exercises and tests** at the end of the book. If your answers are correct you are ready to move to Unit 10. If you found the test difficult, spend more time revising Unit 9.

10

À l'avenir
In the future

In this unit you will learn
- *How to say what you usually do*
- *How to say what you need*
- *How to talk about your future plans*
- *How to use the pronoun y*
- *Two useful verbs sortir and venir*

Before you start

Talking about the future is very easy in French. All you need to do is to use **je vais** followed by the infinitive form of whatever you're going to do. For example to say that you intend to play tennis tomorrow you would say: **demain je vais jouer au tennis.** In this unit you'll learn useful words and expressions to describe your typical day and say what you intend to do in the future.

Essayez! **Have a go!**

1 If you see on a telephone box a notice saying **En dérangement** what does it mean?
2 You want to use the Internet from a post office in France. How would you ask: *What must I do to use the Internet?*

Key words and phrases

demain	*tomorrow*
à l'avenir	*in the future*
qu'est-ce que vous_allez faire?	*what are you going to do?*
je vais …	*I'm going to …*
visiter les monuments historiques	*visit old buildings*
rendre visite à mes_amis	*visit my friends*
voyager	*to travel*
marcher, se promener	*to walk, to go for walks*
faire de longues promenades	*to go for long walks*
faire du tourisme	*to do some sightseeing*
passer quelques jours …	*spend a few days …*
partir pour une semaine …	*go for a week …*
au bord de la mer	*to the seaside*
à la campagne	*to the countryside*
à la montagne	*to the mountains*
en_été, en_automne, en_hiver	*in summer, in autumn, in winter*
au printemps	*in spring*
l'année prochaine	*next year*
en mars	*in March*
pendant le mois d'août	*during the month of August*
j'ai besoin de …	*I need …*
j'ai chaud, froid	*I'm hot, cold*
j'ai soif, faim	*I'm thirsty, hungry*
comment passez-vous votre journée, vos vacances?	*how do you spend your day, your holiday?*
généralement	*generally*
je me lève	*I get up*
je m'habille	*I get dressed*
je me lave	*I wash*
je prends le petit déjeuner	*I have breakfast*
je pars de la maison	*I leave the house*
j'emmène les_enfants à l'école	*I take the children to school*

je vais chez mes_amis	*I go to my friends' house*
je fais des courses	*I do some shopping*
je prépare le déjeuner	*I prepare lunch*
je vais chercher Jean à la gare	*I go and fetch John from the station*
le soir, je vais au cinéma	*in the evening I go to the cinema*
je me couche/je vais au lit	*I go to bed*
louer	*to rent*
se baigner	*to go for a swim*
surtout	*mainly*
se reposer	*to rest*
rester	*to stay*
lire	*to read*
sortir (en boîte)	*to go out (to a nightclub/ private membership club)*
à la maison	*at home*

Insight

This unit introduces few new grammatical structures but quite a lot of new vocabulary. Once you know it you will be able to talk about what you do every day and on holiday.

Dialogue

Les Durand parlent de leurs projets pour les vacances d'été.

The Durands talk about their summer holiday plans.

Listen or read at least twice. How long are they going on holiday for? Where are they going? Note down at least three things M. and Mme Durand intend to do. Does their daughter Rosine enjoy sightseeing?

Jane	Monsieur et Madame Durand, qu'est-ce que vous_allez faire pour vos vacances cet_été?
M. Durand	Nous_allons prendre quatre semaines de vacances: une semaine au bord de la mer au mois de juillet et trois semaines à la montagne en_août.
Jane	Vous_allez rester à l'hôtel ou vous_allez louer une maison?
Mme Durand	Nous_allons d'abord passer quelques jours chez nos_amis au bord de la mer. Ils_habitent à 50 km de Nice. Après ça nous_allons dans notre maison de campagne dans le petit village de Puy-St-Pierre près de Briançon.
Jane	Et comment allez-vous passer vos vacances?
Mme Durand	Au bord de la mer, je vais me baigner tous les jours. À Puy-St-Pierre, je voudrais jouer au tennis, faire de longues promenades et visiter les monuments historiques de la région.
M. Durand	Moi, je vais surtout me reposer, lire et faire un peu de sport comme le tennis ou jouer à la pétanque avec les_enfants. Le soir, j'espère sortir quelquefois pour voir un bon film ou même aller au restaurant.
Rosine	Moi, cette année je ne veux pas faire de tourisme **parce que** c'est **ennuyeux**. Je préfère rester à la maison ou sortir avec mes_amis en boîte.

QV

parce que *because*
ennuyeux *boring*

Insight

Passer les vacances, passer de bonnes vacances .... Vacances is always used in the plural form. The French do like their holidays and have quite a lot of them!

Grammar

1 SAYING WHAT YOU USUALLY DO USING SOME REFLEXIVE VERBS

When describing your typical day you can't avoid using reflexive verbs, i.e. verbs describing things you do to or for yourself such as **se lever** (*to get oneself up*), **s'habiller** (*to get dressed*). While in English *myself, yourself, himself*, etc... is often dropped, in French **me, te, se**, etc... must be kept. Here is the pattern followed by all reflexive verbs in the present:

se laver	*to wash (oneself)*
je me lave	*I wash (myself)*
tu te laves	*you wash (yourself)*
il/elle/on se lave	*he/she/it/one washes (himself, etc...)*
nous nous lavons	*we wash (ourselves)*
vous vous lavez	*you wash (yourself/selves)*
ils/elles se lavent	*they wash (themselves)*

Insight

Perhaps the most useful reflexive verbs is **s'appeler** (lit. *to call oneself*).

Comment vous_appel**e**z-vous? Je m'app**e**lle …
Comment t'app**e**lles-tu? (friendly form) Je m'app**e**lle …
Comment s'app**e**llent-ils? Ils s'app**e**llent …

The letter **e** before a single **l** as in **appeler** is always sounded as **e**. The letter **e** before a double **ll** as in **appellent** is always sounded as **è**.

Pratiquez! **Practise!** To check that you understand reflexive verbs: try to write out **s'habiller** (*to get dressed*). **Me, te, se** will be shortened to **m', t', s'** as **habiller** starts with an **h**.

2 *SAYING WHAT YOU NEED:* **J'AI BESOIN DE ...**

To say what item you need, use **j'ai besoin de (d')** followed by
a noun:

J'ai besoin d'un   *I need a passport*
  passeport pour   *for France.*
  la France.
Il a besoin d'un   *He needs a 0€50*
  timbre de 50   *stamp to send his*
  centimes pour   *letter.*
  envoyer sa lettre.

To say what you need to do, use **j'ai besoin de (d')** followed by a
verb in the infinitive:

J'ai chaud; **j'ai besoin de boire**   *I'm hot; I need to drink a glass of*
  un verre d'eau.   *water.*
Elle n'a plus d'argent. **Elle**   *She has no money left. She needs*
  a besoin d'aller à la banque.   *to go to the bank.*

▶ **J'ai chaud/froid/faim/soif** use **avoir** (not être!).
▶ **Pour** is used before verbs in the infinitive to translate the
  idea of *in order to*: **Pour envoyer sa lettre** il a besoin d'un
  timbre.

Insight
  You can replace **J'ai besoin de ...** with **Il me faut ...** which was
  introduced in Unit 9. It is simpler to use.

3 STATING YOUR INTENTIONS

Just as you use **je voudrais** to say what you would like to do, use
je vais to say what you are going to do followed by the verb in the
infinitive:

Je vais	**me lever** à huit heures.
I'm going	*to get up at eight o'clock.*
Tu vas	**prendre** le petit déjeuner à neuf heures.
You're going	*to have breakfast at nine o'clock.*
Il/Elle va	**partir** de la maison.
He/She is going	*to leave the house.*
Nous_allons	**faire** des courses à midi.
We're going	*to do some shopping at lunchtime.*
Vous_allez	**chercher** Jean à la gare.
You're going	*to fetch John from the station.*
Ils/Elles vont	**se coucher** vers 11 heures.
They're going	*to go to bed around 11 o'clock.*

Insight

Instead of the future tense you can also use the present if it is accompanied by a word which indicates that the action will take place in the future. Thus you can say: **je prends le train demain** instead of **je vais prendre le train demain**.

4 *THE PRONOUN* **Y**

To replace an expression of place preceded by **à**, use the pronoun **y** (*there*):

Vous_allez **à Paris?**	*Are you going to Paris?*
Oui, j'**y** vais.	*Yes, I'm going there.*
Il va travailler **à la pharmacie?**	*Is he going to work at the chemist's?*
Oui, il va **y** travailler.	*Yes, he's going to work there.*

Like other pronouns, e.g. **en, le, la, les**, etc. (Unit 8), **y** is placed just before the verb to which it refers, e.g. **il faut y aller** *we must go there*.

5 SORTIR *TO GO OUT,* **VENIR** *TO COME*

Here are two useful verbs to describe daily activities:

sortir *to go out*	venir *to come*
je sors	je viens
tu sors	tu viens
il/elle/on sort	il/elle/on vient
nous sortons	nous venons
vous sortez	vous venez
ils/elles sortent	ils/elles viennent

6 USING CAPITAL LETTERS

The months, seasons and days of the week do not take a capital letter in French unless they begin a sentence (Unit 5): **en juillet, en_été, le mardi.**

7 *WHEN TO USE* **VISITER** *(TO VISIT) IN FRENCH*

French people talk about visiting museums, old buildings or interesting places but they do not visit the cinema or their relations! They **go** to the cinema or the pub and they **pay a visit** or **see** their relations or friends:

Je vais_aller **visiter** le Louvre l'été prochain.	*I'm going to visit the Louvre next summer.*
Ce week-end je vais **rendre visite** à ma grand-mère.	*This weekend I'm going to visit my grandmother.*
Ils vont **voir** leurs_amis dans le sud de la France.	*They are going to visit their friends in the south of France.*

> **Insight**
> My students often use **visiter** instead of **aller** when discussing their night out at the pub … and I have to remind them that the French only use **visiter** in the context of 'cultural activities'!

ASSESS YOURSELF AND KEEP UP WITH GRAMMAR

Having reached the end of the Grammar section it may be useful to find out how well you're doing with grammar, ways to practise it and, in Units 11–20 of the book, how to build on what you already know.

▶ **How well are you doing with grammar?**
Look at the **Index** of grammar terms and decide which functions you feel are particularly important. Test yourself on two or three of these at a time using the **Activities** of Units 1–10. If you find the exercises difficult, revise the **Grammar** carefully studying the examples.

▶ **Test yourself in a practice activity.**
Once you've completed successfully all the activities in Units 1–10 of **Get started in French** you may feel that you need to test yourself with another book of grammar exercises with the answers at the back. To test yourself you can read the explanations first and do the exercises or try the questions first, check the answers and work out the rule.

▶ **Build up a 'pattern bank'.**
Using the material from Units 11–20 of the book and any other French material, collect examples that can be listed under the structures you've already met. Seeing the structures in various contexts will help you assimilate them.

Activities

1 Imagine you're the man or woman whose typical day is illustrated on the following page. Write underneath the pictures what you do during the day but first have a go at saying it aloud.

a D'abord je …

b puis je …

c ensuite …

d À 8h.30 j'…

e ensuite …

f à midi …

g L'après-midi …

h ou je …

i ou je …

j Le soir je …

k ou j' …

l enfin …

2 Repeat Activity 1. This time pretend that you are describing your friend's, brother's or sister's typical day. Start the sentences with **il ...** or **elle ...** .

3 Your friends Robert and Jeanine have just planned their holidays for this summer. You ask them about it:
  a What does Robert say?
  b What does Jeanine tell you?

	Robert	Jeanine
Tu va partir quand?	in August	on 21st June
Pour combien de temps?	three weeks	ten days
Où vas-tu aller?	to Oxford in England	to Anglet near Biarritz in the south of France
Comment vas-tu passer tes vacances?	▶ learn English ▶ visit old buildings ▶ see some friends ▶ go out in the evening ▶ play tennis	▶ go swimming ▶ read a lot ▶ watch a bit (**un peu**) of TV ▶ go for long walks ▶ go to bed early (**tôt**)

Practise the exercise several times and try memorizing the questions.

4 What questions would you ask Robert and Jeanine if you said **vous** to them?

5 Jane has received a letter from a French friend who is about to visit her in Brighton. Fill in the gaps using each of the words in the box overleaf.

Chère Jane,

Merci (a)........ pour ta gentille lettre.

Oui, mon (b)........, mon fils et moi allons bientôt te rendre visite en (c)........ . Marc (d)........ l'école le 27 juin donc nous allons quitter

Paris le (e)........ 30 juin à midi pour arriver à Gatwick à deux
heures de (f) l' ....

Nous pensons (g)........ avec toi quelques (h)........, puis nous voulons
faire un peu de tourisme à Londres pour (i)........ les monuments
historiques. Ensuite nous voulons aller à Oxford où (j)........ nos
amis Green. Tu n'as pas (k)........ d'aller nous chercher à Gatwick.
Nous pouvons très bien (l)........ le train jusqu'à Brighton et puis un
taxi jusqu'à chez toi. À très bientôt. Amicalement.

prendre	**jours**	**mari**	**Grande-Bretagne**
finit	**habitent**	**samedi**	**rester** **visiter**
beaucoup		**besoin**	**après-midi**

◀) **CD2, TR 1**

6 Michel has a lot of things planned for tomorrow. Listen to the
recording and try to find out what's he's going to do. He has a list
of nine things. If you haven't got the recording, look at the answers
in the **Key to the exercises and tests** to find out about Michel's plans.

◀) **CD2, TR 2**

7 Rôle-play

Now it is your turn to speak about your next holiday. Listen to
Michel and use his prompts to answer.

You have finished the first part of the book with the basic
structures and grammatical points. Before going on to the second
part of the course which deals with everyday situations, do the
Self-test 3 (Units 8–10). Check your written answers in the **Key to
the exercises and tests** and the **Rôle-play scripts**, then record your
score in the box provided after the test. If your score is between 40
and 50 points go straight on to Unit 11. Between 20 and 40 points,
revise the points and areas which require more work. Below 20
points, go back over Units 8, 9 and 10, and take the test again to
see how much you have improved.

SELF-TEST 3

This test covers the main vocabulary and phrases, skills and language points in Units 8–10. **Bonne chance!**

1 Look at the box below and say out loud the likes and dislikes of Sophie and Mohamed. Then write down your own hobbies. One point for each correct answer.

		Sophie	Mohamed	Yourself
a	playing football	1	3	
b	cooking	3	1	
c	watching TV	3	2	
d	listening to music	4	3	
e	swimming	2	4	
f	skiing	4	1	
g	going to restaurants	2	3	
h	playing tennis	1	4	

Adore	Aime beaucoup	N'aime pas	Déteste
4	3	2	1

Points: _____/24

2 Fill in the part of the reflexive verbs which is missing. Half a point for each correct answer.
  a je ..... lève
  b tu ..... habilles
  c il ..... lave
  d nous ..... baignons
  e vous ..... reposez
  f elles ..... couchent

Points: _____/3

3 Talk about the weather in France, incorporating each icon on the map below into a full sentence:

e.g. **chaud** → **il fait chaud.**

a À Lille, ...

b En Bretagne, ...

c Dans le Sud-Ouest ....

d Sur la Côte d'Azur ....

e Dans les Alpes ....

f À Strasbourg ....

g À Paris ....

Points: ____/7

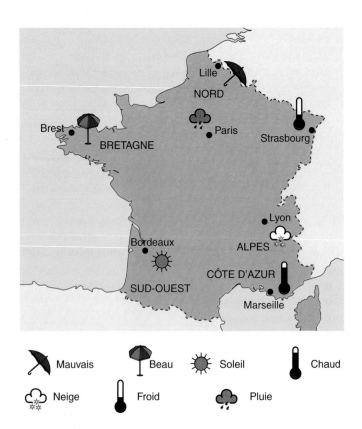

132

4 Talk about the future. Fill in the blanks. One point for each correct answer.

   a Qu'est-ce que vous ...... faire pour vos vacances?
   b Nous ...... passer deux semaines de vacances au bord de la mer.
   c Jane ...... visiter le sud de la France.
   d Tu ...... aller voir le film ce soir?
   e Je ...... me reposer chez moi.
   f Les Durand ...... se baigner tous les jours

Points: ____/6

◀) **CD2, TR 3**

5 Rôle-play

On your last trip to France you stayed with a very nice French family. When you left, you invited them to come and see you. Eva phones you to arrange their visit. Agree on suitable dates. Give yourself one point for each correct answer, and two when your answer consists of two correct sentences.

Points: ____/10

> Self-test 3 score (Units 8–10)
>
> Points: _____/50

11

Les courses
Shopping

In this unit you will
- **Find out about shops in France**
- **Practise buying groceries**
- **Practise buying something to wear**

Before you start, revise
- **Numbers (Appendix)**
- **Asking what's available (Unit 2, Section 3)**
- **Some and any (Unit 2, Section 4)**
- **Asking the price (Unit 2, Section 6)**
- **Saying precisely what you want (Unit 7, Section 2)**
- **Less ..., more ... (Unit 7, Section 4)**
- **Colours (Unit 7, Key words and phrases)**

Les magasins en France *Shops in France*

To find out about French shops read the passage below. Answering the questions in Activity 1 will help you to understand it.

Les magasins, en France, restent ouverts en général jusqu'à 19 heures ou 20 heures. Beaucoup ferment entre 12 heures et 14 heures. Le lundi ils sont souvent fermés dans les petites villes.

La boulangerie ouvre très tôt, vers sept heures du matin, et ferme tard car beaucoup de Français achètent leur pain deux fois par jour. Le dimanche matin, beaucoup de magasins comme les pâtisseries et les charcuteries restent ouverts. Les supermarchés (Monoprix) et hypermarchés (Auchan, Mammouth et Leclerc) sont encore généralement fermés le dimanche.

Dans toutes les grandes villes il y a un marché presque tous les jours et souvent le dimanche. Dans les petites villes ou villages il y a un marché une fois par semaine: le jour du marché. Au marché, on peut acheter des légumes, des fruits, **du poisson, de la viande** et même **des vêtements.**

les légumes *vegetables*
le poisson *fish*
la viande *meat*
les vêtements *clothes*

QV

ACTIVITY 1

a Until what time do shops generally stay open during the week?
b Are they usually open or shut at lunchtime?
c What day of the week do they often shut?
d Which shops are often open on Sunday morning?
e Are supermarkets generally open on Sundays?

ACTIVITY 2

Now read the passage several times and then, without looking at it, try to say out loud in French what you know about French shops. Check back with the passage.

> ## Insight
> As you do the exercise remember that:
>
> ▶ the **-s** at the end of the plural nouns is not pronounced.
> ▶ the **-nt** at the end of the verbs such as **ferment, restent** is not pronounced, so **ferment** sounds like 'fairm' and **restent** like 'rest'.

Key words and phrases

For you to say	
où est la boulangerie la plus proche, s'il vous plaît?	*where is the nearest bakery please?*
où est le supermarché le plus proche?	*where is the nearest supermarket?*
où est-ce que je peux acheter/ trouver un/une/des …	*where can I buy/find a/some …*
je voudrais/il me faut	*I would like/I need*
un/une/des …	*a/some …*
un paquet/une plaquette de …	*a pack of …*
une tranche de …	*a slice of …*
un morceau de …	*a piece of …*
vous avez autre chose?	*do you have anything else?*
c'est trop grand/petit/cher	*it's too big/small/expensive*
je cherche quelque chose de différent	*I'm looking for something different*
vous avez quelque chose de plus grand/petit/moins cher?	*have you got anything bigger/smaller/cheaper?*
je vais prendre une tranche/ un kilo/une livre de plus/ 500 grammes de moins	*I'll take a slice/a kilo/a pound more/500 grams less*
un demi-kilo	*half a kilo*
c'est combien?	*how much is it?*
c'est tout, merci	*that's all, thank you*

Acheter des provisions *Food shopping*

À la boucherie (*butcher's*), on achète:
du veau *veal*
du bœuf *beef*
du porc *pork*
des saucisses *sausages*
un poulet *chicken*

À la charcuterie (*delicatessen*), on achète:
du jambon *ham*
du saucisson *salami-type sausage*

À la boulangerie/pâtisserie (*baker's*), on achète:
une baguette *French 'stick'*
un pain complet *wholemeal loaf*
des petits pains *soft bread rolls*
une tarte aux fraises *strawberry tart*
des croissants *croissants*

À l'épicerie (*grocer's*), à l'alimentation (*foodstore*),
au supermarché (*supermarket*) on achète:
du thé *tea*
du café *coffee*
du beurre *butter*
du lait *milk*
des œufs (rhyming with **deux**) *eggs*
du fromage (de chèvre) *(goat's) cheese*
de la lessive *washing powder*
des pommes *apples*
des pommes de terre *potatoes*

QUICK VOCAB

une laitue *lettuce*
des yaourts à la fraise *strawberry yoghurts*
des boissons (jus de fruit, vins, etc.) *drinks (fruit juice, wine, etc.)*

Insight

The difference between **une charcuterie** and **une boucherie** is simple. A **charcuterie** sells cooked meats such as salami and pâté, while a **boucherie** sells uncooked meats such as pork chops and sausages!

ACTIVITY 3

There is no supermarket around; say in French which shops sell:

a chicken
b bread rolls
c pork
d washing powder
e milk
f salami
g wine

ACTIVITY 4

Below is a dialogue between a grocer and a client. See if you can put the lines in their correct order starting with **Bonjour Madame**.

a Une douzaine (*a dozen*), s'il vous plaît.
b Voilà, Madame, ça fait 6€85.
c **Bonjour Madame.**
d Non, il me faut aussi du jus de fruit.
e Oui … voilà une douzaine d'œufs, c'est tout?
f Bonjour Monsieur, je voudrais des œufs, s'il vous plaît.
g Qu'est-ce que je vous donne: jus de pomme, orange ou ananas (*pineapple*)?
h Vous en voulez combien?
i Je vais prendre le jus d'orange.

Dialogue 1: Au marché *At the market*

Un client achète des provisions pour un pique-nique.

At the market a customer buys some food for a picnic.

Listen to the recording (read the dialogue if you haven't got the recording) then without looking back at the text try Activity 5.

Client	Bonjour, mademoiselle. Je voudrais du beurre, s'il vous plaît.
Vendeuse	Une plaquette comme ça?
Client	Non, quelque chose de plus petit. Et qu'est-ce que vous avez comme fromages?
Vendeuse	Brie, fromage de chèvre, gruyère. Qu'est-ce que je vous donne?
Client	Du gruyère.
Vendeuse	Un morceau comme ça?
Client	Ah non … ça c'est un peu trop gros. Vous pouvez m'en donner un peu moins, s'il vous plaît? C'est pour notre pique-nique.
Vendeuse	Ah bon, d'accord. Voilà … 300 grammes. Et avec ça? Qu'est-ce qu'il vous faut? Des fruits, des yaourts, des biscuits?
Client	Euh, je vais prendre aussi des fruits.
Vendeuse	Alors nous avons des fraises, des bananes, des pommes, des pêches et du melon.
Client	Elles sont bonnes les fraises?
Vendeuse	Délicieuses. Je vous en mets un demi-kilo?
Client	500 grammes! Non, c'est un peu trop. Une demi-livre c'est assez. Ah oui, je voudrais aussi deux grandes bouteilles d'eau minérale … Voilà, c'est tout, c'est combien?
Vendeuse	Alors, ça vous fait 19€83.
Client	Et pour acheter du pain?
Vendeuse	Vous trouverez une boulangerie à 200 mètres sur votre gauche. Et … bon pique-nique Monsieur.

ACTIVITY 5

Look at the three columns below. Can you pick out four items bought by the customer?

a du poulet	**e** des pommes	**i** du lait
b du beurre	**f** du melon	**j** du vin
c du saucisson	**g** des fraises	**k** de la bière
d du fromage	**h** des pêches	**l** de l'eau minérale

ACTIVITY 6

Pretend that you're a customer. Using Dialogue 1 and the **Key words and phrases** earlier in the unit, practise buying a small packet of butter, 300 grams of cheese and half a pound of strawberries. Don't forget to find out where you can buy some bread. (The answers are not given in the **Key to the exercises and tests.**)

Acheter autre chose *Shopping for other things*

Les grands magasins de Paris (*department stores*):
www.paris.org/shops

Saviez-vous que l'on trouve des plans de Paris gratuits dans les grands magasins? Profitez-en (*take advantage of it*) pour en demander un:
«**Vous avez un plan de Paris, s'il vous plaît?**»

Insight

In this second part of the book you will be given many opportunities to put into practice one of the key tips introduced in Unit 9: Learn to guess the meaning of the key words you don't understand by finding out what they mean from the context. Did you understand the French passage above?

ACTIVITY 7

Here is a list of some shops and services in the town of Cauterets.

Alimentation Générale – Primeurs – **Ets. Vaud**
Bijouterie – **Angélique**
Brasserie – *«Au bon accueil»*
Boucherie – Charcuterie – *Bon et fils*
Cave – Marchand de Vin – *Veuve de Bonnet*
Chaussures – *Saint-Etienne*
Confection – MariSol
Droguerie – **Sans souci**
Généraliste – *Dr LeGrand*
Informatique – **infocom**
Librairie – *Blanchard*
Lingerie – Vêtements – *«Chez Madame»*
Pressing – À votre service
Traiteur – *bonne bouche*

Can you identify the French words for:
- **a** Fashion boutique
- **b** Dry-cleaner's
- **c** General practitioner
- **d** Book shop/store
- **e** IT

f Jewellery
g Shoe shop/store
h Ladies' wear
i Delicatessen
j Off-licence/liquor store

À la droguerie (*hardware shop*)
une brosse à dent *toothbrush*
un savon *soap*
un peigne *comb*
de l'huile pour bronzer *suntan lotion*
des kleenex *tissues*
un ouvre-boîte *tin opener*
un tire-bouchon *corkscrew*

Au bureau de tabac (*newsagent's*)
un carnet de timbres *book of stamps*
des journaux *newspapers*
du chewing gum *chewing gum*
une carte postale *postcard*
des magazines *magazines*

Au magasin de vêtements (*clothes shop*)
un pull-over *pullover*
un pantalon *trousers*
une chemise *a shirt*
une paire de chaussures *shoes*
un maillot de bain *swimming costume*
une robe *dress*
une jupe *skirt*
un jean/des jeans *jeans*

QUICK VOCAB

ACTIVITY 8

To make the most of French sales (**les soldes**) read the following paragraph and do the activity. For each word in bold find its English meaning in the box. Then read the rest of the text and say whether the statements are **vrai** or **faux**. Correct the false ones:

Deux fois par an, c'est le rendez-vous tant attendu des **(a) amateurs de bonnes affaires** et des victimes de la mode, quand les prix **(b) baissent**. Il y a alors beaucoup de **(c) remises** importantes et de **(d) promotion**.

| come down | reductions | special offers | bargain lovers |

Les soldes concernent principalement la mode (vêtements, chaussures, accessoires), mais aussi le linge de maison et des milliers d'autres articles. Généralement il s'agit des invendus de la collection précédente. Chaque période de soldes ne peut excéder six semaines. À Paris, elles durent un mois chacune et se déroulent en hiver (janvier/février) et en été (juin/juillet). En période de soldes, les magasins peuvent ouvrir le dimanche.

	vrai	faux
e The sales are only for household linen.	☐	☐
f The new season's collection is sold in the sales.	☐	☐
g The sales last up to eight weeks.	☐	☐
h During the sales, shops sometimes open on Sundays.	☐	☐

Dialogue 2: Dans un magasin de vêtements
In a clothes shop

For this dialogue, you need to understand two new questions:

1 Quelle taille? (*What size?*) when you're buying clothes. (42 is the European equivalent to the woman's size 14 in Britain and 12 in America, 44 is equivalent to size 16 in Britain and 14 in America, etc.). **Quelle pointure?** means *What shoe size?* Size 5 in Britain or 7 in America = 38, size 6 in Britain and 8 in America = 39, etc.

2 Je peux essayer? (*Can I try?*) when you want to try something on.

🎧 CD2, TR 5

Cliente	Bonjour, Madame, je cherche une jupe noire.
Vendeuse	Noire … euh oui d'accord. **Vous faites quelle taille?**
Cliente	40 … 40/42, **ça dépend du modèle.**
Vendeuse	J'ai ce modèle-ci en 40 et 42. C'est une jupe en coton. En 40, je n'ai pas de noir; j'ai du rouge, du gris mais pas de noir.
Cliente	Elles font combien ces jupes?
Vendeuse	63€.
Cliente	Vous n'avez pas quelque chose de moins cher?
Vendeuse	Euh non, sauf ces jupes **en solde** à 47€ mais elles sont grises.
Cliente	Non, il me faut du noir. Bon, eh bien, je vais essayer la jupe à 63€.
Vendeuse	(*pointing to a changing room*) Vous avez **la cabine d'essayage là-bas**.
	(*after a while*)
Vendeuse	Elle vous va bien?
Cliente	Ça va; elle est un peu large mais je crois que je vais la prendre car j'en ai besoin pour ce soir. Vous acceptez les cartes de crédit?
Vendeuse	Mais bien sûr, Madame.

vous faites quelle taille? *what size are you?*
ça dépend du modèle *it depends on the style*
en solde *on sale*
la cabine d'essayage *changing room*
là-bas *over there*

QUICK VOCAB

ACTIVITY 9

Listen to the recording again and try to spot the French version of the following phrases, then write them down:
a I'm looking for a black skirt
b What's your size?
c something cheaper

d I shall try

e the skirt at 63€

f How does it fit?

ACTIVITY 10

You're at the **bureau de tabac** (the **c** in **tabac** is not sounded) and wish to buy a newspaper, stamps, cards and a magazine for your wife.

Vendeur	Bonjour, Monsieur, vous désirez?
a You	*Say you would like a newspaper. Ask him what English newspapers he's got.*
Vendeur	Comme journaux anglais? Nous avons le *Times*, le *Guardian* et le *Daily Telegraph*.
b You	*Say that you will take* The Times *and these three postcards. Ask how much a stamp for England is.*
Vendeur	Un timbre pour l'Angleterre? C'est 70 centimes.
c You	*Say that you will take eight stamps.*
Vendeur	Voilà, Monsieur; huit timbres à 70 centimes. C'est tout?
d You	*Say that you'll also buy the magazine* Elle *for your wife.*
Vendeur	Très bien, Monsieur. Ça vous fait 13€27.

◀) CD2, TR 6

ACTIVITY 11

On the recording you will hear Michel shopping. Listen to the conversation several times and then answer the questions below, in English.

a What does he want to buy?

b What colours does he ask for?

c What's wrong with the first garment?

d What's wrong with the second garment?

e How much is the one he buys?

f Where is he likely to get a street map?

THINGS TO REMEMBER

In this unit you have learnt about French shops and how to buy groceries and other things. Can you remember the key words and expressions? Say in French:

1 Where can I buy ...?

2 Where is the nearest bakery please?

3 I am looking for something less expensive.

4 I need some fruit juice.

5 It is a little too big.

6 I shall also take some fruit.

7 Where is the changing room?

8 Can I try it on?

9 How much is this skirt?

10 Do you have/sell stamps?

You'll find the answers in the **Key to the exercises and tests** at the end of the book. If your answers are correct you are ready to move to Unit 12. If you found the test difficult, spend more time revising Unit 11.

12

Se reposer, dormir
Resting, sleeping

In this unit you will
- *Find out about accommodation in France*
- *Find out how to ask for information at the tourist office*
- *Practise booking into a hotel and a campsite*
- *Complain about things missing/not working*
- *Learn to spell your name*
- *Book accommodation online*

Before you start, revise
- *Saying what you want (Unit 7, Section 2)*
- *Asking what you can do (Unit 5, Section 2)*
- *Different ways to ask a question (Unit 5, Section 3)*
- *Asking the price (Unit 2, Section 6)*
- *Recognizing 'first', 'second', 'third', etc. (Unit 6, Section 7)*
- *Saying that there isn't any (Unit 4, Section 4)*
- *Dates (Unit 5, Section 6)*

Key words and phrases

je cherche ...	*I'm looking for ...*
à louer	*to rent*
un logement	*accommodation*
un appartement	*a flat/apartment*
	(Contd)

un gîte rural	*a self-catering cottage*
meublé et équipé	*furnished and fully equipped*
rester chez l'habitant	*to stay as a paying guest*
le mobil-home	*mobile home*
le terrain de camping	*campsite*
vous avez ... ?	*have you ... ?*
une chambre de libre	*a vacancy*
une chambre d'hôte	*a room in a guest house*
je voudrais réserver	*I would like to book*
une chambre simple/double	*a single/double room*
à deux lits	*with two single beds*
avec un grand lit	*with a double bed*
avec douche et WC	*with shower and WC*
avec salle de bains	*with bathroom*
avec pension complète	*with full board*
avec demi-pension	*with half board*
pour ... personne(s)	*for ... person(s)*
pour ... nuit(s)	*for ... night(s)*
du ... au	*from ... to*
le petit déjeuner est compris?	*is breakfast included?*
c'est en supplément/en plus/en sus	*it's extra*
c'est à quel nom?	*in whose name?*
l'acompte (m), **les arrhes**	*deposit*
c'est complet	*it's full up*

Choisir son logement *Choosing one's accommodation*

Les offices du tourisme et syndicats d'initiative:

- ▶ Maison de la France: www.franceguide.com
- ▶ L'office du tourisme à Paris: www.paris-touristoffice.com
- ▶ FNOTSI (Fédération Nationale des Offices de Tourisme et Syndicats d'Initiative): www.tourisme.fr

Pour louer des logements touristiques:

▶ Syndicat National des Résidences de Tourisme: www.snrt.fr

▶ CléVacances: www.clevacances.com/FR

À L'HÔTEL

Les hôtels sont **homologués** par le gouvernement d'une **étoile** * (hôtel simple) à quatre étoiles luxe ****L (très grand confort, palace). Tous doivent **afficher** leurs prix TTC (toutes taxes comprises) à l'extérieur de l'hôtel et dans les chambres. Les chambres proposent en général un lit deux personnes ou deux lits une personne. On a le choix entre pension complète et demi-pension. Il faut demander si le petit déjeuner est compris dans le prix de la chambre. Il est souvent en supplément. **La taxe de séjour** est toujours en sus. Pour réserver votre chambre, **renseignez-vous** dans les offices de tourisme/syndicats d'initiative ou **auprès des** centrales de réservation sur l'Internet.

AUTRES LOGEMENTS

Pour des séjours généralement plus longs (une semaine, un mois ou plus), il existe plusieurs formules:

▶ la résidence de tourisme/hôtelière. Cette formule propose des logements meublés et équipés avec toutes les **prestations** d'un bon hôtel. Ces résidences sont habituellement situées dans des **lieux** touristiques.

▶ la location en meublé qui propose des villas, appartements, studios, chalets, meublés et tout équipés.

▶ gîte ou la chambre. En louant chez l'habitant (à la nuit ou à la semaine, avec petit déjeuner et, parfois, table d'hôte), le touriste a l'occasion de mieux connaître et **partager** la façon de vivre des Français.

homologué *classified*
une étoile *star*
afficher *display*
la taxe de séjour *tourism tax*
renseignez-vous auprès de *ask for information*
la prestation *service*
le lieu, l'endroit *place*
partager *share*

ACTIVITY 1

The following visitors are looking for accommodation in France. Look at their requirements and decide which of the types of accommodation listed in the box best suits their needs:

a Une famille canadienne veut passer plusieurs semaines calmes dans un joli coin rural de la France.
b Un anglais a un rendez-vous d'affaires à Paris.
c Un couple de personnes âgées cherche un appartement pour un mois au bord de la mer et près d'un golf. Ils n'aiment pas faire la cuisine.
d Un couple américain désire visiter la France. Ils veulent pratiquer leur français et goûter à la cuisine traditionnelle.

> hôtel   résidence de tourisme   chambre d'hôte
> villa meublée et équipée

◀ **CD2, TR 7**

ACTIVITY 2

Study the following icons. They describe the type of services you are likely to find in a four-star hotel and room. Find the matching explanation for each icon then listen to the recording to check your answers.

a   **i** Climatisation

b   **ii** Accès handicapé

c   **iii** Mini-bar

d   **iv** Bureau de change dans l'hôtel

e   **v** Service en chambre

f   **vi** Bagagiste

g   **vii** Sèche-cheveux

h   **viii** Navette aéroport

i   **ix** Coffre-fort

j   **x** Chambre non-fumeur

k   **xi** Piscine

l   **xii** Ascenseur

m   **xiii** Télévision via satellite

n   **xiv** Animaux acceptés

o   **xv** Bar

p 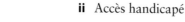   **xvi** WiFi

q   WiFi   **xvii**   Parking privé

Dialogue 1: À la recherche d'un hôtel
Looking for a hotel

À l'office du tourisme une touriste accompagnée de son mari se renseigne sur les hôtels à Paris.

At the tourist office, a tourist accompanied by her husband enquires about hotels in Paris.

What's the tourist's concern regarding the hotel?

Touriste	Bonjour Madame. Je viens d'arriver à Paris et je cherche une chambre. Vous avez une liste d'hôtels, s'il vous plaît?
Hôtesse	Oui Madame, voilà. *(the tourists look at the brochure)*
Touriste	Vous pouvez me réserver une chambre, s'il vous plaît?
Hôtesse	Oui, bien sûr. Vous choisissez quel hôtel?
Touriste	Un hôtel à trois étoiles, l'Hôtel Victor Hugo, dans le 16ème arrondissement. Mais c'est où le 16ème arrondissement?
Hôtesse	Paris est divisé en 20 arrondissements. Le 16ème se trouve au nord-ouest de Paris. C'est un quartier très résidentiel et très calme, et le Bois de Boulogne est tout près.
Touriste	Ah bon, alors c'est d'accord.
Hôtesse	C'est pour combien de personnes?
Touriste	Euh, pour mon mari et moi.
Hôtesse	Et pour combien de nuits?
Touriste	Pour deux nuits.
Hôtesse	Bien. Une chambre à deux lits ou un grand lit?
Touriste	Un grand lit. Nous voulons aussi une douche ou une salle de bains dans la chambre.
Hôtesse	Bon, alors une chambre pour deux nuits, pour deux personnes avec un grand lit et douche ou salle de bains. Très bien, je vais téléphoner et je vous réserve ça tout de suite.

ACTIVITY 3

Listen to the dialogue as often as you need and spot the French version of the following phrases:

a I have just arrived.
b Can you book me a room?
c Where is the 16th district?
d We also want a shower or a bathroom.
e I hope the hotel is not full!
f There are some vacancies.

Dialogue 2: À l'hôtel *In the hotel*

À la réception: les Wilson arrivent à leur hôtel.

At reception: the Wilsons arrive at their hotel. Does the hotel serve meals other than breakfast?

Touriste	Bonjour, Monsieur. Nous avons une réservation au nom de Wilson.
Réceptionniste	Ah oui, vous êtes les Anglais qui ont téléphoné cet après-midi!
Touriste	Oui, c'est ça.
Réceptionniste	Bon, vous avez la chambre 43 au deuxième étage. C'est une chambre très agréable avec grand lit, douche et WC.
Touriste	Le petit déjeuner est compris dans le prix de la chambre?
Réceptionniste	Ah non, Madame, c'est en plus : sept euros par personne.

(Contd)

◈ CD2, TR 9

Touriste	Et à quelle heure servez-vous le petit déjeuner?
Réceptionniste	À partir de 7.30 heures jusqu'à 10 heures.
Touriste	Vous servez le petit déjeuner dans la chambre?
Réceptionniste	Mais oui, Madame, bien sûr.
Touriste	Très bien. Pouvez-vous nous apporter demain matin le petit déjeuner à 8.30, s'il vous plaît?
Réceptionniste	C'est entendu, Madame.
Touriste	Est-ce qu'il y a un ascenseur dans l'hôtel? Nos valises sont très lourdes.
Réceptionniste	Oui, au fond du couloir à droite.
Touriste	On peut prendre un repas dans l'hôtel?
Réceptionniste	Non, je regrette, nous ne servons que le petit déjeuner mais il y a beaucoup de bons restaurants tout près d'ici.

ACTIVITY 4

Answer the following statements with **vrai** or **faux**:

	vrai	faux
a Room 43 is on the third floor.	☐	☐
b Breakfast is included in the price.	☐	☐
c Breakfast is served from eight o'clock.	☐	☐
d Their suitcases are heavy.	☐	☐
e The lift is at the end of the corridor on the left.	☐	☐
f They serve only breakfast.	☐	☐
g There are a lot of restaurants nearby.	☐	☐

ACTIVITY 5

By surfing the Internet you found a central hotel in the 5th district. Judging from its description, it seems quiet and comfortable, which is just what you are looking for. You make your way there to book a room for two.

Hôtel Relais Saint-Jacques

★★★★

3, rue de l'Abbé de l'Epée, 75005 Paris
Metro: Saint-Michel (4)
Luxembourg (RER B)
Tél: 33 (0) 1 43 40 77 79   Fax: 33 (0) 1 70 60 11 30

À deux pas des Jardins du Luxembourg,
de la Sorbonne, du Panthéon, et de la
rue Mouffetard, sur une petite place calme,
cet hôtel de pur style Haussmannien fréquenté
jadis par le célèbre écrivain autrichien
Rilke, conjugue harmonieusement: luxe, confort,
raffinement, spiritualité.

Insight

Rue Mouffetard is in one of Paris's oldest and liveliest neighbourhoods. It was a Roman road running from the Roman **Rive Gauche** city south to Italy. It is closed to normal motor traffic much of the week and is predominantly a pedestrian avenue with a permanent open-air market.

Vous	*Say 'good evening' and ask if they have a room.*
Réceptionniste	Oui, qu'est-ce que vous voulez comme chambre? Une chambre pour une personne?
Vous	*Say 'no, a double room with two beds and a bathroom'.*
Réceptionniste	C'est pour combien de nuits?
Vous	*It's for four nights.*
Réceptionniste	Oui, j'ai une chambre avec salle de bains.
Vous	*How much is it?*
	(Contd)

Réceptionniste	Alors, pour quatre nuits, nous faisons une promotion.
Vous	*Ask what 'promotion' is.*
Réceptionniste	Une promotion? C'est une offre spéciale. Vous restez chez nous quatre nuits, mais vous ne payez que trois nuits. Donc 140€ par nuit multipliés par trois, ça vous fait un total de 420€ au lieu de 560€.
Vous	*Ask if breakfast is included.*
Réceptionniste	Oui, le petit déjeuner est compris.
Vous	*Ask what time breakfast is served.*
Réceptionniste	Entre huit heures et dix heures.
Vous	*Ask if you can have a meal in the hotel.*
Réceptionniste	Mais oui, bien sûr. Le restaurant est au premier étage.
Vous	*Ask who Haussmann is.*
Réceptionniste	Le Baron Haussmann a modernisé Paris au 19ème siècle. C'est lui qui a créé les grandes avenues.

Se plaindre *Complaining*

Insight

While you often find the information on French hotels translated into English, you would certainly not find anything telling you how to complain! So make sure that you learn the key phrases.

Things aren't always as they ought to be and you may have to complain about things not working (**… ne marche(ent) pas**) or things that are missing (**il n'y a pas de …**). If the situation is really bad you can always ask to speak to the **directeur** (*manager*).

ACTIVITY 6

Use the words in the box on the next page and explain to the directeur that some objects in your room are not working (those in the square boxes) and some are missing (those in the circles).

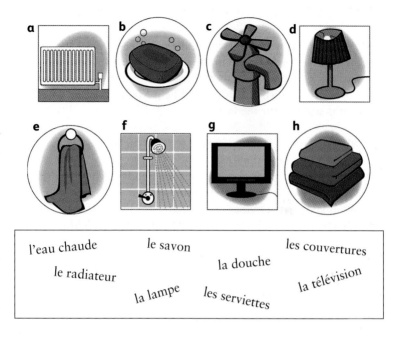

l'eau chaude le savon les couvertures
le radiateur la douche
la lampe les serviettes la télévision

Au camping-caravaning *At the caravan-campsite*

Camping en France: www.campingfrance.com
Fédération Française de Camping-Caravaning: www.ffcc.fr

En France, il y a 9000 terrains de camping aménagés classés de 0 à 4* et 2300 terrains à la ferme. Les offices du tourisme ont la liste des campings; ils peuvent vous aider à réserver un emplacement pour votre tente ou votre caravane.

Le camping sauvage (*camping on unauthorized sites*) est permis avec l'autorisation du propriétaire du terrain, mais interdit sur les plages, au bord des routes ou dans les sites classés. Renseignez-vous auprès des offices du tourisme ou à la gendarmerie.

ACTIVITY 7

Michael Price, his wife and two children, aged eight and six, are on their way to the Pyrénées in the south of France. They stop in a tourist office and enquire about caravan sites. Michael is given a leaflet on 'Le Cabaliros'. Study it and help Michael decide whether or not it is suitable for the family.

a Mr Price wants to know which services for his caravan are provided by Le Cabaliros.
b Mrs Price wants an easy and relaxed holiday. What facilities are there to help housewives and mothers?
c What sporting activities are available for the family?
d What fun activities can Mr and Mrs Price do while the children are occupied?

100 emplacements, dont 88 tourisme

GCC Emplacement avec branchement électrique. Alimentation en eau. Evacuation toutes eaux usées.

LE CABALIROS
65110 CAUTERETS
E-mail: chantal.boyrie@wanadoo.fr
Tel: 05 62 92 55 36
Tel: 05 62 92 55 38 (H.S.)
Fax: 05 62 92 55 36

ÉQUIPEMENTS				LOCATIONS
Restaurant	Ravitaillement	Douche chaude		Mobil-homes
Machine à laver	Salle de repassage	Jeux pour enfants	Jeux pour adultes	Vélos
Animation organisée	Télévision	Aire pour camping-car		

SPORTS ET LOISIRS			LE TERRAIN ET L'EAU
Piscine	Pêche (sur place ou à moins de 5 km)	Minigolf	Accès direct à la rivière

Dialogue 3

Monsieur Price vient d'arriver à l'accueil du Cabaliros.

Mr Price has just arrived at the reception of 'Le Cabaliros'. Is electricity included in the price?

◉ CD2, TR 10

Mr Price	Bonjour Madame. Avez-vous un emplacement pour une voiture et une caravane … pour huit jours?
Femme	Pour huit jours? Oui, c'est possible.
Mr Price	Il nous faut **un branchement électrique**.
Femme	Oui, sans problème.
Mr Price	C'est combien la nuit?
Femme	Alors pour le forfait emplacement, c'est 20€60 la nuit.
Mr Price	Forfait emplacement?
Femme	Oui, **c'est-à-dire** le prix pour l'emplacement de 90 m²; donc pour une voiture, une caravane et deux personnes.
Mr Price	Il faut payer pour l'électricité?
Femme	Oui, c'est en plus: 3€70 par nuit. Mais **par contre** pas de supplément pour l'eau chaude … **ni** pour les douches.
Mr Price	Ah bon … On peut voir l'emplacement?
Femme	Bien sûr. **Il me reste** un **emplacement à l'ombre**, vous le voulez?
Mr Price	Avec plaisir.
Femme	Mais avant, j'ai besoin de noter **la plaque d'immatriculation** de votre véhicule. Vous la connaissez?
Mr Price	Euh, oui. GY53 FKB.
Femme	Merci bien, Monsieur Price. On peut aller voir l'emplacement maintenant.

le branchement électrique *electric connection*
c'est-à-dire *which means*
par contre *on the other hand*
(ni …) ni *(neither …) nor*
il me reste … *I have got … left*
l'emplacement à l'ombre *pitch in the shade*
la plaque d'immatriculation *number plate*

QUICK VOCAB

L'alphabet français *The French alphabet*

ACTIVITY 8

Read the alphabet below several times and practise spelling your name and your address.

A	B	C	D	E	F	G
ah	bé	cé	dé	eux	eff	j'ai
H	I	J	K	L	M	N
ahsh	ee	j'y	kah	elle	emm	enne
O	P	Q	R	S	T	U
oh	pé	ku	erre	ess	té	u*
V	W	X	Y	Z		
vé	doubl'vé	eeks	ee grec	zed		

*as in **du**

▶ To spell double consonants, the French will say **deux** .... For example, to spell **mallet** they'll say: emm - ah - *deux elle* - eux - té; and to spell **poussin**: pé - oh - u - *deux ess* - ee - enne

▶ Be particularly careful when spelling the French letters **e, i, g** and **j** as they can be confusing for English speakers.

Réserver en ligne, envoyer un courriel *Booking online, sending an email*

Si vous avez l'intention de faire du camping ou de réserver un hôtel en France, il vaut mieux (*it's better*) réserver longtemps à l'avance surtout pendant les périodes de vacances. Lorsque la réservation est faite en ligne ou par courriel, il est généralement demandé de l'accompagner d'un versement d'arrhes ou d'un acompte (*an advance*).

ACTIVITY 9

John Osborne decides to book a mobile home online. For his reservation to be accepted, he needs to download it (**télécharger**), sign the contract, add the words **Lu et approuvé** next to his signature and return it to the campsite owner with **les arrhes**.

Read the contract and help John make sense of it by choosing for each highlighted word in the text its equivalent (i–vi on the next page) in English:

CONTRAT de RÉSERVATION de MOBIL-HOME

* Réserver un mobil-home au CAMPING LE GLACIER
  du _____ au _____ à partir de 16h ou avant 10h
* Nombre de personnes: _____
* Au prix net de: _____
* Montant des arrhes (25 % de la location): _____
* Taxe de séjour en supplément: 0.22€ p/jour par adulte _____

  _____

  ▶ **Draps et linge** non fournis.
  ▶ Pour tout **retard** supérieur à 24h, le client s'engage à en **aviser** le camping.
  ▶ En cas de départ anticipé, il n'y aura aucun **remboursement**.
  ▶ Une **caution** de 200€ sera demandée à l'arrivée et restituée au départ si l'**entretien** du Mobil-home a été effectué correctement.
  Signature du client précédée de 'Lu et approuvé' en manuscrit.

---

i   cleaning
ii refund
iii deposit
iv delay
v   sheets and towels
vi inform

ACTIVITY 10

John wrote an email (**un courriel**) to the **directeur du camping Le Glacier** in which he asked several questions. He has received the following reply. Read it and write in French the four questions that John is likely to have asked in his email.

To: **Josborne@hotmail.com**
Cc:
Subject: Réservation mobil-home

Cher Monsieur Osborne,

J'ai le plaisir de confirmer votre réservation du mobil-home du 15 au 22 août.

Je réponds à vos questions:

a) Entre quatre et six personnes peuvent dormir dans le mobil-home.
b) Oui, il faut amener les draps et les serviettes car nous ne les fournissons pas.
c) Oui, nous acceptons les chiens sans supplément.
d) Il faut payer une caution de 200€ à votre arrivée.

À très bientôt le plaisir de vous voir.

Le Directeur du Camping Le Glacier

THINGS TO REMEMBER

In this unit you have found out about accommodation in France, how to ask for information at the tourist office, practised booking into a hotel and a campsite, and complained about things missing or not working. How would you say the following in French?

1 I am looking for a three-star hotel.

2 Can you book me a room for two nights?

3 It is for my husband, my two children and me.

4 Do you have any vacancies?

5 At what time do you serve breakfast?

6 Can you bring us breakfast in our room tomorrow morning at 8.30?

7 The radiator does not work.

8 We have no towels in our room.

9 Do I need to pay a deposit?

10 Do you provide the sheets?

You'll find the answers in the **Key to the exercises and tests** at the end of the book. If your answers are correct you are ready to move to Unit 13. If you found the test difficult, spend more time revising Unit 12.

13

....

Bien manger, bien boire
Eating and drinking well

In this unit you will
- *Find out where to eat*
- *Practise ordering a snack*
- *Choose a menu and order a meal*

Before you start, revise
- *Saying what you want (Unit 7, Section 2)*
- *The verb* prendre *(Unit 5, Section 9)*
- *Some, any (Unit 2, Section 4)*
- *Asking questions (Unit 5, Section 3)*
- *Likes and dislikes (Unit 8, Section 2)*

Bien manger *Eating well*

La cuisine en France est très variée, chaque région offrant ses produits et spécialités gastronomiques. Grâce à sa population importante d'immigrés, la France a une cuisine ethnique riche et relativement bon marché. On peut également acheter un peu partout du fast-food et **des plats à emporter** dans des McDonald's, Pizza Hut etc. Par contre, les restaurants végétariens sont rares, ainsi que les menus qui incluent des plats végétariens.

On peut très bien manger en France dans des restaurants modestes appelés **les petits restaurants du coin**. Au menu ils ont souvent des plats simples mais appétissants comme un pâté maison et **un plat garni**.

On peut aussi manger dans **une brasserie** et commander un plat unique comme **la choucroute** avec de la bière; ou encore dans **un bistrot** où on choisira entre un bifteck-frites, une excellente spécialité et **le plat du jour**; ou pour pas cher dans **une crêperie**, un bar ou un café.

Les restaurants proposent en général plusieurs **menus**, du plus cher, 'le menu gastronomique', au plus modeste, 'le menu touristique' et **la carte**.

Le pourboire est toujours inclus (15%) dans l'addition. Si vous êtes satisfait, vous pouvez laisser quelques euros à la personne qui vous a servi.

le plat à emporter *take-away food*
le petit restaurant du coin *local restaurant offering good but cheap food*
le plat garni *dish with meat and vegetables or salad*
la brasserie *cross between a café and a restaurant*
la choucroute *cabbage, bacon, sausages, potatoes*
le bistrot *cheap restaurant*
le plat du jour *today's special*
la crêperie *pancake house*
le menu *list of dishes served at a fixed price for the whole meal*
la carte *list of dishes individually priced*
le pourboire *tip*

ACTIVITY 1

Without looking at the passage above, choose the correct phrase to complete the following sentences then check your answers in the **Key to the exercises and tests** at the end of the book.

a French cuisine consists *only of regional specialities/a variety of cuisines.*

b Fast-food and take-away food *can easily/cannot be found.*

c Les petits restaurants du coin are usually *cheap/expensive.*

d Un plat garni is a dish with *meat only/meat, vegetables or noodles.*

e In a brasserie one can eat *pancakes/a limited range of dishes.*

f Le plat du jour is *'today's special'/a dish with cold food.*

g If you want a pancake you go to a crêperie/bar.

h If you want the cheapest menu, you choose le menu gastronomique/le menu touristique.

Key words and phrases

vous désirez?	*what will you have?*
vous avez choisi?	*have you made a choice?*
qu'est-ce que vous avez	*what do you have*
à manger?	*to eat?*
à boire?	*to drink?*
qu'est-ce que vous avez	*what do you have in the way*
comme boissons/snacks?	*of drinks/snacks?*
comme parfums?	*of flavours?*
il ne reste plus de …	*there is no … left*
il n'y a plus de …	*there is no more*
des sandwiches au jambon/au fromage	*ham/cheese sandwiches*
une glace à la vanille	*vanilla ice cream*
de la bière en bouteille	*bottled beer*
de la pression	*draught beer*
un café	*a black coffee*
un café crème	*a white coffee* (with milk not cream)
un thé au citron	*lemon tea*
un thé nature	*tea* (without milk, etc…)
un thé avec du lait froid	*tea with cold milk*
une orange pressée	*freshly squeezed orange*
	(Contd)

un jus de fruit	*fruit juice*
un jus de pomme/d'ananas/de pamplemousse	*apple/pineapple/grapefruit juice*
qu'est-ce que c'est le/la/les …?	*what's the …?*
c'est quoi le/la/les …?	*what's the …?*
je vais en prendre un (une)	*I'll take one*
pour commencer …	*to start with …*
comme entrée	*as a starter*
comme plat principal	*as a main course*
ensuite …	*then …*
comme dessert …	*for dessert …*
le plat	*dish, course*
le plat cuisiné	*ready-cooked meal*
plats à emporter	*take-away food*
saignant/bleu	*rare* (lit. *bleeding/blue*)
à point	*medium*
bien cuit	*well done*
l'addition *(f)*	*the bill*

Insight

Understanding a French menu can be difficult! However, using any of the two expressions **Qu'est-ce que c'est …?** or **C'est quoi …?** will get you out of most tricky situations!

Dialogue 1: Commander un snack
Ordering a snack

À la terrasse d'un café deux touristes sont prêts à commander.

Two tourists sitting outside a café are ready to order.

*The man asks the waiter what a **croque-monsieur** is. Listen to or read the waiter's explanations: how would you explain to someone English what a **croque-monsieur** is? What is the woman ordering? What drinks are they having?*

♣ CD2, TR 11

Garçon	Bonjour, Messieurs-dames. Qu'est-ce que vous désirez?
Homme	Qu'est-ce que vous avez à manger?
Garçon	À manger, nous avons des sandwiches au jambon blanc, **rillettes**, pâté de campagne, saucisson sec, hot-dogs, omelettes, croque-monsieur …
Homme	Qu'est-ce que c'est un croque-monsieur?
Garçon	Un croque-monsieur? C'est deux **tranches de pain grillé** avec jambon et fromage **au milieu**.
Homme	**Ça a l'air** délicieux … je vais en prendre un.
Garçon	Et pour vous Madame?
Femme	Moi, je crois que je vais prendre une omelette … qu'est-ce que vous avez comme omelettes?
Garçon	Omelettes au fromage, aux **champignons**, aux herbes …
Femme	Une omelette aux champignons.
Garçon	Et comme boissons, Messieurs-dames?
Homme	Vous avez de la bière?
Garçon	Oui … nous avons de la bière pression et de la Kronenbourg en bouteille.
Homme	Bon, une pression s'il vous plaît.

(Contd)

Garçon	Je vous sers **un demi**?
Homme	Oui, c'est ça.
Femme	Moi, je vais prendre un café crème.
Garçon	Bon, alors une pression, un café crème, une omelette aux champignons et un croque-monsieur.
Homme	Merci bien, Monsieur.

QUICK VOCAB

rillettes *type of potted meat, usually pork, similar to pâté*
tranche de pain grillé *slice of toasted bread*
au milieu *in the middle*
ça a l'air *it seems*
les champignons *mushrooms*
un demi *half (usually half a pint, but sometimes half a litre)*

Insight

Croque-madame can also be ordered. They are like **croque-monsieur** but with an egg on top!

ACTIVITY 2

See if you can unscramble the dialogue below, starting with the sentence in bold:

a Je vais prendre une pression.
b À manger nous avons des sandwiches, des croque-monsieur, des pizzas …
c **Bonjour Monsieur, qu'est-ce que vous désirez?**
d De la pression et de la Kronenbourg en bouteille.
e Qu'est-ce que vous avez à manger?
f Je vais prendre une pizza; et comme bières, qu'est-ce que vous avez?

ACTIVITY 3

You're hungry and decide to go to a café for a snack. Here comes the waiter … be prepared to order:

	Garçon	Qu'est-ce que vous désirez?
a	**Vous**	*Say that you would like a croque-monsieur.*
	Garçon	Je suis désolé, Monsieur, mais il n'y en a plus.
b	**Vous**	*Ask him if he has any omelettes.*
	Garçon	Oui, nous avons omelettes nature, jambon et Parmentier.
c	**Vous**	*Ask what Parmentier is.*
	Garçon	Omelette Parmentier? C'est une omelette avec des pommes de terre.
d	**Vous**	*Say that you'll take the potato omelette.*
	Garçon	Bien, alors une omelette Parmentier; et à boire, Monsieur, qu'est-ce que je vous sers?
e	**Vous**	*Ask him what he has in the way of fruit juice* (the **s** of **jus** is not pronounced).
	Garçon	Comme jus de fruit nous avons du jus d'orange, du jus d'ananas, du jus de pamplemousse …
f	**Vous**	*Say that you would like a pineapple juice and the bill, please.*

ACTIVITY 4

Using the menu on the next page and the dialogue in Activity 3 as a guide, act out similar situations varying the dishes and drinks. (The answers are not given in the **Key to the exercises and tests.**)

Salades composées

Salade mixte..............................7,00
Tomates, salade, œuf

Salade végétarienne.............. 7,80
Tomates, poivron, maïs,
  carotte, concombre,
  salade

Chef salade.....................................9,00
Tomates, pommes à l'huile,
  jambon, gruyère, salade, œuf
  dur

Salade niçoise.................................12,00
Tomates, œuf, thon, poivrons,
  concombre, olives, salade,
  anchois

Buffet chaud

Croque monsieur...................... 5,00
Croque madame.......................5,50
Croque niçois............................5,80
Croque monsieur avec
  tomate et anchois.................5,80
Omelette nature (3 pièces)....5,50
Omelette jambon.....................6,50
Omelette fromage...................6,50
Omelette savoyarde................7,10
Omelette Parmentier.............7,10

Buffet froid

Poulet froid mayonnaise.............8,50
Assiette charcuterie......................9,30
Assiette anglaise...........................9,30
Assiette de viande froide............9,30

Sandwiches

Jambon de Paris............................3,70
Pâté ou rillettes............................4,00
Camembert ou gruyère..............4,00
Saucisson sec ou à l'ail...............4,00

Boissons

Café express.............................2,60
Thé au citron...........................3,60
Jus de fruit...............................3,60
Bière pression..........................3,60
Bière bouteille.........................3,60
Eau minérale............................3,60
Soda...3,60
Apéritif anisé...........................5,00

Dialogue 2: Au restaurant *At the restaurant*

> Menu à 33€
> *En entrée*
> L'œuf cocotte au foie gras,
> La soupe gratinée à l'oignon,
> Le Crottin de chèvre chaud et salade
> _____
> *En plat*
> Le confit de canard
> La poule au pot d'Henry IV garnie maison
> Le steak au poivre avec sa garniture
> _____
> *Dessert*
> La crème brûlée à l'ancienne
> Les profiteroles au chocolat
> La tarte des demoiselles Tatin à la crème

La Poule au Pot
RESTAURANT
Ouvert
de 19 heures à l'aube
DANS LES HALLES

9, rue Vauvilliers
75001 Paris
Tél.: 01 42 36 32 96

Insight

La Poule au Pot is the mythical French dish which King Henry IV had promised all the pots in the kingdom. It embodies, through the person of a good king, the aspiration of the French people to well-being (domestic life, Sunday rest, gastronomy). **La Poule au Pot** has given its name to many French restaurants.

Browsing on the Internet, a tourist finds 'La Poule au Pot', an authentically Art Deco bistro in the centre of Paris. He likes the menu and decides to try it out. Read the menu and listen to the conversation between the tourist and the waiter:

Customer	Vous avez une table pour une personne?
Garçon	Oui, monsieur, il nous en reste juste une près de la fenêtre.

(Contd)

♠ CD2, TR 12

	(later) Alors, qu'est-ce que ce **sera** pour vous, le menu à 33€ ou la carte?
Customer	Je vais prendre le menu.
Garçon	Qu'est-ce que je vous sers comme entrée?
Customer	C'est quoi 'L'œuf cocotte au foie gras'?
Garçon	C'est une spécialité bien française. C'est deux œufs **cuits au four** dans un ramequin. On y ajoute une tranche de foie gras et de la crème en fin de cuisson.
Customer	Je crois que je préfère la soupe à l'oignon.
Garçon	Une soupe gratinée, alors. Bien et ensuite?
Customer	Le steak au poivre.
Garçon	Vous le voulez comment? Saignant, à point ou bien cuit?
Customer	À point. Vous le servez avec quoi le steak?
Garçon	Avec une garniture de légumes de saison, **haricots verts**, carottes et une salade verte. Vous prendrez quelque chose à boire?
Customer	Oui, de l'eau minérale et puis une bouteille de Bordeaux. Vous pouvez **me conseiller** pour le vin?
Garçon	Oui, d'accord, je vous **apporte** un bon Bordeaux. *(later)* C'était bon?
Customer	Très bon, merci.
Garçon	Vous avez choisi un dessert?
Customer	Comme dessert, je vais prendre la tarte des demoiselles Tatin à la crème.
Garçon	Je vous la recommande ... elle est délicieuse et faite maison.
Customer	Vous pouvez expliquer le nom de la tarte?
Garçon	C'est une histoire célèbre. Les demoiselles Tatin avaient un hôtel familial dans la vallée de la Loire. Stéphanie Tatin était spécialiste de la tarte aux pommes. Un jour, **étourdie**, elle cuit la tarte et la sert **à l'envers** ...
Customer	À l'envers?
Garçon	Euh oui ... la tarte était complètement renversée ... comme ça ... Eh bien c'était un tel succès que ce plat est entré dans notre gastronomie nationale. Et voilà, vous prendrez bien un café après la tarte?
Customer	Non merci, et amenez l'addition après le dessert, s'il vous plaît.

sera *will be*
cuit au four *cooked in the oven*
haricots verts *green beans*
me conseiller *advise me*
apporter/amener *bring along*
c'était bon? *was it good?*
étourdi *absent-minded*
à l'envers *upside down*

ACTIVITY 5

Listen to the dialogue again and spot the French version of the following phrases:

a What is 'L'œuf cocotte au foie gras'?
b It is two eggs cooked in the oven.
c I think that I prefer …
d How do you serve the steak?
e Can you advise me about the wine?
f Can you explain the name of the tart?
g Bring the bill after dessert.

ACTIVITY 6

Now it's your turn to order a meal. When you check your answers in the **Key to the exercises and tests,** remember that there are variations to the answers given.

	Serveuse	Bonjour, Monsieur/Madame, vous avez choisi?
a	**You**	*Say that to start with you'll have a* **filet de hareng**.
	Serveuse	Je regrette, il n'y a plus de filet de hareng.
b	**You**	*Say that you'll have an* **avocat à la vinaigrette**.
	Serveuse	Bien, un avocat à la vinaigrette, et ensuite …
c	**You**	*Ask what is* **cassoulet**.
	Serveuse	C'est une spécialité française avec de la viande de porc et haricots blancs.
		(Contd)

d	**You**	*Say that you don't like beans. Say you prefer the* **grillade du jour** *with* **frites**.
	Serveuse	Vous la voulez comment, votre viande?
e	**You**	*Say medium and say that you would also like a bottle of Sauvignon.*
	Serveuse	*(after the starter)* Voilà. Une grillade avec frites.
f	**You**	*Ask what she has in the way of desserts.*
	Serveuse	Fromage, glaces, crème au caramel.
g	**You**	*Say that you'll have a vanilla ice cream.*
	Serveuse	Ah, je regrette mais nous n'avons plus de vanille.
h	**You**	*Ask what other flavours they have.*
	Serveuse	Citron, café, chocolat, fraise.
i	**You**	*Say that you will have a strawberry ice cream.*

ACTIVITY 7

You are on holiday in 'Les Landes' with your friend and her three children. You want to take them out on Friday for a nice meal. Look at the following two restaurants. Which one will you choose? Obviously, price needs to be considered plus the fact the children are boisterous. Luckily they eat any type of food!

BAR – TABACS – AUBERGE

LE PLATANE

Place de la République, 40300 PEYREHORADE
TÉL. 05 57 37 66 54

Service de 12 h à 14.30 et de 19 h à 22 h

MENU du jour 14€
Dimanche menus du jour de 18€30 à 26€ + CARTE

Traiteur – Cuisine régionale
et traditionnelle. Plats à emporter.
Banquets, mariages, séminaires, groupes.

L'AUBERGE AU BON COIN
40230 SAUBRIGUES
TÉL. 05 58 94 71 33

Service de 12 h à 14 h et de 19 h 30 à 22 h

MENUS: 13€ – 18€ – 23€ – 28€
CARTE: 14€ à 25€
MENU ENFANT: 8€

Fermeture: hors saison lundi soir et mardi

Cuisine traditionnelle,
spécialités régionales, dans un cadre typique
et familial au calme de la campagne landaise. Grande
capacité d'accueil, service en terrasse l'été. Grand parking.

Before going on to Unit 14 take the **Self-test 4** (Units 11–13).
Once you have done it, check your answers in the **Key to the
exercises and tests** and **Rôle-play scripts** and write your score in the
box provided after the text. If you score between 40 and 50 points,
you can go straight on to Unit 14. If your score is between 20 and
40 points, you need to spend more time revising the **Dialogues**
and **Key words and phrases**. Below 20 points, go back over Units
11, 12 and 13 and take the test again to see how much you have
improved.

SELF-TEST 4

This test covers the main vocabulary and phrases, skills and language points in Units 11–13. **Bonne chance!**

1 Can you do the following? Say the answers out loud and write them down. Three points for each correct answer.
   a Say that you are looking for a cotton dress.
   b Give the English translation for **Vous faites quelle taille?**
   c Ask whether you can try it on.
   d Say that it is a bit too expensive/big/small.
   e Ask: Do you have anything else?

Points: _____/15

2 Say the following out loud and write them down. Three points for each correct answer.
   a Say good evening and ask if they have a double room with bathroom.
   b Say that it is for two nights.
   c Ask for the price.
   d Ask if breakfast is included.
   e Ask whether there is a restaurant in the hotel.
   f Say that the television does not work.

Points: _____/18

3 Rôle-play

You are on holiday in France. It is lunchtime and you are hungry.
You see a restaurant which looks attractive. You enter and order
some food. Give yourself one point for each correct answer, and
two when your answer consists of two correct sentences.

Points: _____/17

Self-test 4 score (Units 11–13)

Points: _____/50

14

Les transports publics
Public transport

In this unit you will
- *Find out about public transport in France*
- *Learn key expressions to make travelling by bus, taxi, train and underground easier*
- *Find out how to ask for information*

Before you start, revise
- *Finding out what's available (Unit 2, Section 3)*
- *Asking for and understanding directions (Unit 6, Section 1)*
- *Expressions of time, days of the week (Unit 5, Key words and phrases)*
- *Numbers (Appendix)*

Key words and phrases

où est-ce que je peux …?	*where can I …?*
où est-ce qu'il faut …?	*where do you have to …?*
où est-ce que je dois …?	*where must I…?*
il faut monter, descendre	*you have to get on, get off*
arriver, quitter	*arrive, leave*
vous devez changer	*you must change*
composter le billet	*date-stamp the ticket*
réserver une couchette	*book a sleeper*
	(Contd)

le billet/ticket	*ticket*
le carnet (de tickets)	*set of ten tickets*
c'est quelle direction?	*which line (lit. 'direction') is it?*
c'est direct?	*is it direct?*
le trajet, le voyage	*travel, journey*
voyager de jour, de nuit	*travel in the daytime, overnight*
dans la matinée, soirée	*in the morning, evening*
le métro	*the underground*
le RER (réseau express régional)	*fast extension of the métro to the suburbs of Paris*
la banlieue	*the suburbs*
desservir	*to serve*
la station de métro	*tube station*
la correspondance	*connection*
manquer la sortie	*miss the exit*
le taxi	*taxi*
la station de taxis	*taxi rank*
l'autobus (m) (bus)	*town bus*
l'autocar (m) (car)	*coach/long distance bus*
la gare routière	*bus station*
l'arrêt (m) d'autobus	*bus stop*
c'est quelle ligne?	*what number (bus) is it?*
la SNCF (Société Nationale des Chemins de Fer)	*French railways*
la gare	*(train) station*
le guichet	*ticket office*
une place	*a seat (also square, as in* **place du Marché***)*
un aller (simple)	*single ticket*
un aller-retour	*return ticket*
le plein tarif	*full fare*
le bureau de renseignements	*information office*
la consigne	*left luggage*
consigne automatique	*left luggage lockers*
un horaire	*timetable*
la période de pointe	*peak times*
le prochain/dernier train	*the next/last train*
en première/seconde classe	*first/second class*

dans le train	on the train
le quai	platform
la voie	track (often used for *platform* instead of **quai**)
au-delà	beyond

Insight

While there are a lot of new words to learn, these are invaluable as they are irreplaceable. Moreover public transport workers do not usually have much time for tourists, particularly in Paris!

Le Métro et tramway parisiens *The Paris underground and tramway*

RATP: www.ratp.fr

Le métro parisien est très pratique et économique. Avec un seul ticket (1€60), vous pouvez aller n'importe où (*anywhere*) dans Paris pour une durée de deux heures. Si vous achetez les tickets par carnet ils coûtent moins cher (dix tickets pour 11€60).

Pour découvrir Paris et sa région d'Île-de-France en métro, tramway, bus, RER et trains SNCF, achetez 'Paris Visite', un forfait transport (*travel pass*), valable un, deux, trois ou cinq jours consécutifs. Il permet également de bénéficier de réductions sur l'entrée de nombreux sites touristiques de la capitale.

Le métro a 14 lignes identifiables par leur numéro et leurs directions (les deux stations terminus). Pour changer d'une ligne à l'autre, suivez les panneaux oranges 'Correspondance' et le nom de la ligne que vous désirez prendre. Du métro vous pouvez passer facilement au RER. C'est un métro ultra-rapide avec cinq lignes (A, B, C, D et E) qui dessert Paris et sa banlieue. Il faut payer un supplément si vous prenez le RER, au-delà de la zone 2.

Après avoir déserté Paris il y a presque 70 ans, la capitale a retrouvé son métro le 16 décembre 2006! La ligne T3 traverse les 15ème, 14ème et 13ème arrondissements de Paris du sud-ouest au sud-est sur un parcours de 7,9 km ponctué de 17 stations. Depuis, d'autres lignes sont en projet, annonçant un fort développement de ce mode de transport durant les années 2010.

ACTIVITY 1

Answer the following assertions with **vrai** or **faux**:

	vrai	faux
a There is a flat rate in central Paris.	☐	☐
b A set of ten tickets is more expensive than ten single tickets.	☐	☐
c One can buy a tourist pass for ten days.	☐	☐
d Each line is known by one name.	☐	☐
e **Correspondance** is the sign to look for to change line.	☐	☐
f To go on the RER you may pay more.	☐	☐
g The tramway stops every 7.9 km.	☐	☐

ACTIVITY 2

A tourist has just arrived at Charles de Gaulle airport. He needs to go to Orly-Sud to catch an internal flight. Look at the following diagram then complete the dialogue, filling the blank spaces with the words in the box.

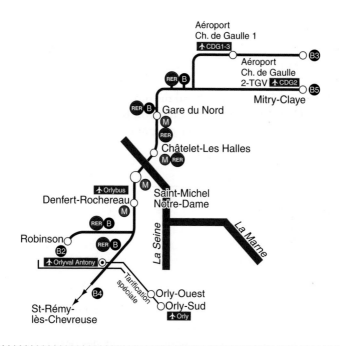

Touriste	Pardon Monsieur, c'est quelle **a** _____ pour l'Aéroport Orly-Sud?
Homme	Orly? Vous **b** _____ la ligne B du RER direction St-Rémy-lès-Chevreuse.
Touriste	C'est direct?
Homme	Non, il faut **c** _____ à la station Antony.
Touriste	Bon, je dois changer à Antony et puis?
Homme	Là, vous avez la liaison Orlyval. C'est un métro automatique qui va vous **d** _____ aux aéroports d'Orly.
Touriste	C'est pas compliqué.
Homme	Non, mais faites bien attention de prendre direction B4 St-Rémy-lès-Chevreuse. Si vous prenez la direction B2, vous **e** _____ la station d'Antony.
Touriste	Ah, merci, Monsieur.

manquerez   mener *(take to)*   changer   prenez   direction

ACTIVITY 3

An American cannot understand the directions he's given to get from the **Orly-Sud** to the **Gare du Nord**. Listen to the recording (if you haven't got it look at the diagram with Activity 2) and tell him in English what to do.

Prendre un taxi *Taking a taxi*

> À Paris, il y a 5300 taxis qui sont jour et nuit à la disposition de la clientèle. Le numéro unique d'appel des stations est le
> **01 45 30 30 30**!

Dans les grandes villes, on peut prendre un taxi à une station de taxi, en le hélant (*hailing*) dans la rue, si son lumineux (*light on the roof*) est éclairé, ou en téléphonant à l'une des principales compagnies.

Il y a un supplément à payer pour le transport d'une quatrième personne adulte ou d'un deuxième bagage dans le coffre.

Dialogue 1: La station de taxis *The taxi rank*

Listen carefully to the recordings, or read the following dialogue, then answer the questions:

The tourist doesn't get any information from the first passer-by: why? How far is the taxi rank? At the crossroads does he have to go right or straight on?

Touriste	Pardon, Monsieur, où est la station de taxis la plus proche?
Homme	Je ne sais pas, je ne suis pas d'ici …
	(Later …)
Touriste	S'il vous plaît, Madame, savez-vous où il y a une station de taxis?
Femme	Mais oui, c'est très simple, vous en avez une, à 500 mètres, à côté de la Gare du Nord.
Touriste	La gare du Nord, c'est où exactement?
Femme	Bon, il faut d'abord monter le boulevard Magenta. Au carrefour, vous allez continuer tout droit et prendre le boulevard Denain et à droite de la Gare du Nord vous allez trouver la station de taxis.

ACTIVITY 4

Would you be able to find the taxi rank? Choose the correct word:

a Il faut monter means
   i turn   **ii** go up   **iii** cross

b Un carrefour is
   i crossroads   **ii** traffics light   **iii** sign post

c Vous continuez tout droit means
   i turn left   **ii** turn right   **iii** carry straight on

Voyager en autobus *Travelling by bus*

RATP: www.ratp.fr
Information on Eurolines: www.eurolines.fr
Gare routière internationale de Paris: 28 Avenue du Général de Gaulle, 93170 Bagnolet, tél: 08 92 90 91 (Métro: Gallieni)

À Paris, on utilise les mêmes tickets pour le métro et pour l'autobus. On peut acheter un billet simple dans l'autobus, mais avec un carnet de tickets, c'est plus économique. Les carnets sont vendus dans certaines stations de métro ou d'autobus. Ils se trouvent aussi dans certains magasins de livres (FNAC) ou de tabac. Avec un ticket d'autobus vous pouvez aller jusqu'au bout de la ligne. Avec deux tickets, vous pouvez aller n'importe où (*anywhere*) dans la ville de Paris.

Insight

Travelling by bus may be a little more complicated than using the underground but it is a nice way to see Paris.

The thing to do is to prepare your bus journey in advance using a bus map. You can download one from www.ratp.fr. You can also usually find a bus map as well as an underground one on the back of Paris street maps.

Dialogue 2: À la gare routière *At the bus station*

A tourist is finding out about buses and tickets. What is she advised to do?

CD2, TR 16

Touriste	Pardon, Monsieur, c'est quelle ligne pour aller à la Gare d'Austerlitz?
Homme	Alors pour la Gare d'Austerlitz le plus simple c'est de prendre la ligne 57 …
Touriste	C'est direct?
Homme	Non, il faut changer au deuxième arrêt, puis vous prenez la ligne 24.
Touriste	C'est loin à pied?
Homme	D'ici? Ah oui, vous ne pouvez pas y aller à pied.
Touriste	Le prochain bus part à quelle heure?
Homme	Dans dix minutes.
Touriste	Et … où est-ce que je peux acheter un ticket?
Homme	Au guichet là-bas …

Touriste	(*later*) Je voudrais acheter un ticket aller-retour pour la Gare d'Austerlitz.
Femme	Il n'y a pas de tickets aller-retour. Achetez deux tickets ou bien alors un carnet, c'est plus pratique et moins cher.
Touriste	Un carnet, qu'est-ce que c'est?
Femme	C'est dix tickets pour le prix de sept.
Touriste	Très bien. Je vais prendre un carnet.

Dialogue 3: Être dans le bon autobus *On the right bus*

The same tourist asks the driver when she should get off. Can you understand where?

CD2, TR 17

Touriste	Ce bus va bien à la Gare d'Austerlitz?
Chauffeur	Oui, c'est bien ça.
Touriste	Vous pouvez me dire où il faut descendre?
Chauffeur	Oui, bien sûr. C'est très facile. C'est le premier arrêt une fois que vous avez traversé la Seine.
Touriste	Euh ... oui mais je ne connais pas Paris. Il faut combien de temps pour arriver à la gare?
Chauffeur	Oh, une bonne demi-heure. Dans trente minutes vous allez passer sur le pont et juste après vous descendrez.

ACTIVITY 5

How would you say:
   a What bus number goes to the Gare d'Austerlitz?
   b Is it direct?
   c Is it far on foot?
   d At what time does the next bus leave?
   e Where can I buy a ticket?
   f I would like to buy a return ticket to les Invalides.
   g I'll take a set of tickets.
   h How long does it take to get to the station?

La SNCF *French railways*

www.sncf.fr
www.voyages-sncf.com

En France, vous devez composter votre billet au moment du départ. Si vous ne le faites pas vous aurez une amende (*fine*). Il faut réserver votre place si vous prenez un TGV (train grande vitesse) ou l'Eurostar. Si vous voyagez

dans d'autres trains SNCF, il est aussi conseillé de le faire surtout au début et à la fin des vacances scolaires.

Dialogue 4: Au bureau de renseignements *At the information office*

*We are in the information office in **la Gare de Lyon** in Paris. A man enquires about trains. Listen to the recording or read the dialogue. Try to answer the following questions: Where does the man want to go? Which train does he want to catch? Where does he want to sit?*

CD2, TR 18

Homme	Bonjour, Madame, je voudrais un aller pour Marseille.
Hôtesse	Marseille … bon. Vous voyagez quel jour?
Homme	Le 10 juin … un samedi.
Hôtesse	À quelle heure voulez-vous quitter Paris?
Homme	Dans la matinée.
Hôtesse	Bon, vous avez quatre TGV : le premier part à 8.20, le deuxième à 9.20, le troisième à 10.20, le quatrième à 11.20.

Homme	**Celui de** 10.20 **me convient** très bien.
Hôtesse	Il quitte Paris Gare de Lyon à 10.20 et arrive à Marseille St Charles à 13.29. La réservation est obligatoire.
Homme	D'accord, bon alors, **il met un peu plus de** trois heures?
Hôtesse	Oui, c'est bien ça.
Homme	C'est combien l'aller simple?
Hôtesse	Vous avez une réduction?
Homme	Non, je n'ai pas de carte.
Hôtesse	OK, alors en 1ère ou en 2ème classe?
Homme	En 2ème classe.
Hôtesse	Alors en seconde classe, l'aller tarif normal coûte 94€, la réservation est incluse dans le prix.
Homme	Oh, c'est un peu cher. Il y a moins cher?
Hôtesse	Le train qui quitte Paris à 9.20 est moins cher. C'est un billet «Découverte Séjour» et l'aller coûte 57€60. Ça vous va?
Homme	Oui, c'est **beaucoup mieux**. Mais, il y a des restrictions?
Hôtesse	Oui, c'est un billet **ni échangeable ni remboursable**.
Homme	Donc je ne peux pas le changer **une fois pris**.
Hôtesse	Oui, c'est tout à fait ça.
Homme	On peut manger dans le train?
Hôtesse	Oui, bien sûr, vous avez une voiture-bar où vous pourrez acheter des sandwiches, des salades ou des **plats cuisinés** ainsi que des boissons chaudes et fraîches.
Homme	Ah bon, et pour ma place?
Hôtesse	Vous avez le choix entre un siège côté fenêtre ou côté couloir?
Homme	Je préfère côté fenêtre.

celui de … me convient *the one at … suits me*
il met un peu plus de … *it takes a bit more than …*
beaucoup mieux *much better*
ni échangeable *neither exchangeable*
ni remboursable *nor refundable*
une fois pris *once taken*
plats cuisinés *hot food*

ACTIVITY 6

Before taking the part of the traveller in this conversation, look at the Marseille–Paris timetable accessible on the SNCF website. How many TGVs are leaving Marseille in the afternoon?

Aller le lundi 08/10 entre 12h12 et 19h29
MARSEILLE St CHARLES–PARIS
prix total pour 1 passager

Départ à	12h12	12h27	13h29	14h31	15h29	19h29
Meilleur prix	77.20€	94.00€	94.00€	94.00€	94.00€	38.90€
Durée	10h37	03h14	03h12	03h00	03h16	03h12

voir les trains suivants

a Vous		*Ask for a return to Paris.*
	Employé	Vous voulez partir quel jour?
b Vous		*Say on the 8th October in the afternoon.*
	Employé	Alors vous avez plusieurs trains qui quittent Marseille St Charles l'après-midi. Il y a un train toutes les heures.
c Vous		*Ask how long the journey lasts.*
	Employé	Environ trois heures, trois heures et quart.
d Vous		*Say that you do not want to arrive in Paris after 19.00.*
	Employé	Alors dans ce cas vous pouvez prendre le train qui quitte St Charles à 13.29, ou à 14.31 ou même à 15.29.
e Vous		*Say that the 15.29 train suits you and ask for the price of the ticket in second class.*
	Employé	Le billet en 2ème classe tarif plein coûte 94€.
f Vous		*Say that it is a little expensive. Ask if there is something cheaper.*
	Employé	Alors, un instant ... Le train de 12.12 est moins cher. Le prix du billet aller-retour ne coûte que 77€20.
g Vous		*Ask if you can change the ticket.*

Employé	Oui, oui tout à fait. Le billet est remboursable et échangeable.
h **Vous**	*Ask at what time the train arrives in Paris.*
Employé	Le train met 10.37 pour arriver à Paris.
i **Vous**	*Say that it is too long and that you will take the 15.20 train.*
Employé	D'accord ...

Insight

There are several ways of asking in French how long the journey takes. The third form using **il faut** is probably the easiest way:

▶ Le trajet dure (*lasts*) combien de temps?
▶ Le train/bus/taxi met (lit. *puts*) combien de temps?
▶ Il faut combien de temps pour le trajet/le voyage?

Le Vélib'

Pour tout savoir sur le Vélib' et son utilisation dans Paris: www.velib.paris.fr/

Le Vélib' est un système de **location** de vélos en libre service très simple à utiliser. Vous prenez un vélo dans une station et vous le déposez dans n'importe quelle autre station Vélib'. Disponibles 24h/24 et 7j/7, les stations Vélib' sont distantes de 300 mètres environ et constituées de **bornes** et de **points d'attache** pour les vélos.

Pour prendre un vélo, rien de plus simple! Il faut vous identifier sur la borne, accéder au menu, et choisir votre vélo **parmi ceux** qui seront proposés à **l'écran.** Vous pouvez **souscrire un abonnement** courte durée par carte bancaire (Ticket Vélib' 1 jour et Ticket Vélib' 7 jours). En plus Vélib' vous offre gratuitement les 30 premières minutes de chaque trajet.

QUICK VOCAB

la location *hiring/renting*
la borne *terminal*
le point d'attache *stand for parking*
parmi ceux *among those*
l'écran *screen*
souscrire/prendre un abonnement *subscribe for an account*

ACTIVITY 7

Answer the following statements with **vrai** or **faux**:

	vrai	faux
a Il faut ramener le vélo à la station où on l'a pris.	☐	☐
b Les stations sont ouvertes jour et nuit et tous les jours de l'année.	☐	☐
c Tout se fait à partir de la borne.	☐	☐
d On ne peut pas prendre un abonnement d'un jour.	☐	☐
e On ne paie pas pour la première demi-heure de chaque trajet.	☐	☐

THINGS TO REMEMBER

In this unit you have found out about public transport in France and learnt key expressions to make travelling by bus, taxi, train and underground easier. Do you remember the French for the following?

1 I would like a set of tickets.

2 I would like a return ticket to Grenoble.

3 Which direction is it for the Gare Austerlitz?

4 The next bus leaves at what time?

5 Where can I buy a ticket?

6 Can you tell me where I must get off?

7 How long does the journey take?

8 Do I need/is it necessary for me to book a seat?

9 You are going to go over a bridge in thirty minutes.

10 Where is the information office?

You'll find the answers in the **Key to the exercises and tests** at the end of the book. If your answers are correct you are ready to move to Unit 15. If you found the test difficult, spend more time revising Unit 14.

15

Faire du tourisme
Sightseeing

In this unit you will
- *Learn how to ask for a town map*
- *Find out about visiting interesting places*
- *Practise buying admission tickets*
- *Find out about museums in France*
- *Book an excursion*

Before you start, revise
- *Saying what you want (Unit 7, Section 2)*
- *Asking for and understanding directions (Unit 6, Section 1)*
- *Asking what you can do (Unit 5, Section 2)*
- *Expressions of time, days of the week (Unit 5, Key words and phrases)*

Key words and phrases

le plan de la ville	*town map*
des renseignements	*information*
les environs	*surroundings*
qu'est-ce qu'il y a à faire?	*what is there to do?*
qu'est-ce qu'il y a à voir?	*what is there to see?*
qu'est-ce qu'on peut visiter?	*what is there to visit*
	(lit. *what can one visit?*)
	(Contd)

une visite guidée	*guided tour*
faire une promenade/balade à pied	*to go for a walk*
les jours fériés/les jours de fête	*public holidays*
l'entrée	*way in, admission charge*
en pleine saison	*in high season*
le tarif réduit, plein tarif	*reduced rate, full rate*
accès (m) gratuit	*free entry*
nocturne	*late-night opening*
hors saison	*out of season*
le musée	*museum*
faire une excursion	*to go on an excursion*
pique-niquer	*to picnic*
l'aire de jeux	*children's playground*
une agence de voyages	*travel agency*

Se renseigner sur les choses à voir *Getting information on things to see*

- ▶ Fédération Nationale des Offices de Tourisme et Syndicats d'Initiative: www.tourisme.fr
- ▶ Office de Tourisme à Paris: www.parisinfo.com
- ▶ Visites guidées en autocar ou en minibus à Paris: www.touringscope.com
- ▶ Croisières sur la Seine: www.vedettesdeparis.com
- ▶ Croisières sur les canaux: www.pariscanal.com
- ▶ D'autres sites utiles:
  www.paris.org
  www.franceguide.com
  www.guideweb.com (sur les régions françaises)
  www.skifrance.fr (informations sur les stations de ski, etc.)

Dès votre arrivée dans une ville ou une région, rendez-vous à l'office de tourisme le plus proche pour demander un plan ainsi que des brochures sur la ville et ses environs. Son personnel multilingue répondra à toutes vos questions sur

les hébergements, visites, musées, loisirs, manifestations
culturelles, circuits touristiques …

En France, il y a de nombreux jours fériés. Il est prudent de les
connaître car les magasins, musées et monuments historiques sont
souvent fermés ces jours-là.

ACTIVITY 1

French public holidays are listed in the right-hand column. Match
the dates with the corresponding holidays:

a	1 janvier	**i**	Toussaint
b	entre le 2 mars et le 25 avril	**ii**	Noël
c	1er mai	**iii**	Assomption
d	8 mai	**iv**	Jour de l'An
e	40 jours après Pâques	**v**	Fête du travail
f	le 7ème lundi après Pâques	**vi**	Victoire 1945
g	14 juillet	**vii**	Ascension
h	15 août	**viii**	Lundi de Pentecôte
i	1er novembre	**ix**	Armistice 1918
j	11 novembre	**x**	Lundi de Pâques
k	25 décembre	**xi**	Fête Nationale

Insight

While you are probably familiar with most French public
holidays, you may find the religious ones more difficult to
guess. Did you know that **La Toussaint (All Saints' Day)** is a
very important day in France when the dead are remembered
and families visit the graves of deceased relatives?

Dialogue 1: À l'office du tourisme *At the tourist office*

*Listen to the recording or read the dialogue on the next page.
Can you name at least three things the tourist could see or do?*

Touriste	Bonjour, Madame, je voudrais un plan de la ville, s'il vous plaît.
Hôtesse	Oui, voilà.
Touriste	Nous ne sommes pas d'ici. Qu'est-ce qu'il y a à voir à Orléans?
Hôtesse	Il y a beaucoup de monuments historiques, surtout dans la vieille ville, comme la maison de Jeanne d'Arc, au numéro 52 sur le plan, à côté de la cathédrale Sainte-Croix; et puis il y a une belle promenade à pied à faire le long de la Loire. Du pont George V, vous avez une vue magnifique sur la Loire.
Touriste	Et qu'est-ce qu'il y a à faire pour les enfants?
Hôtesse	Près d'ici, il y a une piscine couverte ou même le Musée des sciences naturelles qui se trouve rue Émile Zola. Un peu plus loin, vous avez le Parc Floral.
Touriste	Et pour aller au Parc Floral … il y a un bus?
Hôtesse	Oui, vous avez un autobus toutes les 30 minutes. Il part du centre ville, place du Martroi.

ACTIVITY 2

a How would you ask for a town map?
b Ask what there is to see.
c Ask what there is to do for the children.
d Ask if there is an indoor swimming pool.
e Ask if there is a bus to go to the **Parc Floral**.

ACTIVITY 3

The Wilsons want to visit the **Parc Floral**, a 35 hectare designed landscape garden near Orléans, on their way to the south of France. Read the brochure and answer the questions.

a Would the visit be enjoyable for their seven-year-old boy?
b Can they eat there?
c They intend to visit the park in the summer months. What will they be able to see besides the gardens?

LES RENDEZ-VOUS DE L'ANNÉE

- PETIT TRAIN
- PARC ANIMALIER
- AIRE DE JEUX
- GOLF MINIATURE
- BOUTIQUES
- AIRE DE PIQUE-NIQUE

TOUT LE MOIS D'AVRIL
Renaissance du sous-bois !
Floraison exceptionnelle de 200 000 tulipes,
narcisses, jacinthes, muscaris…

DIMANCHE 23 AVRIL
"A la recherche des œufs de Pâques"

- ANIMATIONS
  PÉDAGOGIQUES
- VISITES GUIDÉES
  (sur réservation) :
  15 personnes
  minimum

DE MI MAI À DÉBUT JUIN
Floraison de la Collection Nationale d'iris
(900 variétés), rassemblée dans un jardin
contemporain

SAMEDI 20 ET DIMANCHE 21 MAI
Fête de l'iris - Conseils, vente

DIMANCHE 18 JUIN
La Saint-Fiacre et les Peintres au Jardin

- JARDIN
  DE LA SOURCE

SAMEDI 9 ET DIMANCHE 10 SEPTEMBRE
Journées de découverte du nouveau potager
Conseils, vente

DIMANCHE 17 SEPTEMBRE
Concert par la Musique Municipale d'Orléans

DU 28 OCTOBRE AU 12 NOVEMBRE
31ᵉ Salon du Chrysanthème

DU 1ᵉʳ AVRIL AU 12 NOVEMBRE
La serre aux papillons - Découverte du monde
coloré des papillons exotiques dans un jardin
tropical de 250 m² .
Exposition : l'univers fascinant des couleurs
chez les insectes. Insectes en 3D

www.parcfloral-lasource.fr

PARC FLORAL DE LA *source***, ORLÉANS**

DÉPARTEMENT DU LOIRET, VILLE D'ORLÉANS

45072 Orléans cedex 2 • Tél: 02 38 49 30 17

Dialogue 2: On visite *Let's visit*

Mrs Wilson phones the Parc Floral to find out about opening hours, prices, etc. Listen to the recording or read the dialogue twice and answer the following question: How much would the family pay to visit the park and the butterfly glasshouse?

Touriste	Allô, je voudrais savoir à quelle heure ouvre le parc, s'il vous plaît?
Hôtesse	Le parc est ouvert tous les jours de 10 heures à 19 heures, même les jours fériés! Quant à la serre aux papillons, elle n'ouvre que les après-midi, et les mercredis et dimanches matin.
Touriste	Ah merci. Euh, la serre, c'est quoi?
Hôtesse	C'est un jardin tropical où vivent des papillons exotiques. Nous y avons aussi des projections de films et des expositions thématiques.
Touriste	Et c'est combien l'entrée?
Hôtesse	Alors pour le parc seul, c'est 4 €. Pour le parc et la serre, c'est 6 €80. C'est pour combien de personnes?
Touriste	Trois, deux adultes et un enfant de 7 ans.
Hôtesse	Pour l'enfant, c'est 4 €50 pour le parc et la serre.
Touriste	Ah bon. Et le parc est facile à trouver en voiture?
Hôtesse	Oui, très. Si vous prenez la A71, c'est sortie Orléans – la Source. Vous avez accès à l'Internet?
Touriste	Euh, oui, oui.
Hôtesse	Alors c'est encore plus facile, tapez www.parcfloral-lasource (en un seul mot).fr. Vous y trouverez le plan d'accès au Parc Floral et autres renseignements pratiques.
Touriste	Vous pouvez répéter plus lentement, s'il vous plaît?
Hôtesse	Oui, bien sûr, alors pour le site vous tapez www.parcfloral-lasource.fr. Et voilà!
Hôtesse	Merci beaucoup madame, et au revoir.

ACTIVITY 4

Now it is your turn to buy some tickets for the park. You are accompanied by your daughter, who is 12. She wants to go on the **petit train** and play **mini golf**.

a	**You**	*Ask how much the admission charge is.*
	Hôtesse	L'entrée coûte 4€ par personne, 6€80 avec la serre.
b	**You**	*Ask what the 'serre' is.*
	Hôtesse	C'est pour l'exposition des papillons. Votre fille a quel âge?
c	**You**	*Say her age. Ask if you need to pay for the 'petit train' and the mini golf.*
	Hôtesse	Oui, pour le 'petit train' c'est 1€60 pour elle et 2€ pour vous. Le golf miniature est gratuit.
d	**You**	*Ask if you can have a picnic.*
	Hôtesse	Oui, bien sûr. Je vais vous montrer l'aire de pique-nique sur le plan.
e	**You**	*Thank her and ask what time the park closes.*
	Hôtesse	Nous fermons à 19 heures.

Les musées *Museums*

Les musées et monuments sont généralement ouverts tous les jours, sauf le lundi ou le mardi, de 10 à 12h et de 14 à 18h en été. Ces horaires peuvent varier. La plupart sont fermés les jours fériés. L'entrée est généralement gratuite pour les enfants de moins de 18 ans. Les étudiants, personnes âgées et enseignants actifs ont droit à une réduction (entre 30% et 50%) sur présentation d'un justificatif, et quelquefois l'entrée est gratuite un jour par semaine.

Insight

When touring France it is easy to forget that museums close over lunchtime. So don't get caught! Get up early to see the museums or visit them in the afternoon.

CARTE MUSÉES–MONUMENTS

Musées et monuments en Île-de-France: www.intermusees.com
Musées et monuments en France: www.monuments-france.fr
Paris Museum Pass: www.parismuseumpass.com

Valable deux, quatre ou six jours, la carte musées-monuments permet de visiter librement et sans attente 60 musées et monuments de Paris et d'Île-de-France. Elle est en vente dans les musées et monuments, principales stations de métro, office de tourisme de Paris, **magasins FNAC**. Le forfait pour un jour est de 30€, pour quatre jours consécutifs 45€, et six jours consécutifs: 60€.

Insight

FNAC is the largest French retailer of books, CDs and DVDs, computer software and hardware, television sets, cameras and video games.

ACTIVITY 5

Look at the following information – this is the kind of information you may find on places of interest – then answer the questions:

A   **Art Moderne (Musée National d')**
Centre Georges-Pompidou
Place Georges Pompidou – 75004 Paris
Tél. 01 44 78 12 33   Métro : Hôtel-de-ville, Rambuteau
www.centrepompidou.fr   RER A : Châtelet-Les Halles

Ouvert tous les jours de 11h à 21h sauf mardi (avec possibilité de nocturnes pour les expositions). Plein tarif: 10€ – Tarif réduit: 8€.

Ce billet est valable le jour même pour toutes les expositions en cours, le Musée et l'Atelier Brancusi. Accès gratuit le 1er dimanche de chaque mois.

Collection d'œuvres d'artistes modernes et d'artistes contemporains, sans oublier les architectes, les designers, les photographes ainsi que les cinéastes.

B **Cité des Sciences et de l'Industrie – la Villette**
Centre Parc de la Villette
30, avenue Corentin-Cariou – 75019 Paris
Tél. 01 40 05 80 00   Métro: Porte-de-la-Villette
www.cite-sciences.fr

De 10h à 18h. Le dimanche de 10h à 19h. Fermé le lundi. Plein tarif: 15€. Cité des enfants : 13€. Planétarium: 11€. Tarif réduit : 11€ et 8€.

Située dans le parc de la Villette, la cité présente un panorama complet des sciences et techniques à travers des expositions, des spectacles, des maquettes, des conférences et des jeux interactifs.

C **Louvre (Musée du)**
Entrée principale par la Pyramide
Cour Napoléon – 75001 Paris
Tél. 01 40 20 51 51   Métro : Palais-Royal-Musée-du-Louvre
www.louvre.fr

Ouvert tous les jours de 9h à 18h, sauf le mardi et certains jours fériés. Nocturnes les mercredi et vendredi jusqu'à 22h.

Plein tarif : 9€ – Tarif réduit : 6€ (de 18h à 21.45). Gratuité appliquée aux moins de 18 ans demandeurs d'emploi, enseignants en histoire, handicapés et le 1er dimanche de chaque mois.

Le Musée du Louvre, ancienne demeure des rois de France, et l'un des plus grands musées du monde.

D | **Picasso (Musée National)**
Hôtel Salé
5, rue de Thorigny – 75003 Paris
Tél. 01 42 71 25 21
Métro : Saint-Paul/Saint-Sébastien Froissart/Chemin Vert
Bus : 29 – 96 – 69 – 75 www.musee-picasso.fr

Été: 9h30–18h – Hiver: 9h30–17h30.
Nocturne le jeudi jusqu'à 20h. Plein tarif : 7€70. Tarif réduit
(de 18 ans à 25 ans inclus) : 5€70
Gratuit pour les moins de 18 ans et le premier dimanche de
chaque mois.
Fermé le mardi, le 1er janvier et le 25 décembre.

Installé dans l'Hôtel Salé (XVIIe siècle), le musée rassemble
une importante collection des œuvres de l'artiste.

a If you were in Paris on a Tuesday, what could you visit?
b If you did not have much money, which day would you choose
to visit the attractions above?
c What could you visit late in the evening and when?
d Which museum would most interest a child?

Faire une excursion *Going on an excursion*

ACTIVITY 6

You're interested in French
wines, so you've decided
to go with your partner
on a coach excursion
following **la route des
vins de Bourgogne**. Look
at the information and
answer the questions:

a At what time should you be at the bus stop in the morning?
b How long do you stop at Vézelay?
c Name at least two things you could do from lunchtime
  until 4 p.m.
d How much is the excursion for two people?

LA ROUTE DES VINS
DE BOURGOGNE

EXCURSION EN CAR

1 JOUR

13 mai
3/17 juin
22 juillet
20 oct
11 nov

Aller/retour....92€

**Rendez-vous 7h15.
Départ 7h30.**

Arrivée à Vézelay vers 10h.
Arrêt d'une heure pour visiter
la basilique Sainte-Madeleine.
Continuation vers Beaune. Arrêt
pour déjeuner et temps libre

pour visiter les Hospices et
le Musée du vin. Visite d'une
cave avec dégustation.

Départ à 16h par la route des vins.
(Nuits-Saint-Georges, Gevrey-
Chambertin).
Retour à Paris vers 23h.

ACTIVITY 7

You and your friend decide to book the trip to Beaune. Speak for
both of you.

a	**You**	*Say you would like to go on the excursion of **la route des vins de Bourgogne***.
	Employé	Vous voulez réserver des places pour quel jour?
b	**You**	*Say you'd like two places for the 22nd July.*
	Employé	Le 22 juillet? Bon… ça va, il y a de la place … ça fait 184€.
c	**You**	*Ask if the coach leaves from here.*
	Employé	Non, le car part de la place Denfert-Rochereau, devant le café de Belfort.
d	**You**	*Ask him to repeat.*
	Employé	Oui, place Denfert-Rochereau devant le café de Belfort; mais je vais vous donner tous ces renseignements par écrit.
e	**You**	*Thank him; ask what time the coach leaves.*
	Employé	Le car part à 7.30 mais il faut être là à 7.15.
f	**You**	*Ask if you can buy some wine in the wine cellar.*
	Employé	Oui, vous pouvez déguster et acheter des vins de Bourgogne à un prix spécial.

Insight

Surf www.franceguide.com to find out more about the wine routes in the 17 French wine regions. The site provides useful information on the **caves de dégustation,** French gastronomy, regional recipes and cheese.

◄) CD2, TR 21

ACTIVITY 8

Listen to Michel discussing the possibility of going on a coach excursion to Versailles and Trianon with his friend Agnès. If you haven't got the recording, read the tour description, then answer the questions. You will need to listen to the recording to be able to answer all the questions.

a Jour de l'excursion choisi par Michel et Agnès
b Heure du départ de Paris

c Durée du tour
d Programme de la visite
e Prix de l'entrée de la visite
f Qui paie pour l'excursion et pourquoi

Journée Royale à Versailles 102€

- ► Visite guidée des Appartements Royaux.
- ► Été: Bosquets
- ► Hiver: Promenade en petit train.
- ► Déjeuner face au Grand Canal.
- ► Trianon.
- ► Hameau de la Reine.

 9H15   AUTOCAR   GUIDE INTERPRÈTE   ✗ DÉJEUNER

Départ: 9.15 jeudi et dimanche
Retour approximatif: 16.15
À partir d'avril à septembre

Nous vous proposons de commencer votre journée à Versailles par la visite guidée des Grands Appartements Royaux puis par la visite des jardins (été) ou une promenade en petit train dans le parc (hiver). Le déjeuner sera servi au restaurant 'la Flotille' dans le parc du château en face du Grand Canal.

L'après-midi se poursuivra par la visite guidée des Trianon (vastes pavillons dans lesquels Louis XV et Louis XVI aimaient travailler et séjourner en retrait de la cour) et par la découverte du Hameau de la Reine Marie-Antoinette construit pour son divertissement.

Entrées incluses.

THINGS TO REMEMBER

In this unit you have found out about museums in France and visiting interesting places, and have practised buying admission tickets. How would you say the following?

1 What is there to do?

2 I would like a town map and information on the cathedral.

3 Is there a bus that goes to the Parc Floral?

4 Is the park easy to find?

5 How much is the admission charge?

6 Is the museum open this Tuesday?

7 Does the museum shut between lunchtime and two?

8 The bus leaves from where?

9 One needs to be at the bus stop at what time?

10 What can one visit?

You'll find the answers in the **Key to the exercises and tests** at the end of the book. If your answers are correct you are ready to move to Unit 16. If you found the test difficult, spend more time revising Unit 15.

16

....

Sortir
Going out

In this unit you will
- *Practise finding out what's on*
- *Book tickets for a concert*
- *Find out where you can play tennis and other sports*

Before you start, revise
- *Finding out what's on and where (Unit 15, Key words and phrases)*
- *Saying what you want (Unit 7, Section 2)*
- *Asking what you can do (Unit 5, Section 2)*
- *Talking about your likes and dislikes (Unit 8, Section 2)*
- *Expressions of time, days of the week (Unit 5, Key words and phrases)*

_____

Key words and phrases

qu'est-ce qu'il y a comme …?	*what sort of … is/are there?*
qu'est-ce qu'on peut faire?	*what can I/we/one do?*
un spectacle	*a show*
une soirée	*evening entertainment, party*
un dîner-dansant	*dinner dance*
l'ambiance (f)	*atmosphere*
	(Contd)

la salle	room, hall, auditorium
une boîte (de nuit)	nightclub
un piano-bar	all night restaurant with small band
louer	to book, to hire
la location	hiring
le prêt	lending
le bureau de location	booking office
la place	seat
une séance	performance, film showing
entrée (f) libre	free admission
il/elle doit payer?	he/she must pay?
c'est combien l'heure?	how much is it an hour?
c'est combien la journée?	how much is it a day?
une carte d'abonnement	season ticket
un court de tennis	tennis court
un cours particulier	private lesson
l'inscription (f)	enrolment
faire une randonnée	to go for a walk/hike
faire du vélo	to go cycling
le jeu de société	board game

Insight

Some of the words you will encounter in this unit are already familiar to you from Unit 15 which concentrated on tourist activities. This is because Unit 16 builds on Unit 15 and focuses on social outings.

Où aller? *Where to go?*

Everything you want to know about Parisian outings (theatre, cinema, restaurants, arts, music, visits and walks): www.premiere.fr

Pour connaître le programme des spectacles, adressez-vous à l'office du tourisme – qui vous réservera des places, si vous le leur demandez. Si vous êtes à Paris, achetez un journal spécialisé comme *Pariscope, l'Officiel des Spectacles* ou alors *Zurban*.

Dialogue 1: Sortir le soir *Going out in the evening*

At the tourist office two tourists enquire about activities in the evening.

Touriste	Je passe quelques jours dans la région. Qu'est-ce qu'on peut faire ici le soir?	**◈ CD2, TR 22**
Hôtesse	Il y a beaucoup de choses à faire mais ça dépend, qu'est-ce que vous aimez? Le jazz? La danse?	
Touriste	Oui, nous aimons danser mais surtout … bien manger.	
Hôtesse	Eh bien pourquoi n'allez-vous pas à un dîner-dansant ou dans un restaurant piano-bar?	
Touriste	Un restaurant piano-bar, qu'est-ce que c'est?	
Hôtesse	C'est un restaurant où il y a de la musique avec orchestre. En général, il y a une très bonne ambiance et ça reste ouvert toute la nuit. Mais … si vous aimez danser, vous avez le restaurant 'Raspoutine' tout près d'ici qui organise des soirées dansantes avec repas et orchestre tzigane.	
Touriste	C'est combien pour la soirée dansante?	
Hôtesse	C'est 100 € par personne, tout compris, avec spectacle.	
Touriste	Je peux acheter les billets ici?	
Hôtesse	Non, il faut aller au restaurant qui se trouve au bout du boulevard Victor Hugo; mais … attendez un instant, je vais vous chercher le programme des spectacles de la semaine avec la liste des restaurants et des bars.	

> ## Insight
>
> In the first line of the dialogue the tourist says: **Je passe quelques jours dans la région.** The verb **passer** is very useful in statements and questions such as: **Je passe mes vacances ..., Avez-vous passé de bonnes vacances? Comment avez-vous passé votre week-end?** Don't forget to use it!

ACTIVITY 1

Without looking back at the text say if the following assertions are **vrai** or **faux** and correct the false answers:

		vrai	faux
a	The tourist wants to know what's on in the daytime.	☐	☐
b	They like going to concerts.	☐	☐
c	A piano-bar is a place that is open only at lunchtime.	☐	☐
d	At 'Raspoutine' you can eat and dance.	☐	☐
e	The price for everything including the meal is 100€ per person.	☐	☐
f	The hostess gives the tourist the programme of the week.	☐	☐

ACTIVITY 2

Here are the kinds of night attractions described in a brochure that you can find at the tourist office. Read what is on at each night-spot and say who would enjoy which one most:

a A single lady who likes disco dancing – particularly older tunes – and would love to meet a male friend.

b A couple who like playing bowls with their friends on Sundays.

c A single person who likes betting and socializing on a regular basis.

d A group of students who enjoy Latin music and dancing.

e A man who enjoys tasting different types of beer, has a sweet tooth and likes music.

ACTIVITÉS NOCTURNES

A Saxy Rock Café
Bar glacier   Tél. 05 58 56 21 82
5, avenue Milliès Lacroix
Spécialités: bières du monde, glaces et pâtisseries,
animations musicales.
Ouvert tous les jours de 8h à 2h.

B Havana Café
Bar latino américain   Tél. 05 58 74 09 92
19, rue Georges Chaulet
Spécialités: cubaines. Ambiance salsa. Soirées concerts.
Possibilité de location d'une salle pour soirée privée.
Ouvert du mardi au dimanche à partir de 18h.

C Casino de Dax   Tél. 05 58 56 86 86
Avenue Milliès Lacroix
Roulette, Black-jack, animations (spectacles,
Calas), arts et culture, restaurant, bar.
Ouvert tous les jours à partir de 15h.

D César Palace
Casino   Tél. 05 58 91 52 72
Lac de Christus,
40990 Saint-Paul-lès-Dax – 3 km Ouest
**Boules le dimanche de 16h à 19h et tous les soirs
de 22h à 4h. Machines à sous de 12h à 4h.**

E Club rétro
Le Richelieu – Club   Tél. 05 58 90 20 53
Rue Sainte-Eutrope   ou 05 58 58 49 49
Pour danser sur les souvenirs du temps passé.
Entrée + consommation: 11€. Samedi: 13€
(autres consommations: 8€).
Ouvert du mercredi au dimanche à partir de 21h 30.
Le mercredi entrée gratuite pour tous jusqu'à minuit.
Le jeudi entrée gratuite pour les dames jusqu'à minuit.

ACTIVITY 3

Listen to Michel booking a table by phone at the 'Burro Blanco'
restaurant. Can you answer the following questions? You will need
to listen to the recording to be able to answer all the questions
(**dîner aux chandelles** = *dinner by candlelight*).

Espagnoles

**BURRO BLANCO. 79, rue Cardinale Lemoine (5e)
01 43 25 72 53.**
Tlj jsq 5h du mat. F. Lun. À la Contrescarpe, véritable
flamenco avec chanteurs, guitaristes et danseurs.
Tapas. Menus 50€ à 60€. Carte.

**GRENIER DE TRIANA, 7, rue Mouffetard (5e)
01 43 57 97 33. Tls jsq 4h du mat.**
La meilleure ambiance espagnole de Paris. Chants,
guitare, paëlla, zarzuella. Menus 40€ à 70€ + Carte.
Groupes.

---

a Which day is the restaurant shut?
b What special occasion is Michel celebrating?
c What does he ask for?
d What type of cooking is served?
e At what time does the show finish?
f What is included in the price?

Dialogue 2: Réserver une place *Booking a ticket*

*A student is booking seats for a guitar recital. Why does she get a
cheaper ticket?*

| **Jeune fille** | Pardon Monsieur, je voudrais des places pour le récital de guitare, samedi prochain. |
| **Employé** | Je regrette, samedi c'est complet mais il reste encore des places pour jeudi et vendredi. |

Jeune fille	Bon, eh bien je vais prendre deux places pour jeudi. Ça finit à quelle heure le concert?
Employé	Le concert commence à 19.45 donc je pense qu'il finira vers 22h.
Jeune fille	Bon, ça va, ce n'est pas trop tard. C'est combien la place, j'ai une carte étudiant?
Employé	Alors avec une carte étudiant, c'est tarif réduit à 20€60.
Jeune fille	Ma sœur a 15 ans. Elle doit payer?
Employé	C'est entrée libre jusqu'à 16 ans.

ACTIVITY 4

How do you say:

a I would like some seats for next Sunday.
b At what time does the concert finish?
c How much is it for a ticket?
d It is reduced rate.
e Does my sister have to pay?

ACTIVITY 5

Using the Internet may be a useful way to find out what's on in the cinemas but the information can be a little confusing. Look at the example below and try to work out the address of the cinema, who is entitled to a reduced rate, and on which days. If you find it puzzling, look at the upside-down clues on the next page, then check with the Key to the exercises and tests.

Cinéma Gaumont Opéra Impérial
29, bd des Italiens (2ème arr.)
Métro/accès: Opéra
Tél: 08.36.68.75.55
Place 10€20
Tarif réduit: 8€70 étud., CV, fam. nombr., mil., –18, du lun. au ven. 18h., sf. fêtes et veilles de fête
Carte 5 places: 28€44

Dialogue 3: Réserver un court de tennis
Booking a tennis court

Une touriste veut jouer au tennis. Elle se renseigne à l'office du tourisme.

A tourist wants to play tennis. She enquires at the tourist office. She asks five questions; try to note at least three of them.

CD2, TR 25

Touriste	Où est-ce qu'on peut jouer au tennis?
Hôtesse	Vous avez à Anglet le Club de Chiberta avec 15 courts.
Touriste	Ah très bien, et où est-ce qu'on réserve les courts?
Hôtesse	Vous réservez les courts au club.
Touriste	C'est combien l'heure?
Hôtesse	Je ne sais pas. Il faut vous renseigner là-bas mais si vous jouez souvent, vous pouvez certainement prendre une carte d'abonnement.
Touriste	Je n'ai pas ma raquette de tennis avec moi. On peut louer une raquette au club?
Hôtesse	Je pense que oui.
Touriste	Vous pouvez me donner l'adresse du club, s'il vous plaît?
Hôtesse	Mais oui, la voilà.

29, boulevard des Italiens in the 2nd arrondissement

Tarif réduit: 8€70 étudiants, Carte Vermeille (for seniors), famille nombreuse, militaires, – 18, sauf fêtes, du lundi au vendredi 18h, sauf fêtes et **veilles de fête**

veille de fêtes *the day before public holidays*

ACTIVITY 6

How would you ask:
a Where can I (use **on**) play tennis?
b Where do I (use **on**) book the court?
c How much is it for one hour?
d Can one hire a racket?
e Can you give me the address of the club?

ACTIVITY 7

You are working at the **office du tourisme** in Vittel. An English family comes in. They are all very eager to join in the various activities organized by the town (see below). Can you answer their questions?

● **ACTIVITÉS SPORTIVES ET DE LOISIRS avec JEAN-LOUIS et ANNE**

Jogging: dans le parc en petites foulées sur un rythme progressif.
Gymnastique: en salle, assouplissement et tonification musculaire.
Tir à l'arc: initiation et perfectionnement de la maîtrise du tir.
Promenades et randonnées (pédestre, vélo): parcourir la campagne et les bois environnants.
Self défense: initiation, découverte des gestes d'auto-défense.
Volley et sports collectifs, ✎
Gym, danse et stretching.
Promenade VTT: initiation. ✳ ✎

● **ACTIVITÉS TENNIS et GOLF avec BRUNO**

Usage des cours et du practice, du putting green.
Initiation golf et tennis en groupe. ✎
Cours particuliers. ✳ ✎

● **L'OFFICE DU TOURISME EST À VOTRE DISPOSITION POUR**
ses locations ou prêts de vélos, matériels de golf ✳, de tennis de table, jeux de société;
Son coin lecture (journaux, hebdomadaires).

✳ Activité avec participation financière
✎ Activité avec inscription.

---

a The woman is very keen on playing tennis:
  i Can she have private classes?
  ii Can she hire a tennis racket?

b The husband would like to go for a bicycle ride:
  i Can he hire a bicycle?
  ii Does he need to enrol if he goes on an organized trip?

c Her youngest son would like to try out mountain biking
  (**VTT – vélo tous terrains**).
  i Is it free?
  ii Does he need to enrol?

d Her daughter is very keen on doing archery. They have been told
  that the town runs archery classes:
  i Is it true?
  ii Does she have to pay?

e If it rains what can they do indoors?
  i ....
  ii ....

Before going on to Unit 17 take the **Self-test 5** (Units 14–16). Once
you have done it, check your answers in the **Key to the exercises
and tests** and the **Role-play scripts** and write your score in the box
provided after the text. If you score between 40 and 50 points,
you can go straight on to Unit 17. If your score is between 20 and
40 points, you need to spend more time revising the **Dialogues**
and **Key words and phrases**. Below 20 points, go back over Units
14, 15 and 16 and take the test again to see how much you have
improved.

SELF-TEST 5

UNITS 14–16   POINTS   : /50

This test covers the main vocabulary and phrases, skills and language points in Units 14–16. **Bonne chance!**

1   You are in the **Office de Tourisme** in Paris. Can you do the following? Say the answers out loud and write them down. Three points for each correct answer.
   a Find out whether they can book a room for you.
   b Ask for a town map.
   c Find out how to go to the Eiffel tower.
   d Ask what they've got in the way of excursions.
   e Ask what there is for children to do.
   f Ask for a list of restaurants.
   g Ask the attendant to show you the **grands magasins** on the map.

Points: _____/21

◀) **CD2, TR 26**

2   Rôle-play

You are at the ticket office in the **Gare du Nord** in Paris. You want to go and spend a weekend in Brussels with your partner. Give yourself one point for each correct answer, and two when your answer consists of two correct sentences.

Points:____/15

3   The text overleaf describes the range of excursions available to tourists visiting Paris and the Île-de-France. Read the text and say whether the assertions are **vrai** or **faux**. One point when your assertions are correct. Two points when you give a full answer.

Excursions et balades

Dans un grand autocar de prestige avec climatisation, dans un minibus tout aussi confortable, installés à ciel ouvert sur la plate-forme panoramique du pont supérieur de l'autobus à impériale ou à bord d'un train touristique de quartier, pour deux heures ou pour une journée, découvrez Paris avec des guides polyglottes, des commentaires culturels et des circuits à thème. Les audio-guides fournis disposent de commentaires en plusieurs langues (jusqu'à 14 différentes). Dans les minibus, les chauffeurs sont multilingues. Les programmes sont organisés en journée et en soirée, été comme hiver. Nos fiches vous donnent le détail de leurs offres et vous pourrez réserver auprès des excursionnistes ou par l'intermédiaire de l'Office de Tourisme la formule que vous préférez: une matinée, un après-midi ou une journée, avec ou sans repas.

		vrai	faux
a	The publicity refers to coach and minibus excursions only.	☐	☐
b	Tourists can sit on open-top buses.	☐	☐
c	Tourists have access to films and English books to discover Paris.	☐	☐
d	Tourists are advised to buy audio-guides.	☐	☐
e	Audio-guides are necessary because drivers do not speak foreign languages.	☐	☐
f	Excursions are organized during the daytime in summer and in winter.	☐	☐
g	The Tourist Office is the only place that books the tours.	☐	☐

Points: ___/14

Self-test 5 score (Units 14–16)
Points: _____/50

17

Bonne route
Safe journey

In this unit you will
- *Learn useful information for travelling on French roads*
- *Learn some French road signs*
- *Practise asking for directions*
- *Buy some petrol and get your tyre pressures checked*
- *Find out what to do in case of breakdown*
- *Learn some essential words for describing what's wrong with your car*

Before you start, revise
- *Asking the way and understanding directions (Unit 6, Section 1)*
- *Asking for assistance (Unit 9, Section 1)*
- *Understanding what you need to do (Unit 9, Section 3)*
- *Numbers (Appendix)*

Les routes françaises *French roads*

Pour avoir des informations sur la circulation, les itinéraires conseillés et la météo, consultez les sites suivants:
- ▶ Les autoroutes françaises: www.autoroutes.fr
- ▶ Bison Futé: www.bison-fute.equipement.gouv.fr

(Contd)

▶ Chaînes d'hôtels situés en bord de routes, près des aéroports, aux centres-villes avec réservation automatique de chambre 24h/24.
www.hotelformule1.com
www.etaphotel.com
www.accorhotels.com

Le réseau routier français est l'un des plus denses du monde; il est donc facile de visiter le pays en prenant les autoroutes qui sont payantes ou les petites routes 'de campagne'. Comme dans la plupart des pays, la circulation se fait à droite. N'oubliez pas, avant de partir, de vous munir de la carte verte d'assurance internationale.

Par temps sec, la vitesse est limitée à 50 km/h en agglomération, 90 km/h sur route nationale (N) ou départementale (D), 110 km/h sur route à deux voies séparées et à 130 km/h sur autoroute (A). Par temps de pluie, la vitesse maximale est abaissée à 110 km/h sur autoroute et 100 km/h sur route à deux voies séparées.

Tout au long des autoroutes vous pouvez vous restaurer, faire le plein d'essence ou des achats dans les aires de service. Une quarantaine d'aires disposent de bornes Internet ou d'espaces WiFi pour envoyer les courriels et surfer sur le Web. Les aires de repos, plus nombreuses, sont espacées de 15 kilomètres environ. Elles sont de véritables espaces de détente et sont équipées de tables de pique-nique et d'espaces de jeux pour les enfants.

Les jours fériés en France ne tombent pas nécessairement le lundi. Quand, par exemple, ils tombent un jeudi, beaucoup de Français 'font le pont'. Ils ne travaillent pas le vendredi et prennent un long week-end du mercredi soir au dimanche soir. La circulation à l'entrée et à la sortie des grandes villes, et aux péages des autoroutes devient alors très difficile. Pour éviter les bouchons (longues files de voitures qui avancent très lentement), consultez avant votre départ les sites Internet (voir ci-dessus), et suivez les conseils de Bison Futé.

Insight

Bison Futé (a crafty little Indian) was born in 1958 with the first traffic news. Since then his posters on the French roads where he suggested alternative routes have been taken down, but he can still be found on his website: www.bison-fute.equipement.gouv.fr

ACTIVITY 1

To see how well you've understood the passage above, try to answer the following questions (see **Key words and phrases** before Dialogue 1).

a Do you need to pay a toll on motorways?
b Does the speed limit change according to dry and wet conditions?
c What does N stand for on a French road map?
d What can one do in most **aires de service**?
e Is the Internet accessible on motorways?
f What happens when the French **font le pont**?

ACTIVITY 2

Study the 'Calendrier du trafic routier' prepared by **Bison Futé** and answer the questions:

a Quels sont les mois où la circulation est moins dense?
b À quelles fêtes nationales ou religieuses correspondent les périodes de circulation difficile?

c Quels sont les deux week-ends de l'été où la circulation est extrêmement difficile?

d Quel conseil donneriez-vous à un Anglais qui doit circuler en France pendant les mois de juillet et août?

Calendrier du trafic routier 2008

Légende

- ☐ Circulation habituelle
- ▨ Circulation difficile
- ▦ Circulation très difficile
- ■ Circulation extrêmement difficile

DÉPART Sens départ vers les lieux de vacances.

RETOUR Sens retour depuis les lieux de vacances.

Mai	DÉPART	RETOUR	Juin	DÉPART	RETOUR	Juillet	DÉPART	RETOUR	Août	DÉPART	RETOUR
1 J	Ascension		1 D			1 M			1 V	▨	
2 V			2 L			2 M			2 S	■	▨
3 S		▦	3 M			3 J			3 D		
4 D		▨	4 M			4 V	▨		4 L		
5 L			5 J			5 S	▨		5 M		
6 M			6 V			6 D			6 M		
7 M	▨		7 S			7 L			7 J		
8 J	Victoire 1945		8 D			8 M			8 V		
9 V			9 L			9 M			9 S	▦	▨
10 S			10 M			10 J			10 D		▦
11 D	Pentecôte	▨	11 M			11 V	▨		11 L		
12 L	▨	▨	12 J			12 S	■		12 M		
13 M			13 V			13 D			13 M		
14 M			14 S			14 L	Fête Nationale	▨	14 J	▦	
15 J			15 D			15 M			15 V	Assomption	
16 V			16 L			16 M			16 S		▨
17 S			17 M			17 J			17 D		▨
18 D			18 M			18 V	▨		18 L		
19 L			19 J			19 S	▨	▦	19 M		
20 M			20 V			20 D			20 M		
21 M			21 S			21 L			21 M		
22 J			22 D			22 M			22 V		▦
23 V			23 L			23 M			23 S	▦	▨
24 S			24 M			24 J			24 D		▨
25 D			25 M			25 V	▨		25 L		
26 L			26 J			26 S	▨	▦	26 M		
27 M			27 V	▦		27 D		▦	27 M		
28 M			28 S			28 L			28 J		
29 J			29 D			29 M			29 V		▦
30 V			30 L			30 M			30 S		▦
31 S						31 J			31 D		▨

228

Key words and phrases

quelles sont les directions pour...?	*how do you get to … ? (lit. what are the directions to…?)*
l'autoroute (f)	*motorway*
la rocade	*ring road, bypass*
la sortie	*exit*
la (route) nationale (N)	*similar to an 'A' road in the UK*
à péage	*toll payable*
une aire de repos	*service area*
suivez le panneau	*follow the sign*
c'est indiqué	*it is signposted*
le carrefour	*the crossroads*
les feux (m.pl.) **rouges**	*traffic lights (often shortened to* **les feux***)*
une station-service	*petrol station*
où peut-on se garer?	*where can I park?*
le parking	*car park*
défense de stationner	*no parking*
le parcmètre	*parking meter*
je suis en panne	*I've broken down*
le service de dépannage	*breakdown service*
le moteur ne marche pas	*the engine does not work*
vérifier la pression des pneus	*to check the tyre pressure*
le gonflage des pneus est gratuit	*pumping up the tyres is free*
faire le plein	*filling up the car with petrol*
je vous en remets?	*shall I top it up for you?*
l'essence	*petrol*
le sans plomb	*lead-free (petrol)*
le gazole	*diesel*
l'huile (f)	*the oil*
réparer	*to repair*
la carte	*map*
la route à deux voies séparées	*dual carriageway*
une agglomération	*built-up area*

(Contd)

la (route) départementale (D)	equivalent to a 'B' road in the UK
le jour férié	*bank holiday*
le jour de congé	*day's leave*
le bouchon	*bottleneck, traffic jam*
la plupart de	*most of*
le pompiste	*petrol pump attendant*

Insight

When driving in France, remember that at junctions you normally give way to traffic from the right (**priorité à droite**). But you always have right of way on a priority road marked with a yellow-on-white sign.

Dialogue 1: Les directions pour …? *The way to …?*

You may want to look at the road map of **Bordeaux et son Agglomération** *with Activity 3 before listening to the recording.*

In this telephone conversation a tourist is calling the manager of the **Hôtel Bordeaux Aéroport** *to enquire about accommodation and directions. When is reception open?*

Gérant	Allô, Hôtel Bordeaux Aéroport, j'écoute.
Touriste	Bonjour, Monsieur. Voilà, j'ai l'intention de descendre dans votre hôtel dans deux semaines et je voudrais connaître les directions pour y arriver.
Gérant	Vous viendrez d'où?
Touriste	De Bayonne, donc j'arriverai **soit** par la A63 **soit** la N10.
Gérant	**Il vaudrait mieux** prendre la A63 car la N10 **ne débouche pas sur** la rocade.
Touriste	La rocade?
Gérant	Oui … c'est **la voie rapide** qui **contourne** Bordeaux. Alors c'est très simple. **Une fois sur** la rocade il faut prendre direction aéroport Mérignac puis la sortie 11.

Touriste	Bon, **j'ai compris**. Et après?
Gérant	Après? L'hôtel est très bien indiqué. Suivez les panneaux. Il est dans le grand centre hôtelier de l'aéroport entre le Novotel et le Mercure.
Touriste	Pour avoir une chambre, que faut-il faire?
Gérant	Soit vous réservez directement sur Internet, soit vous nous téléphonez quelques jours à l'avance en nous laissant le numéro de votre carte de crédit, soit vous arrivez le jour même – il y a quelqu'un à la réception à partir de 17 heures – et **vous nous laissez** alors juste votre nom.
Touriste	Et si j'arrive tard?
Gérant	Si vous arrivez au-delà des heures de réception, donc après 22 heures, vous devez insérer dans le distributeur votre carte bancaire. La carte sera débitée du **montant** de la chambre et vous obtiendrez le numéro de votre chambre.
Touriste	Ah bon … ça a l'air très simple … Et c'est combien?
Gérant	31€ la nuit. Le petit déjeuner est en extra: 3€90.
Touriste	Et pour se garer, il y a un parking?
Gérant	Nous avons un parking fermé.
Touriste	Il faut réserver à l'avance?
Gérant	Oh là, là oui, je vous le conseille surtout en périodes de vacances.
Touriste	Bon, alors je vais **m'en occuper** tout de suite.

soit … soit *either … or*
il vaudrait mieux *it would be better*
ne débouche pas sur *does not merge with*
la voie rapide contourne *the expressway goes round*
une fois sur *once on*
j'ai compris *I have understood*
vous nous laissez *you give us (you leave to us)*
le montant *the amount*
s'en occuper *to deal with something*

ACTIVITY 3

Have you understood the conversation between the manager and the tourist? Look at the **Formule 1** brochure below, then read the directions and put them in the right sequence.

a Une fois sorti de la rocade, suivez les panneaux
b puis la sortie 11
c Quand vous arrivez sur la rocade,
d il faut prendre la direction aéroport Mérignac
e Il vaudrait mieux prendre la A63

BORDEAUX ET SON AGGLOMÉRATION

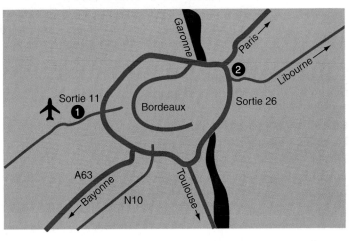

ACTIVITY 4

Looking at the **Formule 1** brochure, you decide that Est-Artigues is the most conveniently placed hotel in the area around Bordeaux for your journey from Bayonne to Paris. You phone the gérante, asking her for the directions. Fill in your part.

a	**You**	*Tell her that you would like to stay one night in the hotel. Ask her how to get to Est-Artigues.*
	Gérante	Vous arrivez d'où?

b	**You**	*From Bayonne.*
	Gérante	De Bayonne? Alors c'est très simple. La A63 vous mène directement sur la Rocade. Prenez la direction est vers Paris, puis sortie 26. Aux …
c	**You**	*Can you repeat, please?*
	Gérante	Oui, alors vous allez prendre la rocade direction est, Paris–Libourne, sortie 26. Une fois sorti, prenez à droite aux feux, sortie CourtePaille, et nous sommes à 500 mètres de là.
d	**You**	*Repeat her instructions from exit 26.*
	Gérante	Voilà, l'hôtel est indiqué. Suivez les panneaux.
e	**You**	*Is there a restaurant?*
	Gérante	Oui, nous avons un restaurant sur place.
f	**You**	*Ask at what time you can arrive.*
	Gérante	Il y a quelqu'un à la réception à partir de 17 heures jusqu'à 22 heures.

Insight

Hotel Formule 1 is an international chain of 'super low budget' or 'no frills' hotels. There are more than 380 hotels in 13 countries worldwide. As with Etap, most are located in France. The rooms are very basic and can sleep up to three. There is a wash basin but no toilet or shower in the room; bathing facilities are shared, but self-cleaned after every use. The advantage is that the hotels are cheap (around €30 per night), usually situated near the motorways, and have enclosed parking.

Stationnement *Parking*

Le stationnement dans la plupart des villes est payant, sous forme d'horodateurs. Le tarif horaire varie en moyenne entre un et deux euros.

ACTIVITY 5

Here are the kind of instructions which are displayed on
horodateurs or **distributeurs** in France. Read them, then answer the
questions with **vrai** or **faux**. Correct the false ones:

▶ Stationnement payant: tous les jours de 9h à 13h et de 14h à 19h
sauf dimanches et jours fériés
▶ Stationnement (de moyenne et longue durée): 8h maximum
▶ Tarifs horaires

30 m = 0,50€	3h = 4€
1h = 1€	4h = 5€
1h30 = 2€	8h = 8€
2h = 2,50€	

▶ Pièces acceptées, 50 centimes, 1€, 2€
▶ Cet appareil ne rend pas la monnaie
▶ Droit de stationnement exclusif de toute garantie
▶ En cas de panne, utiliser l'appareil voisin. Merci

---

		vrai	faux
a	Parking is free after six o'clock and at weekends.	☐	☐
b	You can park your car for short or longer periods.	☐	☐
c	All coins are allowed.	☐	☐
d	Change is given.	☐	☐
e	**Droit de Stationnement exclusif de toute garantie** means that the car is parked at the owner's own responsibility.	☐	☐
f	If the parking ticket machine is out of order, you are advised to use a nearby machine.	☐	☐

Le flash trafic *Traffic news*

◀) **CD2, TR 28**

ACTIVITY 6

Imagine that you are driving in France on the A6 motorway
towards Paris. Your car radio is switched on, and the traffic news

suddenly comes on. Can you get the gist of what is being said?
Look at the map of the area to help you, then answer the questions:

a How would you describe the traffic situation?
b The report recommends caution to the drivers. Why?
c The problem starts at the **barrière de péage** in Fleury-en-Bière.
Give the translation for **barrière de péage**.
d A different itinerary is suggested to reach the east of Paris.
What is it?

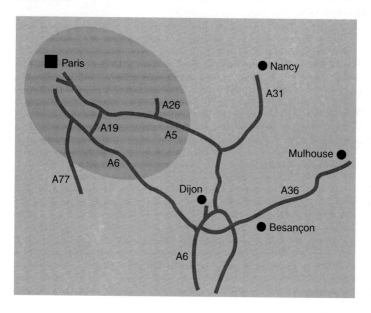

Faire le plein *Filling up with petrol*

When travelling through France you'll probably buy **l'essence** or **le carburant** at a self-service station. If you don't and are faced with an attendant, **pompiste**, ask for **le plein**, to have the tank filled up or buy so many euros' worth, say 50€ or 60€. There is usually a choice between **l'octane 95 sans plomb** (*lead-free petrol with an octane rating of 95*), **l'octane 98 sans plomb** (*super-plus lead-free petrol*) and **le gazole** (*diesel*).

Dialogue 2

A motorist is filling up her car with petrol. The attendant tells her that something is free. What is it?

Pompiste	Bonjour, Madame, qu'est-ce que vous voulez? Du sans plomb?
Cliente	Je prends du sans plomb 95.
Pompiste	Je vous fais le plein?
Cliente	Non, seulement pour 46€ … et vous pouvez aussi vérifier l'huile?
Pompiste	Oui, bien sûr … *(later)* votre niveau d'huile est un peu bas, je vous en remets un peu?
Cliente	Oui, un litre alors.
Pompiste	Et pour la pression des pneus, vous voulez que je regarde? Le gonflage des pneus est gratuit.
Cliente	Oui, je veux bien.
Pompiste	*(after a while)* Voilà, ça fait 53€50 avec l'huile.

ACTIVITY 7

Most of the dialogue above is based on two key structures:

vous pouvez …?	*can you …?*	to ask for help
vous voulez …?	*do you want …?*	to offer something

Read the questions below; can you guess who's asking them? The client or the **pompiste**? Put a tick in the correct column.

	Cliente	Pompiste
a Vous voulez le plein?	....	....
b Vous pouvez regarder le niveau d'eau?	....	....
c Vous voulez du super?	....	....
d Vous pouvez me faire le plein?	....	....
e Vous pouvez vérifier la pression des pneus?	....	....
f Vous voulez 1 litre d'huile?	....	....

ACTIVITY 8

Now it's your turn: you need some unleaded petrol and want to have your oil checked.

a	**You**	*Say hello. Ask for unleaded petrol.*
	Pompiste	Vous voulez le plein?
b	**You**	*Say no. 58€'s worth.*
	Pompiste	C'est tout?
c	**You**	*Ask if he can check the oil.*
	Pompiste	Oui, effectivement, vous avez besoin d'huile. Vous en voulez combien?
d	**You**	*Say one litre.*
	Pompiste	Un litre, bon très bien. Vous voulez que je vérifie la pression des pneus? Le gonflage est gratuit.
e	**You**	*Say no thank you; it's OK (**ça va**).*
	Pompiste	Ça fait 65€. Vous payez à la caisse.

En panne *Breaking down*

In case of accidents and thefts (**accidents et vols**) phone the police. In case of breakdowns look in the yellow pages (**annuaire professions**) under **dépannage** or call the police.

If you break down on the motorway, go to the nearest emergency telephone (tall orange pillars marked 'SOS'). All you need to do is press the emergency button, release it and wait for the operator to connect you.

Dialogue 3

Une femme est tombée en panne sur l'autoroute. Elle appelle le service de dépannage.

A woman has broken down on the motorway. She rings the breakdown service.

Listen to the recording or read the dialogue and try to answer the following questions: On which motorway has the woman broken down? Where is she going? How long is it going to take the mechanic to get there?

Femme	Allô, le service de dépannage?
Mécanicien	Ici, Dépannage Ultra-rapide, j'écoute.
Femme	Voilà, je suis en panne; je ne comprends pas, le moteur ne marche plus. Vous pouvez m'aider?
Mécanicien	Où êtes-vous, Madame?
Femme	Je suis sur l'autoroute A26, entre Reims et St. Quentin.
Mécanicien	Et dans quelle direction allez-vous?
Femme	Vers Calais.
Mécanicien	Elle est comment votre voiture?
Femme	C'est une Peugeot 307 bleue.
Mécanicien	Bon, j'arrive dans une demi-heure.

ACTIVITY 9

Let's hope you won't be so unlucky! But to be prepared for all emergencies practise the following situation: look at the map on the next page; you've broken down with your English Ford and you've just got through to the breakdown service. Fill in your part:

	Homme	Allô, service de dépannage.
a	**You**	*Ask if they can help you – say you've broken down.*
	Homme	Quel est le problème?
b	**You**	*Say that you don't know; the engine is not working.*
	Homme	Où êtes-vous?
c	**You**	*Say you are on the motorway A10 between Orléans and Blois.*
	Homme	Où allez-vous?

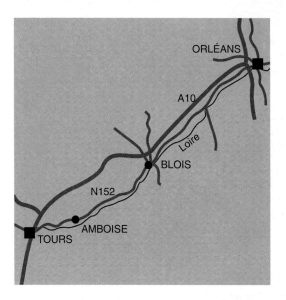

◀) **CD2, TR 31**

ACTIVITY 10

Nothing seems to work in Michel's car. On the next page study the illustrations and explanations describing what's wrong with his car.

Now listen to him explaining his trouble to the mechanic. What he says is not in the same order as overleaf. Fill in the boxes with **1, 2, 3, 4, 5, 6, 7, 8** to show the order in which you hear it. (Check your answers at the back of the book.)

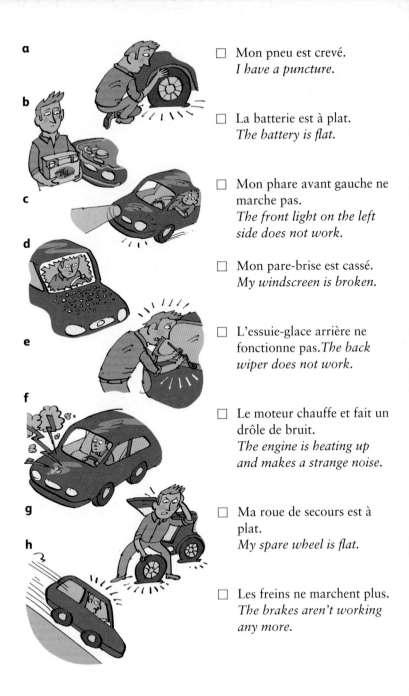

a ☐ Mon pneu est crevé.
I have a puncture.

b ☐ La batterie est à plat.
The battery is flat.

c ☐ Mon phare avant gauche ne marche pas.
The front light on the left side does not work.

d ☐ Mon pare-brise est cassé.
My windscreen is broken.

e ☐ L'essuie-glace arrière ne fonctionne pas. *The back wiper does not work.*

f ☐ Le moteur chauffe et fait un drôle de bruit.
The engine is heating up and makes a strange noise.

g ☐ Ma roue de secours est à plat.
My spare wheel is flat.

h ☐ Les freins ne marchent plus.
The brakes aren't working any more.

THINGS TO REMEMBER

In this unit you have learnt useful information for travelling on French roads, essential words for describing what's wrong with your car and have practised asking for directions and buying petrol.

Say the following in French:

1 How does one get to the motorway?

2 I have broken down near Poitiers.

3 What must I do if I arrive after 10 p.m.?

4 Can you tell me what my room number is?

5 Do you have enclosed parking?

   Translate the following phrases into English:

6 La N10 ne débouche pas sur la rocade.

7 L'hôtel est bien indiqué. Il faut suivre les panneaux.

8 Une fois sur la rocade, il vaudrait mieux prendre direction ...

9 Il (vous) faut/vous devez insérez votre carte bancaire dans le distributeur.

10 La carte sera débitée du montant de la chambre.

You'll find the answers in **the Key to the exercises and tests** at the end of the book. If your answers are correct you are ready to move to Unit 18. If you found the test difficult, spend more time revising Unit 17.

18

L'argent
Money

In this unit you will
- *Find out how to ask for change*
- *Familiarize yourself with French coins and notes*
- *Practise changing traveller's cheques*
- *Learn to say that there is an error in a bill*

Before you start, revise
- *Saying what you want (Unit 7, Section 2)*
- *Asking for help (Unit 9, Section 1)*
- *Expressions of time, days of the week (Unit 5, Key words and phrases)*
- *Numbers (Appendix)*

Pièces et billets de banque en euros
Euro coins and banknotes

En région parisienne, les banques sont principalement ouvertes du lundi au vendredi de 10 à 17h. En province, elles ouvrent du mardi au samedi et ferment entre 13 et 15h.

L'euro est la devise nationale de la France et aujourd'hui de quinze autres pays membres de l'Union européenne. Il y a sept billets de couleurs et de tailles différentes: 5, 10, 20, 50, 100, 200 et 500€.

Sur les billets on peut voir au recto des fenêtres et portails, et au verso des ponts. Ces éléments illustrent différentes périodes de la culture européenne: le classique, le roman, le gothique, la Renaissance, le baroque, etc.

ACTIVITY 1

Il y a huit pièces: 1, 2, 5, 10, 20, 50 centimes, 1€, 2€. Dans un euro il y a 100 centimes. Chaque pièce a deux faces. La première est européenne. Commune avec les autres pays membres de l'Union, elle représente la valeur en euro et douze étoiles, symbole de l'Europe. La deuxième est nationale. Propre à chaque pays, elle représente les symboles caractéristiques de chaque pays. Sur la face française sont représentés trois symboles: la Marianne, symbole de la liberté et de la République, la Semeuse (*sower*), symbole de la fécondité, et l'Arbre, symbole de la vie.

a Do banks shut over lunchtime in France?
b Are euro coins the same throughout the EU?
c In what ways do they differ?

Key words and phrases

If you have not got the recording, check the pronunciation of the words preceded by * in the **Pronunciation tips** overleaf.

* **une pièce**	*coin*
* **un billet**	*banknote*
* **un franc**	*franc* (old currency)
* **un euro**	*a euro*
* **la monnaie**	*small change, currency*
la devise étrangère	*foreign currency*
* **l'argent** (m)	*money*
la livre (sterling)	*(English) pound*
le dollar	*dollar*
* **le cours du change, le taux de change**	*exchange rate*
* **le traveller** (or **chèque de voyage**)	*traveller's cheque*
en bas	*at the bottom*
un stylo	*a pen*
une pièce d'identité	*means of identification*
un changeur de monnaie	*coin changing machine*
une télécarte	*telephone card*
la carte bleue	*the French banker's card*
une carte bancaire	*banker's card*
la note	*hotel bill*
l'addition (f)	*bill* (drinks, snacks)
régler	*to settle* (bill)
une erreur	*a mistake*
le chiffre	*number*
un distributeur automatique	*a cashpoint machine*

(Contd)

For you to say

vous pouvez changer … euros?	*can you change … euros?*
vous avez de la monnaie svp?	*do you have any change please?*
il me faut des pièces de 1€	*I need 1€ coins*
changer, retirer de l'argent	*change, withdraw some money*
la livre est à combien?	*what's the rate of exchange for the pound?*
vous acceptez les cartes de crédit?	*do you accept credit cards?*

Worth knowing

faites (faire) l'appoint	*put in the exact money*
l'appareil ne rend pas l'argent	*no change given*
retirer de l'argent	*to withdraw money*

PRONUNCIATION TIPS

You do not need to know many words when changing money but they need to be pronounced correctly; here is an opportunity to practise saying them:

pièce	pee–esse
billet	bee–yeah
franc	remember not to pronounce the **c**
euro	ir (as in *sir*) – ro
monnaie	mo–nay
argent	make sure the **r** is pronounced otherwise it could sound like **agent (de police)**: *policeman*
cours	don't pronounce the **s**
traveller	as in English but with a French **r**

And now re-read the **Key words and phrases,** checking your pronunciation.

Insight

Mind the difference!

The French use a comma to mark the decimal unit's position and the decimal point to separate sequences of three digits. However, English-speaking countries use the decimal point as the comma is already used to separate sequences of three digits, e.g.: £2,500.15; €3.000,45 €3.000,45.

Faire de la monnaie *Getting small change*

ACTIVITY 2

Try to answer the following, using the key words phrases.

a How would you ask: Can you change 10€ please?
b How would you say: I need 1€ coins?
c What does **la machine ne rend pas l'argent** mean?

Dialogue 1

Listen to the dialogue or read the conversation that takes place between a passer-by and a motorist, who needs some small change for the pay-and-display machine. Then do the activity.

Femme	Pardon, Madame, vous pouvez changer mon billet de 5€, s'il vous plaît?
Passante	Je ne sais pas, mais je vais regarder. Qu'est-ce qu'il vous faut?
Femme	C'est pour l'horodateur. Il me faut cinq pièces de 1€, ou alors une pièce de 1€ et deux pièces de 2€.
Passante	La machine ne rend pas la monnaie?
Femme	Non, et elle **n'**accepte **que** des pièces de 50 centimes, 1€ et 2€.

(Contd)

 CD2, TR 32

Passante	Et vous n'avez pas de carte bancaire?
Femme	Euh, non, je n'en ai pas.
Passante	Eh bien, **vous avez de la chance!** J'ai quatre pièces de 1€ et deux pièces de 50 centimes. **Ça vous va?**
Femme	Merci beaucoup, Madame.

ne … que *only*
vous avez de la chance *you're lucky, you're in luck*
ça vous va? *is that OK (for you)?*

ACTIVITY 3

Dialogue 1

In Dialogue 1 find the French for the following phrases:
a Don't you have a bank card?
b I need five coins of 1€
c it only accepts …
d Can you change …?
e I haven't got any (card)
f I don't know
g Is that OK?
h you're lucky
i I am going to see

Insight
This is a very useful activity to practise these phrases. They are short … but invaluable to get your message across.

ACTIVITY 4

You want to make a phone call but only have a 5€ note on you. Fill in your part of the dialogue.

| **a** **You** | *Stop a man in the street. Ask him if he has any small change for the telephone.* |

	Passant	Qu'est-ce qu'il vous faut?
b	**You**	*Say: I've only got a 5€ note and I need 1€ coins.*
	Passant	Je suis désolé mais je n'ai pas de monnaie. Pourquoi n'achetez-vous pas une télécarte?
c	**You**	*Ask: a 'télécarte'? What is it?*
	Passant	Une carte pour téléphoner. Toutes les cabines téléphoniques marchent avec des télécartes.
d	**You**	*Ask: where can I buy a phone card?*
	Passant	Dans les tabacs, les postes, les gares de métro … un peu partout.

Changer de l'argent *Changing money*

Pour connaître le taux de change:
www.oanda.com/convert/classic www.xe.com

On trouve de nombreux bureaux de change dans les grandes villes (gares, aéroports, grandes agences de banque, points de change). Les grandes postes changent aussi les devises étrangères et les chèques de voyage. Leurs taux sont souvent meilleurs qu'ailleurs. Le nombre de distributeurs automatiques de billets (DAB) augmente régulièrement en France. On y retire de l'argent avec une carte bancaire, la carte Visa/Carte Bleue étant la plus acceptée en France suivie de MasterCard (Eurocard).

Dialogue 2

Un étranger change des chèques de voyages dans une banque.

A foreigner is in a bank changing traveller's cheques.

Listen to the recording or read below and find out: How many dollars does he want to change? What does he need before he can sign his traveller's cheques?

Étranger	Je voudrais changer des chèques de voyage, s'il vous plaît.
Employée	Oui, très bien. Vous avez une pièce d'identité?
Étranger	Oui, voici mon passeport.
Employée	Bon, qu'est-ce que vous voulez?
Étranger	Je voudrais changer 350 dollars en euros.
Employée	D'accord, alors vous allez signer en bas des chèques de voyage.
Étranger	Euh … vous avez quelque chose pour écrire s'il vous plaît?
Employée	Un instant … voici un stylo.
Étranger	Le dollar est à combien aujourd'hui?
Employée	Aujourd'hui le cours du dollar est à 0,68.
Étranger	Il y a une commission à payer?
Employée	Pas pour les chèques de voyage American Express. Mais pour les autres chèques de voyage il y a une commission de 4%.
Étranger	Ah c'est très bien …

ACTIVITY 5

Without looking at the text above, fill in the missing words.

a Je voudrais ……… des chèques de voyage.
b Vous avez une ……… d'identité?

c Vous allez .... en bas des chèques de voyage.

d Vous avez quelque chose pour ....?

e Le dollar est à .... aujourd'hui?

f Il y a une commission à ....?

ACTIVITY 6

Take part in this conversation in **le bureau de change** at the **Gare du Nord** in Paris.

a	**You**	*Say that you would like to change some dollars.*
	Employé	Des dollars américains, canadiens, australiens?
b	**You**	*Say American dollars.*
	Employé	Oui; vous voulez changer des billets ou des travellers?
c	**You**	*Say bank notes.*
	Employé	Combien voulez-vous changer?
d	**You**	*Say 200 dollars. Ask the exchange rate.*
	Employé	Le dollar est à 0,70 aujourd'hui.
e	**You**	*Ask if they are open on Sundays.*
	Employé	Oui, tous les jours de 7h à 21.30. ...*(later)* Voici votre argent!

Une erreur dans la note *An error in the bill*

POUR RÉGLER LA NOTE *PAYING YOUR HOTEL BILL*

▶ It's a good idea to ask for the bill in advance in order to check it.

▶ You ask for **la note** to pay for your hotel bill and for **l'addition** to pay for food and drink.

▶ Remember to check the price of hotel rooms which, by law, should be displayed at the reception and in each room.

▶ Extras (telephone, mini-bar, etc.) should be charged separately.

▶ TTC (**toutes taxes comprises**) means inclusive of tax.

▶ TVA (**taxe à la valeur ajoutée**) means 'VAT'.

◀) **CD2, TR 34**

ACTIVITY 7

Here is some extra practice to help you cope with French prices. Listen to Michel and write down the prices you hear.

a ....
b ....
c ....
d ....
e ....
f ....
g ....
h ....
i ....
j ....

Dialogue 3

A guest is about to leave the hotel. Having asked for the bill, he spots a mistake. Listen to the recording, or read the following dialogue, and say what mistake was made.

Guest	Je voudrais régler ma note, s'il vous plaît.
Réceptionniste	Bien, vous partez aujourd'hui?
Guest	Oui, après le petit déjeuner.
Réceptionniste	Bon, c'est pour quelle chambre?
Guest	Chambre quatorze. Vous acceptez les cartes de crédit?

CD2, TR 35

Réceptionniste	Oui, bien sûr. Alors un instant … nous allons vérifier. Si vous voulez bien repasser après votre petit déjeuner votre note sera prête. *(after breakfast)*
Guest	Pardon, Madame, il y a une erreur. Qu'est-ce que c'est 'mini-bar 10€'?
Réceptionniste	Ce sont les boissons du mini-bar **que vous avez consommées** dans votre chambre.
Guest	Mais **je n'ai rien** pris du mini-bar.
Réceptionniste	Vraiment? Bon, eh bien c'est sans doute une erreur de notre part…! **Nous avons dû nous tromper de chambre**. Je m'excuse Monsieur. Donc ça fait 94€ moins 10€ pour la boisson… euh 84€.
Guest	C'est avec service et taxes?
Réceptionniste	Oui, taxes de séjour et service sont compris.

que vous avez consommées *that you've drunk*
je n'ai rien pris *I haven't taken anything*
nous avons dû nous tromper *we must have made a mistake*

QV

ACTIVITY 8

Have you understood the dialogue well enough to answer the following questions?

a When does the client intend to leave the hotel?
b What was the number of his room?
c Was the bill correct?
d What does the amount of 10€ correspond to?
e Is the bill inclusive of tax and service?

THINGS TO REMEMBER

In this unit you have familiarized yourself with French coins and notes, found out how to ask for change, practised changing traveller's cheques and learnt to say that there is an error in a bill. Say the following sentences:

1 Can you change ... euros?

2 Is there a commission to pay?

3 Do you have any change please?

4 What's the rate of exchange for the pound?

5 Do you have something to sign with?

6 I need 1€ coins.

7 I would like to pay my hotel bill.

8 There is an error.

9 I have taken nothing from the mini-bar.

10 Do you accept traveller's cheques?

You'll find the answers in the **Key to the exercises and tests** at the end of the book. If your answers are correct you are ready to move to Unit 19. If you found the test difficult, spend more time revising Unit 18.

19

Savoir faire face
Troubleshooting

In this unit you will
- *Find out how to ask for medicine at the chemist's*
- *Familiarize yourself with the French health system*
- *Practise making an appointment with the doctor/dentist*
- *Find out about the telephone in France*
- *Learn some key expressions to describe your problems*

Before you start, revise
- *Saying what you want (Unit 7, Section 2)*
- *How to describe things (Unit 7, Section 3)*
- *How to spell in French (Unit 12, Activity 8)*
- *How to say my, your, his, etc. (Unit 4, Section 7)*
- *Expressions of time, days of the week (Unit 5, Key words and phrases)*
- *Numbers (Appendix)*

Sign for a French chemist's

La pharmacie en France *The chemist's in France*

The French chemist's is easily recognizable, with its green neon cross sign outside. For minor ailments you'll find that the trained pharmacist, **pharmacien(-ne)** is usually happy to give you advice. You will not be able to buy medicines (even aspirin!) anywhere except at the **pharmacie**.

Chemist's shops/pharmacies are generally open from 8.00 to 20.00. Some stay open later. Their opening times on Sundays and bank holidays are fixed by a rotating schedule. When they are shut, the address of the nearest duty/night chemist's shop is displayed on the door. In Paris the following chemist's shops stay open all night long:

▶ Pharmacie Dhéry (24h) inside the shopping arcade at 84, avenue des Champs-Elysées (8e), tél: 01 45 62 02 41
▶ Pharmacie Européenne de la Place de Clichy (24h), 6 place de Clichy (17e), tél: 01 48 74 65 18 and 01 42 89 01 04
▶ British and American Pharmacy, 1 rue Auber (9e), tél: 01 47 42 49 40
▶ Pharmacie Anglaise, 62 Avenue Champs Elysées, (8e), tél: 01 43 59 22 52

Le service medical *Medical treatment*

BEFORE LEAVING FOR FRANCE

Check whether your country has signed a bilateral agreement with the French Social Security (**Centre des Liaisons Européennes et Internationales de Sécurité Sociale:** www.cleiss.fr). In all cases, it is more prudent to take out a travel insurance policy.

If you are a EU resident, remember to take your European Health Insurance Card (EHIC) with you. It can be obtained online (www.nhs.uk/nhsengland/Healthcareabroad), by phone (0845 606 2030) or by post (pick up the EHIC form and pre-addressed envelope from the Post Office). With the EHIC you can obtain a refund of generally 70 per cent on the cost of prescriptions and standard doctors' and dentists' fees.

Before making an appointment with a doctor or dentist, make sure that they are **conventionné** and belong to the category **Secteur 1**. **Conventionné** practitioners fall into one of two categories: in **Secteur 1** they charge the official social security rate, in **Secteur 2** an extra charge is added to the official rate.

Show the doctor (general practitioners and specialists) your EHIC before paying him/her directly. He/She will fill out **a feuille de soins** (*treatment form*) and **une ordonnance** (*prescription*) if necessary.

You can obtain your medication from any chemist's shop/ pharmacy on presenting the **feuille de soins** and **ordonnance**. The price of the medicine is printed on a second **feuille de soins** that the chemist will give back to you with the prescription. The **vignettes** (*stickers*) on the medicine packaging must be removed and stuck on the **feuille de soins** in the space provided. The amount left to the patient to pay (approximately 30 per cent) is what the French call the **ticket modérateur**.

Once you have dated and signed the **feuille de soins**, attached the **vignettes** and filled in your permanent address and bank details (name of bank, address, SWIFT code, account number and IBAN or BIC), you should send the form to the nearest Sickness Insurance Office (**Caisse Primaire d'Assurance-Maladie** or **CPAM**) while you are still in France, together with the prescription and a copy of your European Health Insurance Card. The refund will be sent to your home address later. This refund process normally takes around two months.

EMERGENCIES

In an emergency, phone:

- ▶ **SAMU**/24-hour ambulance: 15 or 01 45 67 50 50
- ▶ **SOS Médecins**/Doctors – 24h house calls: 01 47 07 77 77
- ▶ **Urgence Médicales de Paris** (Paris Medical Emergencies): 01 53 94 94 94
- ▶ **SOS Helpline** (in English, 3–11 p.m.): 01 16 21 46 46
- ▶ **SOS Dentaire**/Dental emergency: 01 43 37 51 00
- ▶ **Hôpital Américain de Paris**, 63, boulevard Victor-Hugo, 92 200 Neuilly, tél: 01 46 41 25 25. The hospital provides consultations in English (24/7) for all dental and medical emergencies.

Key words and phrases

For you to say	
la pharmacie	*chemist's*
le pharmacien, la pharmacienne	*chemist/pharmacist*
chez le médecin	*at the doctor's*
chez le dentiste	*at the dentist's*
le cabinet médical/dentaire	*doctor's/dentist's surgery*
prendre rendez-vous	*to make an appointment*
je voudrais … une consultation	*I would like to go to the surgery/ the doctor's office*
une visite du docteur	*a home visit from the doctor*
souffrir	*to suffer, be in pain, feel ill*
depuis quand	*since when*
je voudrais quelque chose pour …	*I would like something for …*
* **la piqûre d'insectes**	*insect bite*
le mal de gorge	*sore throat*
le mal de dents	*toothache*
le mal de tête	*headache*
j'ai mal à la gorge	*I've got a sore throat*

j'ai mal aux dents	*I've got toothache*
j'ai mal à la tête	*I've got a headache*
j'ai mal au ventre	*I've got stomach ache*
il a de la fièvre	*he's got a temperature*
le dentifrice	*toothpaste*
le shampooing	*shampoo*
contre	*against*
j'ai perdu (il a perdu) ...	*I've lost (he's lost) ...*
la perte	*loss*
j'ai laissé (il a laissé) ...	*I've left (he's left) ...*
... est cassé(e)	*... is broken*
... sont cassés(ées)	*... are broken*
on a volé	*... was stolen*
le vol	*theft*
le sac à main	*handbag*
le portefeuille	*wallet*
le porte-monnaie	*purse*
les lunettes	*glasses*
remplir un formulaire, imprimé	*fill in a form*
faire une déclaration par écrit	*to make a statement in writing*

For you to understand

un médicament	*medicine*
une crème	*cream*
une huile	*oil*
une aspirine effervescente	*soluble aspirin*
en comprimés	*in tablet form*
je vous conseille	*I advise you,*
	I recommend to you

* **piqûre** is pronounced 'pic-oore' (with French **u**)

Dialogue 1: À la pharmacie *At the chemist's*

Listen to the recording or read the dialogue: What's wrong with the customer's husband? Has he got a temperature? Name at least three items the customer buys.

Pharmacien	Bonjour, Madame. Vous désirez?
Cliente	Vous avez quelque chose pour le mal de gorge?
Pharmacien	C'est pour vous, Madame?
Cliente	Non, c'est pour mon mari.
Pharmacien	Il a de la fièvre?
Cliente	Non, mais il a aussi mal à la tête.
Pharmacien	Bon, pour le mal de gorge je vous donne des pastilles. Il en prend une quand il a mal. Pour le mal de tête, je vous donne de l'aspirine effervescente, deux comprimés toutes les quatre heures. Il n'est pas allergique à l'aspirine?
Cliente	Non, non … merci. Je voudrais aussi du dentifrice et quelque chose contre le soleil.
Pharmacien	Vous préférez une crème ou une huile?
Cliente	Une crème.
Pharmacien	Alors voici du dentifrice et une crème pour le soleil; c'est tout?
Cliente	Oui, merci.
Pharmacien	Bon, eh bien ça fait 38€15.

ACTIVITY 1

Read the dialogue again and choose the right answers for the patient's medical record card below.

a Patient complains of		**b** Temperature	
i stomach ache	☐		
ii headache	☐	Yes ☐	
iii toothache	☐		
iv sore throat	☐	No ☐	
c Treatment		**d** To be taken	
i antibiotics	☐	....	
ii suppositories	☐	....	
iii aspirin	☐	....	
iv pastilles	☐	....	

Insight

Don't be afraid to ask the pharmacists for their advice. They will do it willingly as they see it as part of the services they offer the customers.

ACTIVITY 2

Now it's your turn to go to the chemist's to get some medicine for your daughter, who has toothache.

Pharmacienne	Bonjour, Monsieur/Madame. Vous désirez?
a You	*Say: my daughter has toothache.*
Pharmacienne	Elle a de la fièvre?
b You	*Say: yes, a little.*
Pharmacienne	Depuis quand souffre-t-elle?
c You	*Say: since yesterday.*
Pharmacienne	Bon, je vais vous donner de l'aspirine vitaminée et si ça continue dans un jour ou deux il faudra aller chez le dentiste.
d You	*Thank her. Ask for something for insect bites.*
Pharmacienne	Pour les piqûres d'insectes? Certainement. Je vous conseille cette crème anti-démangeaisons … elle est très bonne …
e You	*You didn't get everything she said but you understood that she was recommending the cream. Say: I'll take it and ask to pay.*

EU residents are covered for emergency medical treatment throughout the European Union. US visitors with private health insurance are also covered for a limited period. Canadians with a valid **Assurance-maladie du Québec** card can receive reimbursement in some cases. Australian Medicare provides absolutely no coverage in France. However, any foreigner who is sick can receive treatment in the casualty ward of any public hospital.

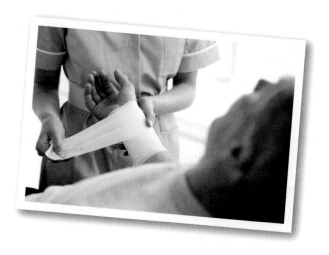

Dialogue 2: Chez le docteur *At the doctor's*

Mrs Jones phones Dr Leroux's surgery to make an appointment. Why does Mrs Jones phone? Who is the patient? Has the patient got a temperature? What other symptom?

◈ CD2, TR 37

Réceptionniste	Allô, le cabinet du docteur Leroux, j'écoute.
Mrs Jones	Je voudrais prendre rendez-vous, s'il vous plaît.
Réceptionniste	Bon, c'est pour une consultation ou une visite?
Mrs Jones	Je ne comprends pas, vous pouvez expliquer?
Réceptionniste	Pour une consultation vous venez ici, pour une visite le médecin va chez vous. Vous êtes la patiente?
Mrs Jones	Non, c'est ma fille. Elle a beaucoup de fièvre …
Réceptionniste	Alors, vous voulez une visite … Écoutez, le docteur **est pris** toute la journée mais il pourrait **passer voir** votre fille dans la soirée vers … peut-être 19.30. Qu'est-ce qu'elle a, votre fille?
Mrs Jones	Je ne sais pas, peut-être **la grippe**. Elle a très mal à la tête.
Réceptionniste	Vous pouvez me donner votre nom et adresse?

Mrs Jones	Jones. J-O-N-E-S et j'habite appartement 2, 10 rue Legrand, à côté de la piscine.
Réceptionniste	Bon, eh bien Mme Jones, le docteur Leroux passera voir votre fille vers 19.30.
Mrs Jones	Merci beaucoup. Au revoir, Madame.

est pris *is busy* (lit. *is taken*)
passer voir *come (go) and see*
la grippe *flu*

Insight

In this dialogue the **réceptionniste** uses the words **la journée**, **la soirée** and not **le jour, le soir**. The common rule is that **journée, soirée, année**, etc. emphasize the notion of duration whereas **jour, soir, an**, etc. merely describe moments in time.

Insight

Using the phone in France may seem like a daunting experience but it doesn't need to be. The most important thing is to speak clearly and open your mouth wide, particularly when pronouncing the vowels **i, o, u, é**. If you don't understand what is being said, don't be afraid to ask the person at the other end to repeat using one of the following expressions:

Vous pouvez répéter, s'il vous plaît?
Vous pouvez parler plus lentement?
Je ne comprends pas.
Vous pouvez expliquer?

ACTIVITY 3

Here are a few French words which appear on the **feuille de soins** and which you may need to recognize in order to fill it in correctly.

Match the words in the left column with their equivalent in the right column, then check your answers at the back of the book.

a la facturation du pharmacien   **i** *the social security office*
b le remboursement   **ii** *signed statement of treatment given*
c les honoraires perçus   **iii** *the GP*
d le médecin traitant   **iv** *keep the original prescription*
e la feuille de soins   **v** *refund*
f conserver l'original de l'ordonnance   **vi** *the chemist's bill*
   vii *the received fee (by the GP)*
g coller les vignettes   **viii** *stick on the (detachable) labels*
h l'organisme d'assurance maladie

ACTIVITY 4

It's your turn to make an appointment at the dentist's. Say your part.

	Réceptionniste	Allô, allô.
a	You	*Say: I would like to make an appointment.*
	Réceptionniste	Oui, très bien; c'est pour vous?
b	You	*Say: no, it's for my son. We are English, on holiday here and he has had toothache since Tuesday.*
	Réceptionniste	Il a quel âge votre fils?
c	You	*Say: he's 12.*
	Réceptionniste	Oui, je vois. Et quand peut-il venir?
d	You	*Say: today, this morning or this afternoon.*
	Réceptionniste	Bon; eh bien cet après-midi, à 3.45. Ça vous va?
e	You	*Ask her to repeat the time.*
	Réceptionniste	À 3.45. Votre nom, s'il vous plaît?
f	You	*Say your name and spell it.*
	Réceptionniste	Merci, nous attendons donc votre fils à 3.45. Au revoir Monsieur/Madame.

La poste, le téléphone et l'Internet en France *Using the post office, the phone and the Internet in France*

LA POSTE

Les bureaux de poste sont ouverts de 8 heures à 19 heures du lundi au vendredi, et le samedi matin de 8 heures à midi. À la poste, on peut acheter des timbres, poster son courrier, changer de l'argent, téléphoner et consulter l'Internet.

> Pour tous renseignements pratiques sur Paris:
> http://en.parisinfo.com/guide-paris

LE TÉLÉPHONE

La plupart des cabines téléphoniques s'utilisent avec des télécartes de 50 ou 120 unités, vendues dans les bureaux de poste, les principales stations de métro et de RER, les tabacs et les caisses des supermarchés.

Pour téléphoner depuis la France, faites les dix chiffres indiqués dans la cabine. Le premier commence toujours par un 0 et le second indique la zone de votre correspondant. La France est divisée en cinq zones. Pour Paris et l'Île-de-France, faites le 01.

Pour téléphoner à l'étranger, composez le préfixe international 00, le code du pays et le numéro de la zone (sans le 0). Pour ne pas payer la communication, vous pouvez vous faire rappeler dans la cabine téléphonique en donnant le code de la France (33), le numéro de la zone sans le 0, puis les huit chiffres de la cabine téléphonique.

L'INTERNET

On peut accéder à l'Internet:

▶ en libre-service en payant la connexion avec une télécarte aux bornes Internet (www.netanoo.com). Ces bornes sont situées dans de nombreux sites publics et privés, galeries marchandes (*shopping centres/malls*), hôtels, points d'accueil des offices de tourisme, etc.

▶ avec WiFi, accessible dans certains hôtels, gares et différents offices de tourisme.

▶ dans les cybercafés. Ceux-ci abondent à Paris et vous en trouverez toujours un situé près de votre lieu de résidence.

ACTIVITY 5

Answer the following statements with **vrai** or **faux**. Correct the false ones:

		vrai	faux
a	The post office is open on Saturday afternoon.	☐	☐
b	Phone cards are only used with public phones.	☐	☐
c	Phone cards are often sold in supermarkets.	☐	☐
d	French numbers have ten digits, the first being o and the second indicating one of the five telephone zones in France.	☐	☐
e	WiFi is only accessible in some hotels.	☐	☐
f	Internet cafés are not so frequent in Paris.	☐	☐

ACTIVITY 6

Look at the call charges opposite and fill in the blanks below, using the correct word from the box.

Pour la France, l'Australie, le Royaume-Uni et les USA, les heures pleines sont de **a** _____ à **b** _____ tous les jours de la **c** _____. Le week-end et jours **d** _____ les heures sont creuses à partir de 12.00. Le tarif est le même que l'on téléphone au Royaume-Uni ou aux **e** _____. Pour **f** _____, le tarif est de 0,49 €/min. pendant les heures **g** _____ et de 0,34 €/min. pendant les heures **h** _____.

fériés   semaine   l'Australie   8.00   creuses   USA   19.30   pleines

JOURS	Heures pleines	Heures creuses
lundi	8–19.30	19.30–8
mardi	8–19.30	19.30–8
mercredi	8–19.30	19.30–8
jeudi	8–19.30	19.30–8
vendredi	8–19.30	19.30–8
samedi	8–12	12–8
dimanche	8–12	12–8
jours fériés	8–12	12–8

PAYS	Tarif par min. Heures pleines	Tarif par min. Heures creuses
France	0,19	0,07
UK	0,23	0,12
USA	0,23	0,12
Australie	0,49	0,34

ACTIVITY 7

Here are some instructions you might see in a **cabine téléphonique** when using a **télécarte**. Can you find the English equivalent for each French instruction?

a décrochez

b introduisez la carte ou faites numéro libre

c patientez SVP

d crédit

e numéro appelé

f retirez votre carte

g appel arrivé

i *incoming call*

ii *credit*

iii *number being connected*

iv *remove card*

v *insert card or dial free number*

vi *wait*

vii *lift receiver*

Au commissariat de police *At the police station*

Pour tout papier d'identité perdu ou volé, vous devez faire **une déclaration** (*statement*) au **commissariat de police** (*police station*) le plus proche. Vous pouvez aussi informer votre consulat. Pour un objet personnel perdu à Paris, présentez-vous en personne au 36, rue des Morillons, 15ème. Pour une carte de crédit, faites une déclaration au commissariat de police après avoir téléphoné au service d'urgence de votre carte.

◄)) **CD2, TR 38**

ACTIVITY 8

To familiarize yourself with some of the vocabulary you need to describe the kind of problems you may experience in France, listen to Michel's various mishaps and fill in the blanks using the correct items from the box. Even without the recording, you may be able to work out what goes where.

a Hier matin, j'ai perdu mes …….. d'appartement dans le métro.
b Après ça, j'ai laissé mon …….. en or et mes …….. à la banque.
c Juste avant midi, on m'a volé au restaurant mon …….. avec tout mon argent et mes …….. de crédit.
d Hier soir, j'ai oublié au commissariat de police ma carte d'…….. et mon parapluie tout neuf.
e Ce matin, j'ai téléphoné au commissariat, mais personne ne m'a répondu. Je crois que mon …….. est cassé.
f Alors j'ai pris ma …….., mais je ne comprends pas, elle ne démarre plus. Mais qu'est-ce que je vais …….. ?

identité	faire	voiture	cartes	téléphone
portefeuille	lunettes	clés	stylo	

Dialogue 3

A man is at the police station reporting the theft of his car. Can you give the make, colour and number plate of his car?

🎧 CD2, TR 39

Agent	Monsieur?
Homme	Je suis anglais, en vacances avec ma famille … On m'a volé ma voiture.
Agent	Quand ça?
Homme	La nuit dernière.
Agent	Où **était** votre véhicule?
Homme	Ma voiture? Dans la rue Gambetta devant l'hôtel du Lion d'Or.
Agent	C'est quoi votre voiture?
Homme	C'est une Volvo S70 rouge.
Agent	Quel est le numéro d'immatriculation?
Homme	Euh … AB08 PLM.
Agent	Bon, nous allons essayer de la retrouver. **En attendant**, il faut faire une déclaration par écrit. Vous pouvez remplir cet imprimé?
Homme	Euh … maintenant?
Agent	Oui, tout de suite car vous en avez besoin pour vos assurances en Angleterre; mais c'est facile … c'est traduit en anglais.

était *was*
en attendant *in the meantime*

QV

ACTIVITY 9

Read the dialogue again and try to spot the French version of the following phrases then write them out:

a my car was stolen ....
b what make of car is it? ....
c what's the registration number? ....

d write a statement ....

e fill in this printed form ....

f you need it for your insurance ....

ACTIVITY 10

In this last exercise, following the examples given, practise saying who lost what, where, and what it looked like. Revise how to say my, your, his, etc. (see Unit 4).

J'ai perdu ma montre en or dans le train.
I have lost my gold watch on the train.

Mon amie a perdu son sac à main en cuir marron dans le bus.
My friend has lost her brown, leather handbag on the bus.

	Who	What	Description	Where
a	you	your pen	gold	office
b	my brother	his suitcase	brown	airport
c	your sister	her purse	leather white	park
d	his father	his passport	British	street
e	my friend	her scarf	in silk	bus

Take the **Self-test 6** (Units 17–19). Once you have done it, check your answers in the **Key to the exercises and tests** and the **Rôle-play scripts** and write your score in the box provided after the test. If you score between 40 and 50 points, congratulate yourself. You are now a truly competent speaker of basic French. If your score is between 20 and 40 points, you need to spend more time revising the **Dialogues** and **Key words and phrases**. Below 20 points, go back over Units 17, 18 and 19, and take the test again to see how much you have improved.

SELF-TEST 6

This test covers the main vocabulary and phrases, skills and language points in Units 17–19. **Bonne chance!**

1 You are staying in 'Les Edelweiss', 7, Boulevard Latapie-Flurin in the centre of Cauterets. Some French friends from Paris phone you and want to go hiking with you. Can you do the following? Look at the information below and say the answers out loud. Three points for each correct answer.

  a Ask whether they are coming by car or train (translate: *take the car or train*).
  b Give directions if they choose to come by train.
  c Give directions if they choose to come by car and tell them that they can park the car opposite the hotel.
  d Give them the address of the hotel and say that it is in the centre of Cauterets.
  e Fix a date and time: Friday 22nd April around seven o'clock in the evening.

Points: _____/15

CAUTERETS

Hautes-Pyrénées (65) - Midi-Pyrénées – Altitude 932 m –
1336 habitants – Paris 899 km – Capacité d'accueil: 22 000 lits

Accès par avion: Aéroport de Tarbes: 35 km de Cauterets
Accès par train: Gare SNCF à Lourdes puis bus jusqu'à Cauterets (30 km)
Accès par voiture: Autoroute jusqu'à Tarbes, puis la N21 et la D921

---

2 Match up the words in the left-hand column with the correct English translation in the right-hand column. One point for each correct answer.

a	la monnaie	**i**	*banknote*
b	un changeur de monnaie	**ii**	*banker's card*
c	un distributeur automatique	**iii**	*bill (drinks, snacks)*
d	une carte bancaire	**iv**	*exchange rate*
e	la pièce	**v**	*coin changing machine*
f	la télécarte	**vi**	*a cashpoint machine*
g	un billet	**vii**	*means of identification*
h	le cours du change	**viii**	*bill (hotel)*
i	l'addition	**ix**	*telephone card*
j	la note	**x**	*coin*
k	la pièce d'identité	**xi**	*small change*

Points: _____/11

◀) **CD2, TR 40**

3 Rôle-play

You want to change some money in a French bank. Follow the prompts. One point for each correct sentence. Two points when your answer consists of two correct sentences.

Points: ___/10

4 You have damaged your knee after two days of skiing in Cauterets. As you need to see the doctor you speak to the hotel receptionist. Say the answers out loud and write them down. Two points for each correct answer.

   a Tell the receptionist that you need to see a doctor.
   b Ask for his/her address.
   c Ring the doctor and say that you want an appointment.
   d Explain that your knee (**le genou**) is sore.
   e Say that you have been suffering for three days.

f Say that you cannot walk.
g Tell the receptionist that you can come tomorrow morning at ten o'clock.
h Say your name and spell it.

Points: _____/14

Self-test 6 score (Units 17–19)

Points: _____/50

Taking it further

In the **Introduction** and **Unit 4** we emphasize how important it is for language learners to create every opportunity to speak the language with other learners or French speakers, listen to some French regularly and read French material. If the idea at first seems a little daunting we give some tips in **Unit 7** to help you get the gist of what you read or listen to, or make the most of your conversations in French. Ideally you should find a 'study buddy' with whom you could work through the course and try your French out. Learning French would then become more meaningful and fun as speaking a language is about communicating with others. Going to France or one of the francophone countries would also be a most valuable experience to try the language out whilst getting direct feedback from the people you talk to. Anyhow, if this is not possible you can still get a real flavour of French in your own home by using the following:

▶ Newspapers (*Libération; Le Parisien* – found in Paris and easy to read; *Le Figaro* – the weekend issue is particularly interesting).
▶ Magazines (*Paris-Match, Marie-Claire, Elle, Cosmopolitan*).
▶ Satellite and/or cable TV channels (e.g. *TV5 Europe, Canal +, La 5ème*. For news: *CNN* and *Euronews*).
▶ Radio stations on long wave (*France Inter, RTL, Europe 1*), or via satellite.
▶ Websites:

a to find out information relating to France: www.yahoo.fr or www.google.fr
b to familiarize yourself with French society and institutions: www.diplomatie.gouv.fr (a site prepared by Le Ministère des Affaires Étrangères)
c to read the French press online: www.lemonde.fr, www.lefigaro.fr, www.liberation.fr, www.leparisien.fr

d to listen to French news in easy French with their transcription: www.rfi.fr/lffr/statiques/accueil_apprendre.asp

▶ In London you can also get information and activities at l'Institut Français, 17 Queensberry Place, London SW7 2DT (telephone 020 7073 1350 or visit www.institut-francais.org.uk).

Key to the exercises and tests

Unit 1
Activities: 1 a Bonjour Madame/Mademoiselle b Bonjour Monsieur
c Bonsoir Madame Mademoiselle d Bonjour Messieurs-dames
e Bonne nuit, Monsieur f Bonsoir Messieurs-dames 2 Bonsoir
Monsieur 3 c 4 Bonne nuit 5 Comment ça va? Très bien merci.
6 a s'il vous plaît b ça va c au revoir d madame e bonsoir f non
merci 7 a iii, b ii, c iii, d iii

Things to remember: 1 Bonjour, Madame 2 Comment ça va? Ça va
3 Vous parlez_anglais? 4 Parlez plus lentement 5 Pardon?

Unit 2
Have a go: Bonjour Madame. Je voudrais une baguette, s'il vous
plaît.

Dialogue: Beer, wine and two bottles of mineral water; no, she
doesn't get any beer

Activities: 1 a un café b une bière c un journal d des bouteilles e un
euro f un timbre 2 une chambre, un café, un journal 3 a Je voudrais
quatre cartes, s'il vous plaît b Vous_avez quatre timbres? c Et de
l'aspirine, s'il vous plaît? d C'est combien? 4 trois 5 a iii, b iv, c ii,
d i 6 a Messieurs-dames b café c bière d voudrais e addition
7 a cinq b neuf c dix d neuf e deux f quatre g neuf h huit

Things to remember: 1 Je voudrais 2 du pain 3 de l'eau 4 de la
limonade 5 des timbres 6 Vous_avez ...? 7 un journal 8 un paquet
de café 9 C'est combien? 10 C'est six euros

Unit 3
Have a go: Je voudrais deux bouteilles de bière et un kilo d'oranges.

Dialogue: Yes, part-time in a travel agency; 3 children – a girl and
2 boys; Jane is not married, she has a boyfriend.

Practise: travaille, travailles, travaille, travaillons, travaillez, travaillent

Activities: 1 a 13 b 18 c 4 d 12 e 7 f 19 g 5 h 15 i 11 j 9 2 a treize b quinze c vingt d treize e dix-neuf f onze g cinq h six i quatre j douze 3 a est b ont c Elles d enfants, un e n'a pas f n'est pas g dix h a, ans 4 a n'ai pas de timbres b n'a pas de café c n'est pas marié d n'est pas secrétaire e n'ai pas de chambre f n'ont pas d'enfants g n'est pas dans le nord de l'Angleterre h ne parle pas français i n'a pas 18 ans 5 a Je m'appelle Anne b Non, je suis mariée c Oui, j'ai deux_enfants d Une fille et un garçon e Ils_ont douze et dix_ans f J'habite Chaville g Oui, je suis secrétaire 6 a Vous_êtes marié? b Vous_avez des_enfants? c Vous travaillez? d Vous_habitez Paris? e Vous_avez des frères et sœurs? f Ils_ont quel âge? g Vous_êtes français? h Vous parlez anglais?

Self test 1 (Units 1–3): 1 a Je m'appelle … et vous? b Vous vous_appelez comment?/Comment vous_appelez-vous?/Quel est votre nom? c Comment vas-tu? d Je vais (très) bien et toi? e Je suis dentiste/Je travaille pour Air France/dans_une banque f Vous travaillez?/Qu'est-ce que vous faites dans la vie? g J'habite Brighton en_Angleterre (dans le sud de l'Angleterre) h Je suis_anglais(e) et je parle anglais et allemand i Je suis marié(e) et j'ai trois_enfants/Je ne suis pas marié(e) et je n'ai pas d'enfants j Je ne comprends pas k Vous parlez anglais? (raise the voice on the last syllable) l Parlez plus lentement m J'ai … ans 2 a suis b est c sont d ai e sont f a g ont h avons i sommes j ai

Unit 4
Have a go: Vous_êtes français(e)? Vous_êtes marié(e)? Je m'appelle … et vous? Vous travaillez?

Dialogue: Yes; Yes; Yes; 3 children

Activities: 1 a v b i c vii d viii e iii f ii g vi h iv 2 (Note that there are alternative ways of asking these questions) a Il y a un restaurant dans l'hôtel? b Il y a une pharmacie près d'ici? c Il y a des magasins près d'ici? d La banque est ouverte? e Il y a un train direct pour Paris? f C'est loin la gare? g Où sont les toilettes? 3 a Il y a une pharmacie mais_il n'y a pas d'aspirine b Il y a une pâtisserie mais_il n'y a pas de croissants c Il y a une gare mais_il n'y a pas de trains d Il y a un arrêt d'autobus mais_il n'y a pas de bus e Il y a un bar mais_il n'y a pas de bière f Il y a une cabine téléphonique mais_il n'y a pas de téléphone 4 a Vous_êtes en vacances? b Vous_êtes mariée? c Vous_avez des enfants? d Vous_habitez Londres? e Vous travaillez? 5 a combien b où c quand d où e où f comment 6 a 49€50 b 3€75 c 8€60 d 56€15 e 68€

Things to remember: (Note that there are alternative ways of asking these questions)
1 Vous vous_appelez comment? 2 Vous_avez quel âge? 3 Vous_habitez où? 4 Vous_avez des_enfants? 5 Il y a une banque près d'ici? 6 C'est loin? 7 C'est où, l'arrêt d'autobus? 8 C'est combien, le billet? 9 C'est à quel étage? 10 Ma fille n'a pas d'enfants 11 Mon fils a vingt-deux ans 12 Mes enfants travaillent à Paris

Unit 5

Have a go: Vous_avez un plan, s'il vous plaît? Il y a une banque et une cabine téléphonique près d'ici? You can find more questions to ask in Key words and phrases of Unit 4.

Practise: l'avion part quand: le bus arrive quand: on rentre quand? on peut prendre le petit déjeuner quand? il y a un métro quand? le concert finit quand? Dialogue: 8.30 a.m. and 5.30 p.m.; school canteen

Activities: 2 a prends b commencent c arrive d apprend e déjeune f prenez g fais h est i finit j faites k attendons l comprennent
3 a iii, b vii, c v, d i, e ii, f iv, g vi 4 f, e, a, c, g, d, h, b 5 a prends b prennent c commence d travaille e déjeune f finit g fait h regardent
6 le 1er mai, le 10 juin, le 3 février, le 13 octobre, le 21 mars, le 30 septembre, le 15 juillet, le 6 août 7 a mercredi b vendredi c dimanche d lundi e jeudi f samedi g mardi 8 a il est neuf heures dix (du matin) b midi moins vingt c une heure et demie (de l'après-midi) d six heures vingt-cinq (du soir) h minuit moins dix

Things to remember: 1 lundi, mardi, mercredi, jeudi, vendredi, samedi, dimanche 2 janvier, février, mars, avril, mai, juin, juillet, août, septembre, octobre, novembre, décembre 3 a Vous_êtes français? b Est-ce que vous_êtes français? c Êtes-vous français? 4 er, ir, re 5 Aujourd'hui, c'est le 12 août 6 dix heures du matin/du soir 7 tous les jours de la semaine sauf le samedi et le dimanche 8 aujourd'hui, demain, quelquefois, souvent, toujours

Unit 6

Have a go: 1 Vous pouvez parler plus lentement? Vous pouvez répéter, s'il vous plaît? 2 Use the dialogue and Key words and phrases of Unit 5

Dialogue: As you leave the house turn left, go to the end of rue Vaugirard, turn right into rue Vincennes and the park is 200 metres on your left. It takes approximately 25 minutes.

Activities: 1 a Pour aller à la piscine? b Pour aller à la gare? c Pour aller à l'église St. Paul? d Pour aller au musée? e Pour aller à l'office du tourisme? 2 a C b E c A d D e B 4 à Brighton, en France, l'Allemagne, à Berlin, à Bonn, au Danemark, aux_États-Unis, au Japon, à Londres 5 a en face du b à côté de la c au coin de d entre e au bout de f grands magasins g bar h pâtisserie i dans la rue j sur la place

Unit 7

Have a go: 1 dans 2 sur 3 entre 4 à côté du 5 sous 6 devant 7 derrière

Dialogue: the big scarves are too expensive, Vous pouvez me faire un paquet-cadeau, s'il vous plaît?

Activities: 1 cet, ces, ce, ces, ce, cet, cette, cette 2 Mme Durand a 35 ans. Elle a les cheveux blonds et longs. Elle a les_yeux verts. Elle fait 1,70 mètre et pèse 65 kg. Elle porte des lunettes rondes. Elle porte un ensemble vert uni, des chaussures légères et une chemise blanche. Jane a 23 ans. Elle a les cheveux bruns et courts. Ses_yeux sont bleus (Elle a les_yeux bleus). Elle fait 1,62 mètre et pèse 55 kg. Elle porte un jean bleu pâle et un pull-over blanc. Elle a (porte) des bottes noires. 3 a une boîte de petits pois français b une tarte aux pommes c un baba au rhum d une glace à la vanille e un sorbet au citron f un grand verre de vin rouge g un café au lait sans sucre h un poulet à 6€80 i un petit café noir j un sandwich au fromage k une bouteille de lait 4 a Chère b famille c tout d sympathique e bonnes f grande/confortable g grande/confortable h longues i jours j meilleure k anglaise l mieux m prochaine 5 a un grand café noir b deux pressions c et un petit crème d non, deux pressions, un petit crème et un grand café noir e Vous_avez des croissants? f J'en voudrais quatre

Self-test 2 (Units 4–7): 1 a C'est loin? b Non, ce n'est pas loin c Il y a une banque près d'ici? d Non, il n'y a pas de banque près d'ici e Avez-vous/Vous_avez un timbre? f Non, je n'en_ai pas g C'est comment le film?/Le film est comment? h C'est où/Où est l'arrêt d'autobus? i C'est_à dix minutes d'ici à pied j Le magasin ouvre quand?/Quand est-ce que le magasin ouvre? 2 a v b iv c i d iii e ii 3 a le dimanche trente et un mars b le mercredi deux juin c le vendredi dix-huit janvier, d le mardi vingt-quatre octobre e le samedi onze mai f le lundi vingt-trois août g le jeudi dix-neuf septembre 4 a Je prends le petit déjeuner à huit heures du matin b Ma mère fait la cuisine/cuisine tous les jours c Mon mari et moi prenons souvent le train le lundi d Qu'est-ce que tu fais/vous faites ce week-end? e Elle travaille toujours jusqu'à midi f À quelle heure finis-tu/finissez-vous le travail? g Aujourd'hui il rentre à la maison vers 20 heures h Tu regardes la TV depuis 10 heures du matin i Je ne travaille jamais le dimanche

Unit 8
Have a go: Je cherche quelque chose pour ouvrir les bouteilles de vin.

Dialogue: Cooking French dishes; squash, swimming, windsurfing.

Activities: 1 a Comment vous_appelez-vous? Je m'appelle Roger Burru b Quel âge avez-vous? J'ai 35 ans c Vous_êtes marié? Oui, je suis marié d Vous_avez des_enfants? Non, je n'ai pas d'enfants e Qu'est-ce que vous faites dans la vie? Je suis professeur f Depuis quand? Depuis 10 ans g Où habitez-vous? J'habite Lille h Qu'est-ce que vous faites comme sport? Je fais de la natation i Vous faites quoi pendant vos loisirs? J'aime beaucoup faire la cuisine 2 e, c, a adore, d, g aime beaucoup, f, h n'aime pas, b déteste 3 b le prends c le connaissez d les a e l'ai f l'aiment g la fais h l'attendons i la regarde j les_écoutons 4 a viii, b vii, c iv, d ii, e ix, f x, g iii, h vi, i v, j i 5 a F b F c V d V e V f F g V h V i F j F k V l F

Things to remember: 1 Qu'est-ce que vous faites comme sport? 2 Je fais de la planche à voile quand_il fait beau en_été 3 Quand le temps est mauvais, je joue au squash 4 Vous faites quoi pendant vos loisirs? 5 J'aime beaucoup faire la cuisine 6 Je ne regarde jamais la télévision 7 Mon fils joue de la trompette à l'école 8 Le samedi j'adore sortir avec mes amis 9 Je ne le connais pas bien 10 Savez-vous/Est-ce que vous savez à quelle heure commence le film/le film commence?

Unit 9
Have a go: 1 a Vous pouvez répéter, s'il vous plaît? b Vous pouvez parler plus lentement s'il vous plaît?

Activities: 1 a v, b vii, c ix, d vi, e iii, f viii, g ii, h iv, i i 2 a iv, b v, c i, d vi, e ii, f iii 3 a C b F c B d D e A f E; i 7 ii add pepper and salt iii 30 g of butter iv when the butter is hot v a fork 4 c, a, f, b, e, d

Practise: It is strictly forbidden to take photographs using a tripod or flash; to damage the sculptures or the vases; to pick flowers or fruit; to climb on the sculptures; to walk on the lawn and to climb on the seats; to lunch outside the area reserved for the cafeteria; to bring animals into the museum's grounds; to ride a bicycle; to play ball games; to drop rubbish except in the litter baskets.

Things to remember: 1 Je ne sais pas 2 Je ne comprends pas 3 Vous pouvez m'aider, s'il vous plait? 4 La machine ne marche pas 5 Qu'est-ce qu'il faut faire? 6 Il me faut un passeport pour aller en France 7 Il faut boire beaucoup

Unit 10
Have a go: 1 Out of order 2 Qu'est-ce qu'il faut faire pour utiliser l'Internet?

Dialogue: 4 weeks; to the seaside and to the mountains;
Mrs Durand: swimming, play tennis, go for long walks and see
regional historic monuments; Mr Durand: have a rest, read, do some
sport (e.g. tennis), play pétanque, go to the cinema or restaurant.
No, she prefers to stay at home or go out to a night club with friends.

Practise: Je m'habille, tu t'habilles, il/elle/on s'habille, nous nous_
habillons, vous vous_habillez, ils s'habillent

Activities: Activities 1, 2, 3, 4, 5, could have alternative answers
to the ones given below: 1 a D'abord je me lève à 7 heures b puis
je me lave c ensuite je prends le petit déjeuner avec les_enfants d À
8h30, j'emmène les_enfants à l'école et ensuite je fais des courses
f À midi, je prépare le déjeuner g L'après-midi, je joue au tennis
h ou je vais chez mes_amis i ou je vais au cinéma j Le soir, je
regarde la télévision k ou j'écoute la radio l enfin je me couche à
23 heures. 2 a ...il/elle se lève ... b ...il/elle se lave ... c ...il/elle
prend ... d il/elle emmène ... e ...il/elle fait ... f ...il/elle rentre,
prépare ... g il/elle joue ... h ...il/elle va chez ses_amis ... i il/elle
va ... j il/elle regarde ... k il/elle écoute ... l il/elle se couche ...
3 Robert: a en août b 3 semaines c à Oxford en_Angleterre d Je
vais apprendre l'anglais, visiter des monuments historiques, voir
des_amis, sortir le soir, jouer au tennis. Jeanine: a le 21 juin b 10
jours c à Anglet près de Biarritz dans le sud de la France d Je vais
me baigner, lire beaucoup, regarder un peu la télévision, faire de
longues promenades, me coucher tôt. 4 Vous allez partir quand
en vacances? Où allez-vous aller? Comment allez-vous passer vos
vacances? 5 a beaucoup b mari c Grande-Bretagne d finit e samedi
f après-midi g rester h jours i visiter j habitent k besoin l prendre
6 a téléphoner à Marc b aller chez le dentiste c aller à la banque
d faire des courses et acheter 2 steaks, une bouteille de vin et une
glace à la fraise e écrire une lettre à sa mère f poster la lettre g jouer
au tennis h faire la cuisine i inviter Anne à dîner

Self-test 3 (Units 8–10): 1 a Sophie déteste, Mohamed aime
beaucoup, je n'aime pas jouer au football b Sophie aime beaucoup,
Mohamed déteste, j'adore faire la cuisine c Sophie aime beaucoup,
Mohamed n'aime pas, j'adore regarder la télévision d Sophie
adore, Mohamed aime beaucoup, j'adore écouter de la musique

e Sophie n'aime pas, Mohamed adore, j'aime beaucoup faire de la natation f Sophie adore, Mohamed déteste, je n'aime pas faire du ski g Sophie n'aime pas, Mohamed aime beaucoup, j'adore aller au restaurant h Sophie déteste, Mohamed adore, et je n'aime pas jouer au tennis 2 a me b t' c se d nous e vous f se 3 a il fait mauvais b il fait beau c le soleil brille d il fait chaud e il neige f il fait froid g il pleut 4 a allez b allons c va d vas e vais f vont

Unit 11
Activities: 1 a 7/8 p.m. b shut c Monday d pâtisseries, charcuteries e No 3 a, c boucherie, d, e, g épicerie, b boulangerie, f charcuterie 4 c, f, h, a, e, d, g, i, b 5 b, d, g, l 7 a Confection b Pressing c Généraliste d Librairie e Informatique f Bijouterie g Chaussures h Lingerie – Vêtements i Traiteur/Charcuterie j Cave – Marchand de Vin 8 a bargain lovers b come down c reductions d special offers e F – also for fashion and thousands of other items f F – the previous season's g F – they cannot exceed six weeks h V 9 a Je cherche une jupe noire b Vous faites quelle taille? c quelque chose de moins cher d Je vais essayer e la jupe à 63€ f Elle vous va bien? 10 a Je voudrais un journal, s'il vous plaît. Vous avez/vendez quels journaux anglais? b Je vais prendre le *Times* et ces trois cartes postales. C'est combien un timbre pour l'Angleterre? c Je vais prendre huit timbres d Je vais aussi acheter le magazine *Elle* pour ma femme 11 a a pullover b white/pale yellow c it's too big d he doesn't like the colour e 68€50 f at the cash desk

Things to remember: 1 Où est-ce que je peux acheter...? 2 Où est la boulangerie la plus proche, s'il vous plaît? 3 Je cherche quelque chose de moins cher 4 Il me faut du jus de fruit 5 C'est un peu trop gros 6 Je vais aussi prendre des fruits 7 Où est la cabine d'essayage? 8 Je peux essayer? 9 Elle fait combien/C'est combien cette jupe? 10 Vous avez/vendez des timbres?

Unit 12
Activities: 1 a villa meublée et équipée b hôtel c résidence de tourisme d chambre d'hôte 2 a ii b xiv c xii d vi e xv f iv g viii h xvii i xi j i k x l ix m iii n v o vii p xiii q xvi 3 a Je viens d'arriver b Vous pouvez me réserver une chambre? c C'est où le seizième arrondissement? d Nous voulons aussi une douche ou une salle de

bains e J'espère que l'hôtel n'est pas complet f Il y a des chambres
de libre 4 a F – on the second b F – it is on top c F – from 7.30
d V e F – at the end of the corridor on the right f V g V 5 Bonsoir,
vous avez une chambre, s'il vous plaît? Non, une chambre double
à deux lits et avec salle de bains. C'est pour quatre nuits. C'est
combien? C'est quoi, une promotion? Est-ce que le petit déjeuner
est compris? À quelle heure servez-vous le petit déjeuner? On
peut prendre un repas dans l'hôtel? Haussmann, c'est qui? 6 a Le
radiateur ne marche pas b Il n'y a pas de savon c Il n'y a pas d'eau
chaude d La lampe ne marche pas e Il n'y a pas de serviettes f La
douche ne marche pas g La télévision ne marche pas h Il n'y a pas
de couvertures 7 a electricity, water facilities, water sewage
b restaurant, food shop, launderette, ironing, television, children's
playground, organized entertainment c cycling, swimming in the
pool, fishing, mini-golf d bowling 9 i l'entretien ii remboursement
iii caution iv retard v draps et linge vi aviser 10 Suggestions:
a Combien de personnes peuvent dormir dans le mobil-home?
b Faut-il/Est-ce qu'il faut amener les draps et les serviettes?
c Acceptez-vous/Est-ce que vous acceptez les chiens sans
supplément? d Quand faut-il/est-ce qu'il faut payer la caution/Il
faut payer la caution quand?

Things to remember: 1 Je cherche un hôtel à trois étoiles 2 Vous
pouvez me réserver une chambre pour deux nuits? 3 C'est pour
mon mari, mes deux enfants et moi 4 Vous avez des chambres de
libre? 5 À quelle heure servez-vous/vous servez le petit déjeuner?
6 Pouvez-vous nous apporter demain matin le petit déjeuner dans
notre chambre à 8.30? 7 Le radiateur ne marche pas 8 Nous
n'avons pas de serviettes dans notre chambre 9 Il (me) faut/Je dois
payer une caution? 10 Vous fournissez les draps?

Unit 13
Activities: 1 a a variety of cuisines b can easily be found c usually
cheap d meat, vegetables or noodles e a limited range of dishes
f today's special g a crêperie h le menu touristique 2 c e b f d a
3 a Je voudrais un croque-monsieur b Vous avez des omelettes?
c Qu'est-ce que c'est 'Parmentier'? d Je vais prendre l'omelette
Parmentier e Qu'est-ce que vous avez comme jus de fruit? f Je

voudrais un jus d'ananas et l'addition, s'il vous plaît 5 a C'est quoi
'L'œuf cocotte au foie gras'? b C'est deux œufs cuits au four c Je
crois que je préfère … d Vous le servez avec quoi le steak?
e Vous pouvez me conseiller pour le vin? f Vous pouvez expliquer
le nom de la tarte? g Amenez l'addition après le dessert 6 a Pour
commencer je vais prendre un filet de hareng b Alors je vais
prendre un avocat à la vinaigrette c Qu'est-ce que c'est le cassoulet?
d Je n'aime pas les haricots. Je préfère la grillade du jour avec frites
e À point. Je voudrais aussi une bouteille de Sauvignon f Qu'est-
ce que vous avez comme desserts? g Je vais prendre une glace à la
vanille h Qu'est-ce que vous avez comme autres parfums? i Je vais
prendre une glace à la fraise 7 L'Auberge Au bon coin. It provides
special menus for children and offers a family type atmosphere in
the country.

Self-test 4 (Units 11–13): 1 a Je cherche une robe en coton
b What size are you? c Je peux essayer? d C'est un peu trop cher/
grand/petit e Vous avez autre chose? 2 a Bonsoir. Vous avez une
chambre double avec salle de bains? b C'est pour deux nuits c C'est
combien? d Le petit déjeuner est compris? e Il y a un restaurant
dans l'hôtel?/On peut manger dans l'hôtel? f La télévision ne
marche pas.

Unit 14

Activities: 1 a V b F c F d F e V f V g F 2 a direction b prenez
c changer d mener e manquerez 3 He needs to take the
underground link to Antony, then the RER B direction Charles
de Gaulle or Mitry-Claye and get off at the station Gare du Nord
which is after Châtelet-Les Halles 4 a go up b crossroads c carry
straight on 5 a C'est quelle ligne pour aller à la Gare d'Austerlitz?
b C'est direct? c C'est loin à pied? d Le prochain bus part à quelle
heure? e Où est-ce que je peux acheter un ticket? f Je voudrais
acheter un (ticket) aller-retour pour les Invalides g Je vais prendre
un carnet h Il faut combien de temps pour arriver à la gare?
6 a Je voudrais un (billet) aller-retour pour Paris b le 8 octobre
dans l'après midi c Il (le train) met combien de temps? d Je ne veux
pas arriver à Paris après 19 heures e Le train de 15.29 me convient.
C'est combien le billet en deuxième classe? f C'est un peu cher.

Il y a (quelque chose de) moins cher? g Je peux changer le billet?
h Le train arrive à Paris à quelle heure? i C'est trop long/Il met trop
de temps. Je vais prendre le train de 15.20 7 a F – to any Vélib'
station b V c V – from the terminals you can access information,
hire a bicycle and take a short-term subscription using your bank
card d F e V

Things to remember: 1 Je voudrais un carnet 2 Je voudrais un
aller-retour pour Grenoble 3 C'est quelle direction pour (aller à)
la Gare d'Austerlitz? 4 Le prochain bus part à quelle heure? 5 Où
est-ce que je peux acheter un billet? 6 Pouvez-vous me dire où il
faut **descendre**? 7 Il faut combien de temps pour le trajet/voyage?
8 Il faut que je réserve/je dois réserver une place? 9 Vous allez
passer sur un pont dans trente minutes 10 Où est le bureau de
renseignements?

Unit 15
Activities: 1 a iv b x c v d vi e vii f viii g xi h iii i i j ix k ii 2 a Je
voudrais un plan de la ville b Qu'est-ce qu'il y a à voir? c Qu'est-ce
qu'il y a à faire pour les enfants? d Il y a une piscine couverte?
e Pour aller au Parc Floral, il y a un bus? 3 a Yes. There are
animals, a children's play area, a miniature golf and a little train
for a ride around the park. b Yes. There is a picnic area. c Exotic
butterflies in a glasshouse and an exhibition on insects. 4 a C'est
combien l'entrée? b C'est quoi la serre? c douze ans; il faut payer
pour le 'petit train' et le golf miniature? d On peut pique-niquer?
e Merci Madame. À quelle heure ferme le parc? 5 a B b A, C and
D: on the 1st Sunday of each month c A: every evening except
Tuesdays until 9 p.m. + late-night openings with some exhibitions;
C: late-night opening on Wednesdays and Fridays; D: late-night
opening on Thursdays; d B because of its dynamic approach in
teaching sciences and techniques: interactive games, spectacles,
etc. 6 a 7.15 a.m. b one hour c have lunch, visit the Hospices, the
wine museum and the wine cellar d 184€ 7 a Nous voulons faire
l'excursion de la route des vins de Bourgogne b Nous voulons
deux places pour le 22 juillet c Le car part d'ici? d Vous pouvez
répéter, s'il vous plaît? e Merci. À quelle heure part le car?
f On peut acheter du vin dans la cave? 8 a dimanche b 9.15

c 7 heures environ d le matin: visite des appartements du château et des jardins, déjeuner dans le restaurant du Château, l'après-midi: visite du Grand Trianon et du petit village construit pour la Reine Marie-Antoinette e Le prix de l'entrée est compris dans le prix de l'excursion f Michel offre l'excursion à Agnès parce que c'est son anniversaire

Things to remember: 1 Qu'est-ce qu'il y a à faire? 2 Je voudrais un plan de la ville et des renseignements sur la cathédrale 3 Il y a/Est-ce qu'il y a un bus pour aller au Parc Floral? 4 Le parc est facile à trouver? 5 C'est combien l'entrée? 6 Est-ce que le musée est ouvert ce mardi? 7 Est-ce que le musée ferme entre midi et deux heures? 8 Le bus part d'où? 9 Il faut être à l'arrêt du bus à quelle heure? 10 Qu'est-ce qu'on peut visiter?

Unit 16
Activities: 1 a F in the evenings b F they like to dance and eat well c F it is a restaurant with music, open all night d V e V f V 2 a E b D c C d B e A 3 a Monday b his wedding anniversary c dinner by candlelight d Spanish e 2 a.m. f a dozen red roses 4 a Je voudrais des places pour dimanche prochain. b Ça finit à quelle heure le concert? c C'est combien la place? d C'est tarif réduit. e Ma sœur doit payer? 5 29, boulevard des Italiens, those who are students, seniors, from large families, servicemen, under 18. From 18.00 Monday to Friday except on public holidays and the days before. 6 a Où est-ce qu'on peut jouer au tennis? b Où est-ce qu'on réserve le court? c C'est combien l'heure? d On peut louer une raquette? e Vous pouvez/Est-ce que vous pouvez/Pouvez-vous me donner l'adresse du club, s'il vous plaît? 7 a i yes ii no; b i yes ii no; c i no ii yes; d i yes ii no; e i play table tennis ii board games

Self-test 5 (Units 14–16): 1 There are alternative answers to the ones given below: a Vous pouvez me réserver une chambre, s'il vous plaît? b Vous avez un plan de Paris? c Pour aller à la Tour Eiffel, s'il vous plaît? d Qu'est-ce que vous avez comme excursions? e Qu'est-ce qu'il y a à faire pour les enfants? f Vous avez une liste de restaurants? g Vous pouvez me montrer les grands magasins sur le plan? 3 a F – also to tourist trains b V – and also on air-conditioned coaches, comfortable minibuses and tourist trains c F – audio-guides, cultural commentaries and theme tours d F – they are provided e F – drivers are multilingual f F – also during the evenings g F – also tour companies

Unit 17

Activities: 1 a Yes b Yes, in wet conditions the speed limit is lowered to 110 km/h on motorways and 100 km/h on dual carriageways c route nationale d get some food, fill up the vehicle with petrol, do some shopping e Internet and WiFi facilities are provided in 40 service areas f they extend the weekend (between a public holiday and the weekend) 2 a mai, juin, b Ascension, Victoire 1945, Pentecôte, Fête Nationale, Assomption c 11–13 juillet, 1–3 août d avoid travelling at the weekend 3 e, c, d, b, a 4 a Je voudrais passer une nuit dans votre hôtel. Quelles sont les directions pour Est-Artigues? b De Bayonne c Vous pouvez répétez s'il vous plaît? d Une fois sorti, il faut prendre à droite aux feux, sortie CourtePaille, et c'est à 500 mètres e Il y a un restaurant? f Je peux (on peut) arriver à quelle heure? 5 a F it is free from 1 to 2 p.m., after 7 o'clock, on Sundays and bank holidays b V c F only 50 centimes, 1€, 2€ d F e V f V 6 a quite difficult b because of a 4 kilometre long tailback on the A6 on the outskirts of Paris c toll gate d leave the A6 at Courtenay, divert onto the A19, then join the A5 to reach the eastern part of Paris 7 pompiste a, c, f; cliente b, d, e 8 a Bonjour, je voudrais de l'essence sans plomb, s'il vous plaît b Non, pour 58€ c Vous pouvez vérifier l'huile? d Un litre e Non, merci, ça va 9 a Vous pouvez m'aider, je suis en panne b Je ne sais pas, le moteur ne marche pas c Je suis entre Orléans et Blois sur l'autoroute A10 d direction/vers Tours e C'est une voiture anglaise: une Ford Focus blanche. Vous arrivez quand? 10 a 2 b 1 c 4 d 3 e 5 f 8 g 6 h 7

Things to remember: 1 Quelles sont les directions pour l'autoroute? 2 Je suis en panne près de Poitiers 3 Qu'est-ce que je dois faire si j'arrive après 22 heures? 4 Vous pouvez/Est-ce que vous pouvez/ Pouvez-vous me dire quel est le numéro de ma chambre? 5 Vous avez un parking fermé? 6 The N10 does not merge with the ring road 7 The hotel is well signposted. You need to follow the signs 8 Once

on the ring road it would be better to take direction ... 9 You need to
insert your banker's card into the cash point machine 10 The card
will be debited with the amount of the room

Unit 18

Activities: 1 a not in the Paris region but outside Paris they do b the
side with the € is common, the other is not c each country shows its
national symbols 2 a Vous pouvez changer 10€, svp? b Il me faut
des pièces de 1€ c No change given 3 a vous n'avez pas de carte
bancaire? b il me faut cinq pièces de 1€ c elle n'accepte que ... d vous
pouvez changer ... e je n'en ai pas f je ne sais pas g ça vous va?
h Vous avez de la chance i Je vais regarder 4 a Pardon Monsieur,
vous avez de la monnaie pour le téléphone, s'il vous plaît? b Je n'ai
qu'un billet de 5€ et il me faut des pièces de 1€ c Une télécarte,
qu'est-ce que c'est? d Où est-ce que je peux acheter une télécarte?
5 a changer b pièce c signer d écrire e combien f payer 6 a Je voudrais
changer des dollars b des dollars américains c des billets d 200
dollars; il est à combien le dollar? e Vous êtes ouverts le dimanche?
7 a 5€40 b 7€22 c 19€75 d 22€ e 89€56 f 172€ g 315€40
h 632€15 i 918€30 j 72 centimes 8 a after breakfast b 14 c no
d drinks from the mini-bar e yes

Things to remember: 1 Vous pouvez changer... euros? 2 Il y a une
commission à payer?/Il faut payer une commission? 3 Vous avez de
la monnaie, s'il vous plaît? 4 Quel est le taux/le cours d'échange de
la livre?/La livre est à combien? 5 Vous avez quelque chose pour
signer? 6 Il me faut des pièces de 1€ 7 Je voudrais payer ma note
d'hôtel 8 Il y a une erreur 9 Je n'ai rien pris du mini-bar 10 Vous
acceptez les chèques de voyage?

Unit 19

Activities: 1 a ii, iv b No c iii, iv d iii two every four hours and
iv one when needed 2 a Ma fille a mal aux dents b Oui, un peu
c Depuis hier d Merci; vous avez quelque chose pour les piqûres
d'insectes? e Je vais la prendre; c'est combien? 3 a vi, b v, c vii,
d iii, e ii, f iv, g viii, h i 4 a Je voudrais prendre rendez-vous b Non,
c'est pour mon fils. Nous sommes anglais, en vacances ici et il
a mal aux dents depuis mardi. c Il a 12 ans d aujourd'hui, ce matin

ou cet après-midi e À quelle heure, s'il vous plaît? f Monsieur/
Madame … 5 a F – it shuts at 12 b F – also with the **Netanoo**
Internet terminals c V d V e F – WiFi is also accessible in some
stations and tourist offices f F – they are plentiful 6 a 8h b 19.30h
c semaine d fériés e USA f l'Australie g pleines h creuses 7 a vii, b v,
c vi, d ii, e iii, f iv g i 8 a clés b stylo, lunettes c portefeuille, cartes
d identité e téléphone f voiture, faire 9 a on m'a volé ma voiture
b C'est quoi votre voiture? c quel est le numéro d'immatriculation?
d faire une déclaration par écrit e remplir cet imprimé f vous en
avez besoin pour vos assurances 10 a J'ai perdu mon stylo en or
au bureau b mon frère a perdu sa valise marron à l'aéroport c ma
sœur a perdu son porte-monnaie en cuir blanc au parc d son père
a perdu son passeport britannique dans la rue e mon amie a perdu
son foulard en soie dans l'autobus

Self-test 6 (Units 17–19): 1 a Vous prenez la voiture ou le train?
b En train vous descendez à la gare de Lourdes, puis vous prenez
l'autobus jusqu'à Cauterets. Cauterets est à 30 km de Lourdes
c En voiture, vous prenez l'autoroute jusqu'à Tarbes, puis la
N 21 et la D 921. Vous pouvez garer la voiture en face de l'hôtel
d 'L'Edelweiss' est situé au 7, Boulevard Latapie-Flurin, au centre
de Cauterets e le vendredi 22 avril vers sept heures du soir 2 a xi
b v c vi d ii e x f ix g i h iv i iii j viii k vii 4 a J'ai besoin de voir un
docteur/Il me faut voir un docteur b Quelle est son adresse?/Vous
pouvez me donner son adresse? c Allô, je voudrais prendre rendez-
vous d J'ai mal au genou e J'ai mal/Je souffre depuis trois jours f Je
ne peux pas marcher g Je peux venir demain matin à dix heures
h Check with the French alphabet in Unit 12.

Appendix: numbers

0	zéro	21	vingt et un	70	soixante-dix
1	un	22	vingt-deux	71	soixante et onze
2	deux	23	vingt-trois	72	soixante-douze, etc.
3	trois	24	vingt-quatre	80	quatre-vingts
4	quatre	25	vingt-cinq	81	quatre-vingt-un
5	cinq	26	vingt-six	82	quatre-vingt-deux, etc.
6	six	27	vingt-sept	90	quatre-vingt-dix
7	sept	28	vingt-huit	91	quatre-vingt-onze
8	huit	29	vingt-neuf	92	quatre-vingt-douze, etc.
9	neuf	30	trente	100	cent
10	dix	31	trente et un	101	cent un
11	onze	32	trente-deux, etc.	102	cent deux, etc.
12	douze	40	quarante	200	deux cents
13	treize	41	quarante et un	210	deux cent dix
14	quatorze	42	quarante-deux, etc.	300	trois cents
15	quinze	50	cinquante	331	trois cent trente et un
16	seize	51	cinquante et un		
17	dix-sept	52	cinquante-deux, etc.		
18	dix-huit	60	soixante		
19	dix-neuf	61	soixante et un		
20	vingt	62	soixante-deux, etc.		

1,000 mille

2,000 deux mille

1,000,000 un million

2,000,000 deux millions

Rôle-play scripts

Unit 3

ACTIVITY 3

Man	Vous êtes_anglaise?
You	Non, je suis_américaine. (1)
Man	Vous_habitez en Angleterre?
You	J'habite à Cambridge,/mais je suis de Chicago. (2)
Man	Et qu'est-ce que vous faites à Cambridge? Vous étudiez? Vous ...
You	Parlez plus lentement, s'il vous plaît. (1)
Man	Vous travaillez à Cambridge?
You	Oui, je travaille pour les touristes américains. (1)
Man	Vous êtes mariée avec un Anglais?
You	Je ne suis pas mariée/mais j'ai un petit_ami anglais. (2)
Man	Il travaille aussi à Cambridge?
You	Il travaille à Londres./Il est comptable. (2)
Man	Et vous avez des_enfants?
You	J'ai deux_enfants. (1)
Man	Des filles ou des garçons?
You	Une fille et un garçon. (1)
Man	Ils_ont quel âge?
You	Ils_ont dix_ans et cinq_ans. (1)
Man	Et vos parents, ils_habitent avec vous?
You	Non, ils_habitent aux_USA. (1)
Man	Vous parlez bien le français?
You	Non, seulement un peu. (1)

Unit 4

ACTIVITY 7

Tourist	Pardon, euh ... vous parlez français?
You	Seulement un petit peu.
Tourist	Je cherche une pharmacie. C'est loin d'ici?
You	Parlez plus lentement, s'il vous plaît.
Tourist	Il y a une pharmacie près d'ici?
You	Oui, Boots est à_dix minutes à pied.
Tourist	Elle est_ouverte maintenant?
You	Oui. Vous_êtes_en vacances?
Tourist	Oui, je suis_en vacances avec mon fils depuis une semaine. Il y a une piscine ici?
You	Oui, il y en_a une, mais_elle est fermée.
Tourist	Quel dommage! Et il y a peut-être un cinéma?
You	Oui, il y en_a un. Il est loin, mais l'arrêt d'autobus est au bout de la rue.
Tourist	C'est quel numéro pour l'autobus?
You	C'est le 27.

Unit 5

ACTIVITY 9

Journalist	Bonjour, je voudrais vous poser des questions sur vos occupations pendant la semaine. Vous travaillez?
You	Je travaille à Londres pour une compagnie d'assurances.
Journalist	Vous prenez le train pour aller à Londres?
You	Je prends le train à 7.20.
Journalist	Et vous commencez le travail à quelle heure?
You	Je commence à 9 heures du matin.
Journalist	Et où déjeunez-vous? À la cantine? En ville?

(Contd)

You	À midi, je déjeune toujours dans un restaurant avec mes collègues.
Journalist	Et le soir, vous finissez le travail à quelle heure?
You	Je finis souvent à 17.30 et quelquefois à 18.30.
Journalist	Et vous travaillez le soir chez vous?
You	Non, je regarde la télé avec ma femme.
Journalist	Ah bon. Et le week-end qu'est-ce que vous faites?
You	Le samedi après-midi, je vais_à la piscine avec mes deux enfants.

Unit 6

ACTIVITY 7

Passer-by	Je ne suis pas d'ici. Vous pouvez m'aider, s'il vous plaît? Où est la banque?
You	La banque est_à côté de la pharmacie.
Passer-by	Merci beaucoup. Je voudrais acheter quelques souvenirs pour ma famille. Où sont les grands magasins?
You	Ils sont_en face du supermarché.
Passer-by	Il faut combien de temps pour aller au supermarché?
You	Il faut_environ 15 minutes à pied.
Passer-by	Merci. Et ... où est la poste?
You	Elle est_en face du café.
Passer-by	Elle est_ouverte maintenant?
You	Elle est fermée mais_elle ouvre à 2 heures.
Passer-by	Et où est la piscine à Chatou?
You	Il faut aller tout droit jusqu'au pont, tourner à gauche, prendre la première à droite. La piscine est en face du parc.
Passer-by	Ah merci beaucoup.

Unit 7

ACTIVITY 6

Paul	Allô Rosine, c'est Paul ici. Tu arrives quand à Paris?
You	J'arrive le 13 février.
Paul	Le mardi 13 février?
You	Non, le 13 février c'est un mercredi.
Paul	Ah pardon. Et tu arrives comment?
You	Je prends l'Eurostar de Londres à Paris.
Paul	Ah très bien. Tu arrives mercredi matin?
You	Non, l'après-midi. Le train arrive à 17.19 à la Gare du Nord.
Paul	Bon je viendrai te chercher à la gare. Je suis grand et mince et j'ai les yeux bleus. Et toi, tu es comment?
You	Je suis petite et mince et je porte des lunettes.
Paul	Tu as les cheveux comment?
You	Ils sont longs et blonds.
Paul	Écoute, je porterai un jean et un T-shirt rouge, et toi?
You	Des bottes noires, une chemise verte et un pantalon blanc.
Paul	D'accord, et j'aurai aussi le journal *Le Monde* à la main. Eh bien, à mercredi Rosine, et bon voyage.

SELF-TEST 2

ACTIVITY 5

Man	Vous connaissez déjà Paris?
You	Non, c'est la première fois/que je vais_à Paris. (2)
Man	Et vous restez combien de temps à Paris?
You	Une semaine. (1)
Man	Vous_allez dans_un hôtel?
You	Non, j'ai des_amis américains/qui habitent Paris. (2)
Man	Qu'est-ce qu'ils font dans la vie?
You	Il est journaliste/et elle ne travaille pas. (2)
Man	Ah, c'est bien ... et ils_habitent où à Paris?

(Contd)

You	Ils_habitent dans le seizième arrondissement près du Bois de Boulogne. (2)
Man	Quelle coïncidence! J'habite aussi dans le seizième. Vous prenez_un taxi pour_aller chez vos_amis?
You	Non, les taxis sont trop chers. (1)
Man	Eh bien, ma femme m'attend à la gare avec la voiture. Venez_avec nous!
You	Merci beaucoup, Monsieur.

Unit 8

ACTIVITY 6

Presenter	Alors vous faites beaucoup de sport?
You	Je déteste le sport, mais mon petit_ami fait du sport trois fois par semaine.
Presenter	Et la cuisine vous_aimez la faire?
You	Je n'aime pas faire la cuisine. Je cuisine pendant la semaine et mon petit_ami toujours le week-end.
Presenter	Bien. Et vous faites quoi pendant vos loisirs?
You	J'adore écouter de la musique classique.
Presenter	Et votre ami, qu'est-ce qu'il aime?
You	Il écoute du jazz et regarde la télé.
Presenter	Et vous la télé, vous la regardez?
You	Je ne la regarde plus, parce qu'il n'y a rien à regarder.
Presenter	Et vous sortez ensemble? Vous_allez au cinéma?
You	J'aime le cinéma français, mais mon petit_ami ne regarde que les films américains.
Presenter	Et le restaurant vous_y allez souvent?
You	Nous adorons aller au restaurant et nous_y allons deux ou trois fois par mois.
Presenter	Quelles cuisines aimez-vous?
You	J'aime la cuisine française, mais il aime la cuisine italienne.
Presenter	Eh bien, il me semble qu'il faut vous trouver un autre petit_ami!

Unit 9

ACTIVITY 5

You	Pardon, Monsieur, je voudrais utiliser l'Internet. Vous pouvez m'aider?
Man	Mais bien sûr. Alors il faut d'abord mettre l'ordinateur en marche. Puis après ça, il faut aller dans « menu » et …
You	Je ne comprends pas. Vous pouvez parlez plus lentement s'il vous plaît?
Man	Il faut_appuyer sur le bouton « marche/arrêt » sur le clavier et puis il faut_aller dans « menu » et …
You	Où est l'Internet?
Man	L'Internet? Il faut_aller dans « menu », sélectionner Internet et cliquer dessus.
You	C'est quoi « cliquer "?
Man	"Cliquer"? Ça veut dire que vous appuyez dessus avec la souris.
You	Mais ça ne marche pas.
Man	Vous avez dû mal cliquer. Il faut cliquer deux fois avec le doigt …
You	Vous pouvez me montrer?
Man	Euh … je suis_occupé pour le moment. Donnez-moi cinq minutes et je viens vous aider.
You	D'accord, je vais_attendre.

Unit 10

ACTIVITY 7

Michel	Qu'est-ce que vous allez faire pour vos vacances cet été?
You	Je vais_aller au Portugal.
Michel	Vous_y allez seul ou avec votre famille?
You	Avec ma femme et mes deux_enfants qui ont treize et onze ans.

(Contd)

Michel	Quand partez-vous_au Portugal?
You	Nous_y allons pendant le mois d'août.
Michel	Et vous_y resterez combien de temps?
You	Nous_allons passer deux semaines au bord de la mer.
Michel	Vous_allez descendre à l'hôtel? Vous_allez faire du camping?
You	Nous_avons de très bons_amis anglais au Portugal.
Michel	Ah c'est bien. Et comment allez-vous passer vos vacances?
You	Les enfants vont jouer au tennis le matin et se baigner l'après-midi.
Michel	Et vous et votre femme, qu'allez-vous faire pendant la journée?
You	Nous_allons nous reposer et nous promener.
Michel	Et le soir?
You	Nous_allons lire ou parler avec nos_amis.
Michel	Et les_enfants? Ils vont sortir le soir?
You	Oui, ils peuvent sortir en boîte avec leurs_amis.

SELF-TEST 3

ACTIVITY 5

Eva	Allô, c'est Eva ici. Lionel et moi aimerions vous rendre visite pour nos vacances. Vous pouvez nous recevoir cet été?
You	Je ne parle pas très bien français./Vous pouvez parler plus lentement? (2)
Eva	Est-ce que nous pouvons rester chez vous pendant le mois d'août?
You	Vous voulez venir quand au mois d'août? (1)
Eva	Nous souhaitons venir du 1er au 15 août.
You	Je suis vraiment désolée/mais je ne peux pas en août. (2)
Eva	Ah quel dommage!
You	Mon mari et moi sommes_au Canada du 20 juillet au 20 août. (1)
You	Je voudrais beaucoup vous voir./Vous pouvez changer les dates de vos vacances? (2)
Eva	Si vous préférez, on peut venir au début du mois de septembre?

You	Ces dates sont plus pratiques pour nous. (1)
Eva	Alors c'est parfait. Je peux prendre le billet pour septembre?
You	Oui. Vous pouvez acheter le billet. (1)

SELF-TEST 4

ACTIVITY 3

You	J'ai très faim/et je voudrais manger. (2)
Waiter	Alors … c'est pour une personne? Suivez-moi. Cette table vous convient?
You	Oui, c'est parfait./Qu'est-ce que vous_avez comme menus? (2)
Waiter	Nous avons le menu touristique à 15€ et le menu gastronomique à 21€.
You	Je vais prendre le menu à 15€. (1)
Waiter	Très bien. Alors comme entrée il y a l'assiette de crudités et comme plat principal du magret de canard.
You	C'est quoi le magret de canard? (1)
Waiter	C'est du filet cuit selon notre recette maison. Vous la voulez comment la cuisson?
You	Bien cuite./Je déteste la viande saignante. (2) Qu'est-ce que vous servez comme légumes? (1)
Waiter	Alors le canard est servi avec du riz et de la ratatouille. Vous voulez boire quelque chose?
You	Une bouteille d'eau minérale. (1)
Waiter	Très bien. Je vous apporte cela tout de suite.
You	Vous pouvez/me donner le menu? (2)
Waiter	D'accord je vous amène ça …
You	Je voudrais une glace à la vanille et au chocolat. (1)
Waiter	Ah, je regrette, mais nous n'avons plus de chocolat.
You	Qu'est-ce que vous_avez/comme autres parfums? (2)
Waiter	Fraise, citron et café.
You	Je vais prendre citron./Vous pouvez m'apporter l'addition avec le café? (2)
Waiter	Mais, bien sûr.

ACTIVITY 2

You	Bonjour. Je voudrais_un billet aller-retour/pour Bruxelles pour deux personnes. (2)
Ticket clerk	C'est pour quel jour?
You	Je voudrais partir le 17 janvier/et revenir le 21 janvier. (2)
Ticket clerk	Très bien. Alors sans réductions, le billet aller-retour pour deux personnes coûte 372€.
You	C'est_un peu trop cher./Vous avez quelque chose de moins cher? (2)
Ticket clerk	Oui, justement nous avons en ce moment une promotion: un aller-retour Paris-Bruxelles pour deux personnes pour 148€.
You	Le prix est meilleur./Quelles sont les conditions? (2)
Ticket clerk	Il faut voyager du vendredi au dimanche, et le billet n'est ni échangeable, ni remboursable.
You	À quelle heure le train part de Paris? (1)
Ticket clerk	Vous désirez voyager le matin ou l'après-midi?
You	Le matin entre 9.30 et 10.30. (1)
Ticket clerk	Vous avez plusieurs trains. Il y en a un à 9.25, un autre à 10.25 …
You	Je vais prendre le train de 10.25. (1)
Ticket clerk	Très bien. Pour le retour, il y a un train à 14.43. Un autre à 16.13 …
You	Je voudrais prendre le train de 16.13. (1)
You	Il faut combien de temps/pour aller de Paris à Bruxelles? (2)
Ticket clerk	Le train met 1 heure 22 minutes. Alors le billet vous va?
You	D'accord. Je peux payer avec ma carte de crédit? (1)
Ticket clerk	Oui, tout à fait.

ACTIVITY 3

You	Je voudrais changer de l'argent, s'il vous plaît. (1)
Bank clerk	Oui, bien sûr. Vous avez une carte de crédit?
You	J'ai une carte Visa. (1)
Bank clerk	Eh bien, c'est facile. Utilisez le distributeur automatique de billets.
You	Il ne marche pas/et l'hôtel n'accepte pas les cartes bancaires. (2)
Bank clerk	Vous avez des chèques de voyage?
You	Non, je n'en_ai pas. (1)
Bank clerk	Bon, eh bien ... je vais vous faire une avance sur votre carte Visa. Vous voulez changer combien?
You	Il me faut 300 euros pour payer l'hôtel. (1)
Bank clerk	Pas de problème. Vous avez une pièce d'identité avec vous? Votre passeport?
You	J'ai laissé mon passeport dans ma chambre à l'hôtel. (1)
Bank clerk	Ah ... malheureusement il me le faut pour cette transaction.
You	La banque ferme à quelle heure? (1)
Bank clerk	Elle ferme dans 45 minutes. Il est loin votre hôtel?
You	Il est à quinze minutes à pied. (1)
Bank clerk	C'est bon. Vous avez juste le temps d'y aller et de revenir.
You	D'accord. Merci beaucoup, Madame. (1)

French–English vocabulary

à *to, in*
abord *see* **d'abord**
abricot *(m) apricot*
accord *see* **d'accord**
achat *(m) shopping;* **faire des achats** *to do some shopping*
acheter *to buy*
addition *(f) bill, sum*
adorer *to adore, to love*
adresse *(f) address*
affaires *(f pl) business;* **homme d'affaires** *businessman*
âge *(m) age*
agence de voyages *(f) travel agency*
aider *to help*
aimer *to like, to love*
aire *(f)* **de pique-nique** *picnic area*
alcool *(m) spirit*
alimentation *(f) grocer's shop*
aller *to go*
aller *(m)* **simple** *single ticket*
aller-retour *(m) return ticket*
allô *hello (on phone)*
alors *well, then*
ambiance *(f) atmosphere*
ami *(m),* **amie** *(f) friend*
amende *(f) fine*
an *(m) year*
ancien(ne) *ancient, former*
anglais(e) *English (often used for British)*
Angleterre *(f) England*

année *(f) year*
août *August*
apparaître *to appear*
s'appeler *lit. to be called;* **je m'appelle** *my name is*
apprécier *to appreciate*
apprendre *to learn*
après *after*
après-midi *(m) afternoon*
argent *(m) money*
arrêt *(m) stop*
arrivée *(f) arrival*
arriver *to arrive*
arrondissement *(m) district in large towns*
ascenseur *(m) lift*
aspirine *(f)* **effervescente** *soluble aspirin*
assez *enough, fairly*
assiette *(f) plate*
attendre *to wait for*
aujourd'hui *today*
au revoir *goodbye*
aussi *also, too, as well*
autobus *(m) bus;* **en autobus** *by bus*
autocar *(m) coach;* **en autocar** *by coach*
automne *(m) autumn;* **en automne** *in autumn*
autoroute *(f) motorway*
autre *other;* **autre chose** *something else*
avec *with*

avion *(m) aeroplane*
avoir *to have;* **avoir l'air** *to seem*
avril *April*

baguette *(f) 'French stick'*
  (bread)
se baigner *to go for a swim*
balle *(f) ball*
banlieue *(f) suburb*
banque *(f) bank*
bar *(m) bar*
bas(se) *low*
bas *(m) bottom, lower part*
bâtiment *(m) building*
battre *to beat*
beau (belle) *handsome,*
  beautiful
beaucoup (de) *much, a lot*
belle *see* **beau**
besoin *(m) need;* **avoir**
  besoin *to need*
beurre *(m) butter*
bien *well;* **bien sûr** *certainly*
bientôt *soon;* **à bientôt**
  see you soon
bière *(f) beer*
billet *(m) ticket,* (bank) *note*
blanc (blanche) *white*
bleu(e) *blue;* **bleu marine**
  navy blue; **bleu pâle** *pale blue*
blond(e) *blond*
bœuf *(m) beef, ox*
boire *to drink*
boisson *(f) drink*
boîte *(f) box, can, tin*
boîte *(f)* **aux lettres** *letter box*
boîte *(f)* **(de nuit)** *disco,*
  nightclub
bol *(m) bowl*

bon(ne) *good;* **bon marché**
  cheap
bonjour *good day, hello*
bonsoir *good evening*
botte *(f) boot*
boucherie *(f) butcher's*
bouchon *(m) cork, bottleneck*
boulangerie *(f) baker's*
boulevard *(m) boulevard*
bout *(m) end;* **au bout de**
  at the end of
bouteille *(f) bottle*
brasserie *(f) pub-restaurant*
briller *to shine*
britannique *British*
brouillard *(m) fog*
bruit *(m) noise*
brun(e) *brown* (hair, complexion)
bureau *(m)* **de location** *box*
  office
bureau *(m)* **de renseignements**
  information office
bureau *(m)* **des réservations**
  booking office
bus *(m) see* **autobus**

cabine téléphonique *(f)*
  telephone box
cabinet de toilette *(m) small*
  room containing wash basin
  and bidet
cadeau *(m) present*
café *(m) coffee, café;* **café au lait**
  white coffee; **café crème** *coffee*
  served with cream
caisse *(f) cash desk, cashier's*
  ticket office
ça *that, it;* **ça va?** *how are*
  things?; **ça va** *things are OK*

cabine (f) **d'essayage** fitting room

campagne (f) country; **à la campagne** in (to) the country

camping (m) camping, campsite

car (m) see **autocar**

carnet (m) book (of tickets), ten metro tickets

carrefour (m) crossroads

carte (f) map, card, menu; **carte bancaire** banker's card; **carte d'abonnement** season ticket; **carte de crédit** credit card; **carte d'identité** identity card; **carte postale** postcard

cassé(e) broken

ce, cet, cette this, that (adjective)

ceci see **ce**

célèbre famous

célibataire (m and f) single, bachelor

cent a hundred

centime (m) centime

centre (m) centre; **au centre de** in the centre of; **centre ville** town centre, **centre commercial** shopping centre

certain(e) certain

certainement certainly

ces these, those

c'est it is, this is

c'est ça that's it

cet, cette see **ce**

chambre (f) bedroom

champignon (m) mushroom

chance (f) luck

changer to change

changeur (m) **de monnaie** coin changing machine

chaque each, every

charcuterie (f) shop selling cooked meats

chaud(e) hot; **avoir chaud** to be hot

chauffer to heat up

chaussure (f) shoe

chemise (f) shirt

chèque (m) **de voyage** see **traveller**

cher (chère) expensive, dear

chercher to look for; **aller chercher** to go and fetch

cheveux (m pl) hair

chez at the home of; **chez moi** at my house, at home

chocolat (m) eating or drinking chocolate

choisir to choose

choix (m) choice

chose (f) thing

cinq five

cinquante 50

circulation (f) traffic

citron (m) lemon

classe (f) class

classique classical

clé (f) key

coin (m) corner

combien (de)? how much? how many?

commander to order

comme as, like, in the way of

commencer to start, to begin

comment how, how to, what

complet(ète) full

composer *to dial (a telephone number)*
composter *to date-stamp (a ticket)*
comprendre *to understand*
comprimé *(m) tablet*
compris *understood, included*
connaître *to know (a person or a place)*
connu(e) *known*
conseiller *to advise*
consigne *(f) left luggage;* **consigne automatique** *luggage lockers*
content(e) *pleased*
continuer *to continue*
copain/copine *(boy, girl) friend*
correspondance *(f) connection*
costume *(m) suit for men*
côté *(m) side;* **à coté de** *next to;* **de l'autre côté** *on the other side*
se coucher *to go to bed*
couchette *(f) couchette*
couleur *(f) colour*
coup *(m)* **de fil** *telephone call*
cours *(m)* **particulier** *private lesson*
cours *(m)* **du change** *exchange rate*
courses *(f pl) shopping*
court(e) *short*
court *(m)* **de tennis** *tennis court*
coûter *to cost*
couverture *(f) blanket, cover*
cravate *(f) tie*
crème *(f) cream*
crêperie *(f) pancake house*

croire *to believe*
croissant *(m) croissant*
croque-monsieur *(m) toasted cheese sandwich with ham*
en cuir *in leather*
cuisine *(f) kitchen, cooking*
cuit(e) *cooked*

d'abord *firstly*
d'accord *OK, agreed*
dans *in, into*
danser *to dance*
date *(f) date*
de *of, from*
décembre *December*
décider *to decide*
décrocher l'appareil *to lift the receiver*
déjeuner *to lunch, lunch;* **petit déjeuner** *(m) breakfast*
demain *tomorrow*
démarrer *to start*
demi(e) *half;* **demi-kilo** *(m) half a kilogram;* **demi-heure** *(f) half an hour*
dent *(f) tooth*
dentifrice *(m) toothpaste*
dépannage: le service de dépannage *breakdown service*
dépendre de *to depend on*
depuis *since;* **je suis marié depuis dix ans** *I've been married for ten years*
déranger *to disturb, to inconvenience;* **en dérangement** *out of order*
dernier(ière) *last*
descendre *to go down*

désirer to wish for
desservir to serve
détester to hate
deux two
deuxième second
devoir must, should, ought
différent(e) different
dimanche Sunday
diminuer to decrease
dîner (m) dinner, to have dinner
dire to say
direct(e) direct
directement directly
direction (f) direction
disque (m) record
dix ten
dix-huit 18
dix-neuf 19
dix-sept 17
doit, ça doit see **devoir**
donner to give
dormir to sleep
douche (f) shower
douze 12
droit(e) straight; **tout droit**
  straight on
avoir droit to be entitled
à droite right (hand)

eau (f) water
eau (f) **minérale** mineral water
école (f) school
écouter to listen
écrire to write
par écrit in writing
église (f) church
élève (m and f) pupil
émetteur(trice) issuing

emmener to take (someone
  somewhere)
emplacement (m) pitch
en in, on, of it, of them
enfant (m and f) child
ensemble together
ensemble (m) outfit, suit (woman)
ensuite then
entre between
entrée (f) way in, admission
  charge
environ about
environs (m pl) surroundings
envoyer to send
équitation (f) riding
erreur (f) mistake
espérer to hope
essayer to try
essence (f) petrol
essuie-glace (m) windscreen
  wiper
est (m) east
et and
étage (m) floor
été (m) summer; **en été** in
  summer
étoile (f) star
être to be
eux them (people)
éviter to avoid
excursion (f) excursion, trip;
  faire une excursion to go on an
  excursion
excuser to excuse
expliquer to explain

en face (de) facing
facile easy

faim *(f) hunger;* **avoir faim**
  to be hungry
faire *to do, to make*
famille *(f) family*
il faudra *it will be necessary*
il faut *it is necessary, one has to*
faux (fausse) *false*
favori (favorite) *favourite*
femme *(f) wife, woman*
fenêtre *(f) window*
fermé(e) *closed*
fermer *to close*
fête *(f) feast-day, celebration*
feux *(m pl)* **(rouges)** *traffic lights*
février *February*
fièvre *(f) fever, temperature*
figurer *to appear*
fille *(f) daughter, girl*
fils *(m) son*
finalement *finally*
finir *to finish*
fleur *(f) flower*
fois *(f) time;* **une fois** *once*
fond *(m) back, far end;* **au fond**
  du couloir *at the far end of the*
  corridor
fondre *to melt*
forme *(f) shape*
formidable *great*
foulard *(m) scarf*
fourchette *(f) fork*
fraise *(f) strawberry*
franc *(m) franc*
français(e) *French*
France *(f) France*
frère *(m) brother*
frein *(m) brake*
frite *(f) chip; (adjective) fried*

froid(e) *cold;* **avoir froid** *to be*
  cold
fromage *(m) cheese*
fruit *(m) fruit*

garçon *(m) boy, waiter*
garder *to keep*
gare *(f) station;* **gare routière**
  bus, coach station; **gare SNCF**
  railway station
garer *to park*
garni(e) *served with vegetables,*
  salads, etc.
à gauche *left*
généralement *generally*
glace *(f) ice cream*
gonflage *(m)* **des pneus**
  pumping up the tyres
gorge *(f) throat*
gourmet *(m) gourmet*
grand(e) *big, tall*
Grande-Bretagne *(f) Great Britain*
gratuit(e) *free*
grillade *(f) grilled meat*
grippe *(f) flu*
gros (grosse) *fat, large*
guichet *(m) ticket office*

(s')habiller *to dress*
habiter *to live*
haricot *(m) bean;* **haricot vert**
  green bean
heure *(f) hour;* **quelle heure**
  est-il? *what time is it?*
hiver *(m) winter;* **en hiver**
  in winter
homme *(m) man;* **homme**
  d'affaires *businessman*

hôpital (m) hospital
horaire (m) timetable
hors outside; **hors-d'œuvre**
  starter; **hors de service** out
  of service
hôtel (m) hotel; **hôtel de ville**
  town hall
huile (f) oil
huit eight

ici here
île (f) island; **Île de France**
  Paris area
indicatif (m) dialling code
indiquer to indicate
ingénieur (m) engineer
inscription (f) enrolment
intéressant(e) interesting
introduire to insert
inviter to invite

jamais never
jambon (m) ham
janvier January
jardin (m) garden
jardinage (m) gardening
jaune yellow
jean (m) or **jeans** (m pl) jeans
jeu (m) game; **jeu de société**
  parlour game
jeudi Thursday
jeune young
joli(e) pretty
jouer to play
jour (m) day; **jour férié**
  bank holiday
journal (m) newspaper
journée (f) day, day-time
joyeux(se) joyful, merry

juillet July
juin June
jupe (f) skirt
jus (m) **de fruit** fruit juice
jusqu'à until, as far as

kilo(gramme) (m) kilogram

la the, her, it
là(-bas) (over) there
lait (m) milk
laisser to leave; **laissé** left
large wide, big
(se) laver to wash
le the, him, it
léger (légère) light
légume (m) vegetable
lentement slowly
lequel, laquelle who, which;
  sur laquelle on which
lettre (f) letter
leur(s) their, to them
se lever to get up
libre free (but for free of charge
  use **gratuit**); **libre service** (m)
  small supermarket
ligne (f) number (bus), line
  (metro)
lire to read
lit (m) bed; **à deux lits** twin-
  bedded; **le grand lit** double bed
litre (m) litre
livre (m) book; (f) pound
location (f) hire
loin far
loisir (m) hobby
long (longue) long
louer to let, to hire, to book
lourd(e) heavy

lui *to him, to her, he, as for him*
lundi *Monday*
lunettes *(f pl) glasses*

Madame *Madam, Mrs*
Mademoiselle *Miss*
magasin *(m) shop;* **grand magasin** *department store*
mai *May*
maillot *(m)* **de bain** *swimming costume, swimsuit*
maintenant *now*
mais *but*
maison *(f) house;* **à la maison** *at home*
mal *badly;* **avoir mal** *to have a pain;* **mal** *(m)* **de dos** *backache*
malheureusement *unfortunately*
manger *to eat*
manquer *to be lacking, missing*
marché *(m) market;* **bon marché** *cheap*
marcher *to walk, to work (for a machine)*
mardi *Tuesday*
mari *(m) husband*
marié(e) *married*
marron *brown*
mars *March*
matin *(m) morning*
mauvais(e) *bad*
médecin *(m) doctor, physician*
médicament *(m) medicine*
meilleur(e) *better*
mélange *(m) mixture*
mélanger *to mix*
même *same, even*
menu *(m) set meal*

mer *(f) sea;* **au bord de la mer** *at the seaside, by the sea*
merci *thank you*
mercredi *Wednesday*
mère *(f) mother*
Messieurs-dames *ladies and gentlemen*
mesurer *to measure*
métro *(m) underground*
mettre *to put*
midi *midday, lunchtime*
mieux *better*
milieu *(m) middle, milieu*
mille *a thousand*
mince *thin*
minuit *midnight*
moi *me, I*
moins *less*
mois *(m) month*
moitié *(f) half*
mon, ma, mes *my*
monde *(m) world;* **tout le monde** *everybody*
monnaie *(f) small change*
Monsieur *Sir, Mr*
montagne *(f) mountain;* **à la montagne** *in, to the mountains*
monter *to go up*
montre *(f) watch*
montrer *to show*
monument *(m) monument*
morceau *(m) piece*
moteur *(m) engine*
motif *(m) pattern, design*
moyen(ne) *medium, average*
musée *(m) museum*

natation *(f) swimming*
neiger *to snow*

neuf *nine*
neuf (neuve) *new*
niveau *(m) level*
nocturne *late-night opening*
Noël *(m) Christmas*
noir(e) *black*
nom *(m) name*
non *no*
nord *(m) north*
note *(f) bill* (hotel, telephone)
notre, nos *our*
nouveau(elle) *new;* **à nouveau** *again*
novembre *November*
nuit *(f) night*
numéro *(m) number;* **numéro d'immatriculation** *number plate*

occupé(e) *busy*
s'occuper *to deal with, to attend to*
octobre *October*
œil *(m) eye*
œuf *(m) egg*
œuvre *(f) work of art*
office du/de tourisme *(m) tourist office*
omelette *(f) omelette*
on *one* (used also for *we* and *I*)
onze *11*
(en) or *(made of) gold*
ou *or;* **ou … ou** *either … or*
où *where*
ouest *(m) west*
oui *yes*
ouvert(e) *open*
ouvrir *to open*

pain *(m) bread*
panne *(f) breakdown*
panneau *(m) sign*
pantalon *(m) trousers*
paquet *(m) packet*
paquet-cadeau *(m) gift-package*
parcmètre *(m) parking meter*
pardon *pardon, sorry, excuse me*
parfum *(m) perfume, flavour* (ice cream)
parking *(m) car park*
parler *to speak*
en particulier *particularly*
partir *to go, to leave*
à partir de *from, as*
pas *not;* **pas du tout** *not at all*
passant(e) *passer-by*
passer *to pass*
pâté *(m) pâté;* **pâté de campagne** *country pâté*
pâtisserie *(f) a cake shop, pastry, cake*
payer *to pay*
pays *(m) country, area*
à péage *toll payable*
pendant *during*
penser *to think*
perdre *to lose;* **perdu** *lost*
père *(m) father*
personne *(f) person;* **personne (+ ne)** *nobody*
peser *to weigh*
pétanque *(f) pétanque* (kind of bowls)
petit(e) *small;* **petit déjeuner** *(m) breakfast*
(un) peu *(a) little, few*
pharmacie *(f) chemist's*

pharmacien(ne) *(m, f)* chemist

pièce *(f)* room, coin; **pièce d'identité** *identification*

pied *(m)* foot; **à pied** *on foot*

pique-nique *(m)* picnic

piscine *(f)* **(couverte)** *(indoor) swimming pool*

place *(f)* square, space, seat

plaisir *(m)* pleasure; **faire plaisir** *to please;* **avec plaisir** *with pleasure*

plan *(m)* **(de la ville)** *(town) map*

planche *(f)* **à voile** *windsurfing board*

plat *(m)* dish, course

plein(e) *full;* **le plein, s'il vous plaît** *(at the garage) fill it up, please*

il pleut *it is raining*

sans plomb *(m)* lead-free petrol

(la) plupart *most*

plus *more, plus;* **plus … que** *more than;* **en plus** *in addition, extra;* **ne … plus** *no longer, no more*

pneu *(m)* tyre

poêle *(f)* frying pan

poids *(m)* weight

à point *medium done* (meat)

pointure *(f)* shoe size

pois, petits pois *(m pl)* peas

poisson *(m)* fish

poivre *(m)* pepper; **poivrer** *to pepper*

pomme *(f)* apple; **pomme de terre** *potato;* **pommes frites** *(f pl)* chips

pompiste *(m)* pump attendant

pont *(m)* bridge

portefeuille *(m)* wallet

porte-monnaie *(m)* purse

porter *to carry, to wear*

poste *(f)* post, post office

poulet *(m)* chicken

pour *for, in order to*

pourboire *(m)* tip

pouvoir *can, be able to;* **vous pouvez** *you can*

pratique *practical, convenient*

pratiquer *to practise, to do*

préférer *to prefer*

premier(ière) *first*

prendre *to take;* **pris** *taken*

près (de) *near;* **près d'ici** *nearby*

pression *(f)* pressure (tyre); *draught (beer)*

presque *nearly*

printemps *(m)* spring; **au printemps** *in spring*

prix *(m)* price

prochain(e) *next*

proche *near*

professeur(e) *(m, f)* teacher

profession *(f)* profession

promenade *(f)* **(à pied)** *walk*

se promener (à pied) *to go for a walk*

puis *then*

pull-over *(m)* pullover

quai *(m)* platform

quand? *when?*

quarante *40*

quatorze *14*

quatre *four*

quatre-vingt-dix 90
quatre-vingts 80
que that, than
(ne) … que only
quel(le)? which?, what?
quelque(s) some (a few);
  quelque chose something
quelquefois sometimes
quelqu'un someone
qu'est-ce que what
qui who, which
quinzaine (f) 15 or so
quinze 15
quitter to leave
quoi? what?

raide straight (hair)
randonnée (f) hike
rapide rapid
raquette (f) racket
regarder to watch
régler to settle (bill)
regretter to be sorry
remplir to fill in
rendez-vous (m) appointment
rendre to give back
rendre visite to pay a visit
renseignement (m) (piece of)
  information
se renseigner to inquire
rentrer to go back, to go home
réparer to repair
repas (m) meal
répéter to repeat
se reposer to rest
RER (m) fast extension of the
  underground in the suburbs
restaurant (m) restaurant
réserver to reserve, to book

rester to stay
retourner to go back, to return
rien nothing; **de rien** don't
  mention it
robe (f) dress
rocade (f) ring road, bypass
rouge red
route (f) road
rue (f) street

sac (m) **à main** handbag
saignant(e) bleeding, rare
  (meat)
saison (f) season; **hors saison**
  out of season; **en pleine saison**
  in high season
saler to salt
salle (f) hall, auditorium, room;
  salle de bains bathroom; **salle
  à manger** dining room
sandwich (m) sandwich
sans without
saucisson (m) kind of salami
savoir to know (a fact or how to
  do something e.g. **je sais faire
  la cuisine** I know how to cook)
savon (m) soap
scène (f) scene
séance (f) session
secrétaire (m and f) secretary
seize 16
sel (m) salt
selon according to
semaine (f) week
sept seven
septembre September
servir to serve
serviette (f) towel, napkin;
  serviette de toilette hand towel

shampooing *(m) shampoo*
s'il vous plaît *please*
situé(e) *situated*
six *six*
ski *(m) ski;* **ski de fond** *cross-country skiing;* **ski de piste** *downhill skiing*
SNCF *(f) French railways*
sœur *(f) sister*
soie *(f) silk;* **en soie** *made of silk*
soif *(f) thirst;* **avoir soif** *to be thirsty*
soir *(m) evening*
soirée *(f) evening, evening entertainment*
soixante *60*
soixante-dix *70*
en solde *in the sale*
soleil *(m) sun*
son, sa, ses *his, her, its*
sortie *(f) exit*
sortir *to go out*
souffrir *to suffer*
source *(f) spring* (of water)
souvenir *(m) souvenir, memory*
souvent *often*
spectacle *(m) show*
sport *(m) sport*
station *(f)* **de métro** *underground station,* **station thermale** *spa*
stationnement *(m)* **(interdit)** *(no) parking*
stationner *to park*
station-service *(f) petrol station*
stylo *(m) pen*
sucre *(m) sugar;* **sucreries** *(f pl) sweet things*
sud *(m) south*

suivre *to follow*
supermarché *(m) supermarket*
sur *on*
surtout *mainly, especially*
svp (s'il vous plaît) *please*
sympathique *friendly, pleasant*
syndicat d'initiative *(m) tourist office*

tabac *(m) tobacconist's-cum-newsagent's*
taille *(f) size, waist*
tarif *(m) price list, rate;* **tarif réduit** *reduced rate*
tarte *(f) pie*
taxi *(m) taxi*
télécarte *(f) phone card*
téléphone *(m) telephone*
téléphoner (à) *to phone*
temps *(m) time, weather*
tête *(f) head*
T.G.V. *(m) high speed train*
thé *(m) tea*
ticket *(m) ticket*
timbre *(m) stamp*
tir à l'arc *(m) archery*
tire-bouchon *(m) corkscrew*
toi *you (familiar)*
toilette *(f),* **faire sa toilette** *to wash and dress;* **les toilettes** *lavatory*
ton, ta, tes *your*
tonalité *(f) dialling tone*
toujours *always*
touriste *(m and f) tourist*
tourner *to turn*
tout(e), tous, toutes *all;* **tout de suite** *immediately;* **tout droit** *straight ahead;* **tout le monde**

everybody; **tous les deux** both of them; **tous les jours** every day

train (m) train; **en train** by train

trajet (m) journey

tranche (f) slice

travail (m) work, job

travailler to work

traveller (m) traveller's cheque

traverser to cross

treize 13

trente 30

très very

trois three

troisième third

se tromper to make a mistake

trop too, too much, too many

trouver to find; **se trouver** to be (situated)

TTC all taxes included

un(e) a, an, one

uni(e) plain

va, vas see **aller**

vacances (f pl) holiday(s)

valise (f) suitcase

vanille (f) vanilla

vase (m) vase

il vaut it costs, it is worth

veau (m) veal

vélo (m) bicycle

vendeur (m), **vendeuse** (f) sales assistant

vendredi Friday

vent (m) wind

ventre (m) stomach

vérifier to check

verre (m) glass

vers towards

verser to pour

vert(e) green

vêtement (m) garment

viande (f) meat

vie (f) life, cost of living

vieux (vieil, vieille) old

ville (f) town

vin (m) wine

vingt 20

visite (f) **guidée** guided tour

visiter to visit (a place)

vite quickly

vitesse (f) speed

voie (f) track

voilà there is, here is, there you are

voir to see

voiture (f) car; **voiture-restaurant** restaurant-car; **en voiture** by car

voler to steal; **volé** stolen

votre, vos your

je voudrais I'd like

vouloir to want; **vous voulez** you want

voyager to travel

vrai(e) true

V.T.T. (m) mountain biking

WC (m) (pronounced **vé-cé**) toilet

week-end (m) weekend

y there, to it

yaourt (m) yoghurt

yeux (m pl) see **œil**

zéro zero

English–French vocabulary

a **un, une**
about **environ**
address **l'adresse** *(f)*
admission charge **l'entrée** *(f)*
after **après**
afternoon **l'après-midi** *(m)*
again **encore, de nouveau**
age **l'âge** *(m)*
agency **l'agence** *(f); travel agency* **l'agence** *(f)* **de voyages**
all **tout, toute, tous, toutes**
also **aussi**
always **toujours**
and **et**
appear **apparaître**
apple **la pomme**
appointment **le rendez-vous**
April **avril**
arrival **l'arrivée** *(f)*
arrive **arriver**
as **comme**
aspirin **l'aspirine** *(f)*
at **à, chez;** *at the corner* **au coin;** *at home* **à la maison**
August **août**
autumn **l'automne** *(m);* *in autumn* **en automne**

bad **mauvais(e);** *badly* **mal**
baker's **la boulangerie**
bank **la banque;** *bank holiday* **le jour férié**
bath **le bain;** *to have a bath* **prendre un bain;** *bathroom* **la salle de bains**

be **être**
be able to **pouvoir**
bean **l'haricot** *(m)*
beautiful **beau, belle**
bed **le lit;** *double bed* **le grand lit;** *twin-bedded* **à deux lits**
beer **la bière;** *draught* (beer) **la pression**
before **avant**
behind **derrière**
believe **croire**
better **meilleur(e), mieux**
between **entre**
bicycle **le vélo**
big **grand(e)**
bill (food, drinks) **l'addition** *(f)*
bill (hotel) **la note**
black **noir(e)**
blue **bleu(e)**
book **le livre**
book **louer, réserver**
bottle **la bouteille**
box **la boîte;** *box office* **le bureau de location**
boy **le garçon**
bread **le pain**
break **casser;** *broken* **cassé(e)**
breakdown **la panne;** *breakdown service* **le service de dépannage**
breakfast **le petit déjeuner**
bridge **le pont**
British **britannique**
brother **le frère**
brown **marron**

bus l'**autobus** (m), **le bus**; bus
  stop l'**arrêt** (m) **d'autobus**
busy **occupé(e)**
but **mais**
butcher's **la boucherie**
butter **le beurre**
buy **acheter**

cake, cake shop une **pâtisserie**
camping, campsite **le camping**
can **peux, peut, pouvez**
car **la voiture**; by car **en voiture**
car park **le parking**
carry **porter**
cash desk, cashier's **la caisse**
catch **prendre**
certainly **bien sûr**
change **changer**
change (small) **la monnaie**
cheap **bon marché**; cheaper
  meilleur marché
check **vérifier**
cheese **le fromage**
chemist **le pharmacien, la**
  pharmacienne
chemist's **la pharmacie**
chicken **le poulet**
child l'**enfant** (m and f)
chips **les frites** (f pl)
choose **choisir**
church l'**église** (f)
close **fermer**; closed **fermé(e)**
clothes **les vêtements** (m pl),
  la tenue
coach l'**autocar** (m), **le car**
coffee (black) **le café**
coin **la pièce**
cold **froid(e)**; to be cold **avoir froid**
colour **la couleur**
come **venir**; come home **rentrer**

cook **faire la cuisine**
cooking **la cuisine**
corkscrew **le tire-bouchon**
cost **coûter**
country **le pays**
course **le plat**
credit card **la carte de crédit**
cross **traverser**

dance **danser**
daughter **la fille**
day **le jour**; the whole day **toute**
  la journée
dear **cher, chère**
December **décembre**
dinner **le dîner**
dish **le plat**
do **faire**
doctor **le médecin**
dress **la robe**; s'**habiller**
drink **boire**; **la boisson**
during **pendant**

easy **facile**
eat **manger**
egg l'**œuf** (m)
end **le bout**; at the end
  au bout
engine **le moteur**
England l'**Angleterre** (f)
English **anglais(e)**
Englishman l'**Anglais**;
  Englishwoman l'**Anglaise**
enough **assez**
evening **le soir, la soirée**
every **tout, toute**; every day **tous**
  les jours; everybody **tout le**
  monde everything **tout**
excuse me **pardon**
exit **la sortie**

expensive **cher, chère**
eye **l'œil** *(m)*

false **faux, fausse**
family **la famille**
far **loin**
fat **gros(se)**
father **le père**
February **février**
fill in **remplir;** *fill it up*
  (with petrol) **faire le plein**
find **trouver**
finish **finir**
first **premier, première**
firstly **d'abord**
fish **le poisson**
floor **l'étage** *(m)*
follow **suivre**
foot **le pied;** *on foot* **à pied**
for **pour**
France **la France**
free (costing nothing) **gratuit(e)**
French **français(e)**
Frenchman **le Français;**
  Frenchwoman **la Française**
French railways **la S.N.C.F.**
Friday **vendredi**
friend **l'ami** *(m)*, **l'amie** *(f)*
friendly **sympathique**
from **de, à partir de**
fruit juice **le jus de fruit**
full **complet, complète, plein(e)**

gardening **le jardinage**
get up **se lever**
girl **la fille**
give **donner**
glasses **les lunettes** *(f pl)*
go **aller, partir;** *go up* **monter;**
  go down **descendre**

go and get **aller chercher**
go out **sortir;** *go home* **rentrer à**
  la maison
good **bon, bonne**
goodbye **au revoir**
good evening **bonsoir**
good night **bonne nuit**
Great Britain **la Grande-Bretagne**
green **vert(e)**
grocer's shop **l'alimentation** *(f)*

hair **les cheveux** *(m pl)*
half **demi(e);** *half an hour* **demi-**
  heure
ham **le jambon**
handbag **le sac à main**
hate **détester**
have **avoir**
head **la tête**
headache **le mal de tête**
hear **entendre**
heavy **lourd(e)**
hello **bonjour, allô** *(on the phone)*
help **aider**
here **ici**
here is **voilà**
hike **la randonnée**
hire, hiring **louer, la location**
hobby **le loisir**
holiday(s) **les vacances** *(f pl)*
home, at home **à la maison;**
  at my home **chez moi**
hope **espérer**
hospital **l'hôpital** *(m)*
hot **chaud(e);** *to be hot* **avoir**
  chaud
hotel **l'hôtel** *(m)*
hour **l'heure** *(f)*
house **la maison**
how **comment**

how much/how many **combien**
hundred (a) **cent**
hunger **la faim**; *to be hungry* **avoir faim**
husband **le mari**

I **je, moi**
ice cream **la glace**
identification **la pièce d'identité**
ill **malade**
immediately **tout de suite**
in, into **à, en, dans**
in front of **devant**
information (piece of) **le renseignement**
information office **le bureau de renseignements**
inquire **se renseigner**
insert **introduire**
interesting **intéressant(e)**
invite **inviter**
it's **c'est, il est, elle est**

January **janvier**
jeans **le jean, les jeans**
journey **le trajet**
July **juillet**
June **juin**

key **la clé**
know **savoir, connaître**

ladies and gentlemen **Messieurs-dames**
large **gros(se), grand(e)**
last **dernier, dernière**
late-night opening **le nocturne**
learn **apprendre**
leave **quitter**
left, on the left **à gauche**

left luggage **la consigne**
lemon **le citron**
less **moins**
letter **la lettre**
letter box **la boîte aux lettres**
lift **l'ascenseur** (m)
like **aimer**
like **comme**
line (underground) **la ligne**
listen **écouter**
litre **le litre**
little **petit(e)**; *(a) little* **(un) peu**
live **habiter**
long **long, longue**
look for **chercher**
lose **perdre**; *lost* **perdu(e)**
lot, a lot (of) **beaucoup (de)**
love **aimer**
lunch **le déjeuner**

Madame, Mrs **Madame, Mme**
make **faire**
man **l'homme** (m)
many **beaucoup**
map **la carte**; *map (town)* **le plan (de la ville)**
March **mars**
market **le marché**
married **marié(e)**
May **mai**
me **moi**
meal **le repas**
measure **mesurer**
meat **la viande**; *well done* **bien cuit(e)**; *medium* **à point**
medicine **le médicament**
menu **la carte**
midday **midi**
middle **le milieu**; *in the middle* **au milieu**

midnight **minuit**
milk **le lait**
Miss **Mademoiselle**
Monday **lundi**
money **l'argent** (m)
month **le mois**
more **plus**; no … more
  ne … plus
morning **le matin, la matinée**
mother **la mère**
motorway **l'autoroute** (f)
mountain **la montagne**; in/to the
  mountains **à la montagne**
much **beaucoup**
museum **le musée**
must; one must **il faut** + infinitive

name **le nom**
near **près (de)**
nearby **près de**; near here **près
  d'ici**
nearly **presque**
need **avoir besoin**
never **jamais**
new **neuf, neuve, nouveau,
  nouvelle**
newspaper **le journal**
next **prochain(e)**
next to **à côté de**
night **la nuit**
nightclub **la boîte (de nuit)**
no **non**
nothing **rien**
November **novembre**
now **maintenant**
number **le numéro**; (bus) number
  la ligne

October **octobre**
of, off **de**

often **souvent**
oil **l'huile** (f)
OK **d'accord**
old **vieux, vieil, vieille**
omelette **l'omelette** (f)
on **sur, à, en**; on foot **à pied**
once **une fois**
one **un, une, on**
only **seulement**
open **ouvrir**; opened **ouvert(e)**
opposite **en face de**
or **ou**
order **commander**
other **autre**
out of **hors de**

packet **le paquet**
pain **la douleur**; to have a pain
  avoir mal
park **garer**
parking meter **le parcmètre**
particularly **particulièrement**
passer-by **le/la passant(e)**
pay **payer**
peas **les petits pois** (m pl)
pepper **le poivre**
person **la personne**
petrol **l'essence** (f); petrol station
  la station-service
petrol: lead-free **le sans plomb**
phone card **la télécarte**
picnic **le pique-nique**; to have a
  picnic **faire un pique-nique**
pie **la tarte**
piece **le morceau**
platform **le quai**
play **jouer**
please **s'il vous plaît**
pleased **content(e)**
post; post office **la poste**

postcard **la carte postale**
potato **la pomme de terre**
pound (sterling) **la livre
(sterling)**
prefer **préférer**
pressure (tyre) **la pression**
pretty **joli(e)**
price **le prix**
price list **le tarif**
pullover **le pull-over**
pump attendant **le pompiste**
purse **le porte-monnaie**
put **mettre**

quick **rapide**; quickly **vite**

rain **la pluie**; it's raining **il pleut**
rare (meat) **saignant(e)**
read **lire**
record **le disque**
red **rouge**
repair **réparer**
repeat **répéter**
reserve **réserver**
rest **se reposer**
right, on the right **à droite**
road **la route**
room **la pièce, la salle**; bathroom
la salle de bains; dining room
la salle à manger

sale (on) **en solde**
sales assistant **le vendeur,
la vendeuse**
salt **le sel**
same **même**
sandwich **le sandwich**
Saturday **samedi**
say **dire**
school **l'école** (f)

sea **la mer**; by the sea **au bord
de la mer**
season **la saison**; out of …
hors …; in high … **en pleine …**
seat **la place**
secretary **le/la secrétaire**
see **voir**
send **envoyer**
September **septembre**
serve **servir**
serve (transport) **desservir**
shampoo **le shampooing**
shine **briller**; the sun shines **le
soleil brille**
shirt **la chemise**
shoe **la chaussure**; shoe size **la
pointure**
shop **le magasin**
shopping **les courses** (f pl); to
do some shopping **faire les
courses**
shopping centre **le centre
commercial**
show **montrer**
show **le spectacle**
shower **la douche**; to have a
shower **prendre une douche**
sign **le panneau**
since **depuis**
single/bachelor **célibataire**
Sir, Mr **Monsieur, M.**
sister **la sœur**
situated **situé(e)**
size **la taille**
skirt **la jupe**
sleep **dormir**
slice **la tranche**
slow **lent**; slowly **lentement**
small **petit(e)**
snow **neiger**

soap **le savon**
some **quelque(s)**
someone **quelqu'un**
something **quelque chose**
something else **quelque chose
d'autre**
sometimes **quelquefois**
son **le fils**
soon **bientôt**
sorry **pardon; désolé(e)**
speak **parler**
spend (time) **passer**
sport **le sport**; to do a sport
pratiquer un sport
spring **le printemps;**
in spring **au printemps**
square **la place**
stamp **le timbre**
star **l'étoile** (f)
start **commencer**
station (rail) **la gare (SNCF);**
bus/coach station **la gare
routière;** underground station
la station de métro
straight **raide, droit(e)**
straight on **tout droit**
street **la rue**
surburbs **la banlieue**
sugar **le sucre**
suitcase **la valise**
summer **l'été** (m)
sun **le soleil**
Sunday **dimanche**
supermarket **le supermarché**
surroundings **les environs** (m pl)
swim **nager**
swimming **la natation;**
swimming pool **la piscine;**
swimming costume, swimsuit
le maillot de bain

take, taken **prendre, pris**
tall **grand(e)**
taxi **le taxi**
tea **le thé**
teacher **le professeur, la
professeure**
tell **dire**
telephone **téléphoner, le
téléphone**
telephone box **la cabine
téléphonique**
than **que**
thank you **merci**
that's all **c'est tout**
the **le, la, les**
then **ensuite, puis, alors**
there **y**
these, those **ces**
thin **mince**
thing **la chose**
think **penser**
thirst **la soif;** to be thirsty
avoir soif
this, that **ce, cet, cette**
this is **c'est**
thousand **mille**
throat **la gorge**
Thursday **jeudi**
ticket **le billet, le ticket**
ticket office **le guichet**
time **l'heure** (f); what time is it?
quelle heure est-il?
time **le temps;** spend time
passer le temps
timetable **l'horaire** (m)
tip **le pourboire**
to **à, en, pour, jusqu'à**
tobacconist's/newsagent's
le tabac
today **aujourd'hui**

together **ensemble**
toilet **les toilettes** *(f pl)*
toll payable **à péage**
tomorrow **demain**
too; too much; too
  many **trop**
tooth **la dent**; *toothpaste* **le
  dentifrice**
tour **la visite**; *guided tour* **la
  visite guidée**
tourist **le/la touriste**
tourist office **l'office** *(m)* **du/
  de tourisme, le syndicat
  d'initiative**
towards **vers**
towel **la serviette**
town **la ville**
traffic **la circulation**
train **le train**; *by train* **en
  train**; *on the train* **dans
  le train**
travel **voyager, le voyage**
traveller's cheque **le traveller**
trip **l'excursion** *(f)*
trousers **le pantalon**
true **vrai**
try **essayer**
Tuesday **mardi**
turn **tourner**
tyre **le pneu**

underground **le métro**
understand **comprendre**
until **jusqu'à**

very **très**
visit **visiter**

wait **attendre**

walk **marcher**; *a walk* **une
  promenade**; *to go for a walk*
  se promener
wallet **le portefeuille**
wash (oneself) (**se**) **laver**
watch **regarder; la montre**
water (mineral) **l'eau** *(f)* **minérale**
wear **porter**
weather **le temps**
Wednesday **mercredi**
week **la semaine**
weigh **peser**
well **bien**
what **que(le); qu'est-ce que; quoi**
when **quand**
where **où**
which **quel(le)**
white **blanc, blanche**
white coffee **le café crème**
who **qui**
wife **la femme**
windsurf board **la planche à voile**
wine **le vin**
winter **l'hiver** *(m)*; *in winter*
  en hiver
wish **désirer**
with **avec**
without **sans**
woman **la femme**
work **travailler, marcher** *(machine)*
work **le travail**
write **écrire**

year **l'an** *(m)*, **l'année** *(f)*
yellow **jaune**
yes **oui**
yoghurt **le yaourt**
you **tu, toi**
young **jeune**

Index

References are to units followed by section or task numbers (e.g. 13:1). The **Pronunciation guide** is referenced by the initials PG, followed by the section number.